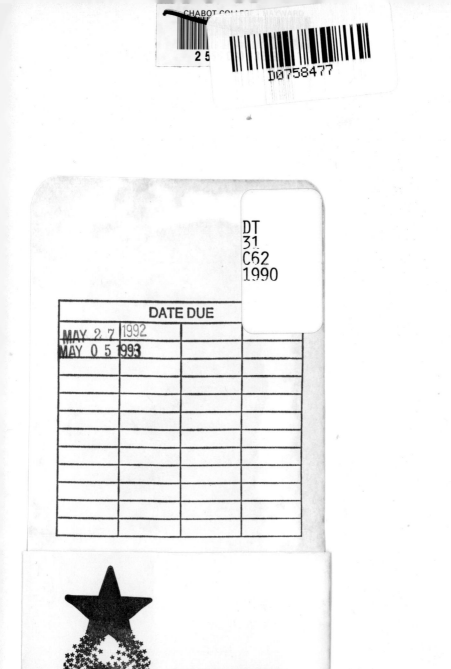

AFRICA'S WAY

A journey from the past

AFRICA'S WAY

A journey from the past

LAURENCE COCKCROFT

I.B.TAURIS & Co Ltd
Publishers
London

Published by
I.B.Tauris & Co Ltd
110 Gloucester Avenue
London NW1 8JA

British Library Cataloguing in Publication Data
Cockcroft, Laurence
  Africa's Way: a journey from the past.
  1. Africa. Economic development. Effects of tribal customs
  I. Title
  330.96

ISBN 1–85043–195–7

Typeset in 10/12 Century by Columns of Reading
Printed and bound in Great Britain by
Redwood Press Limited, Melksham, Wiltshire

Contents

List of Maps vi

Preface ix

1 Introduction 1

2 The Peopling of Africa 9

3 Patterns of Allegiance 21

4 States Beyond the Clan 36

5 The Colonial Impact 63

6 Torn Between Two Worlds 84

7 Chiefs Without a Tribe 97

8 The Politics of Development 119

9 The Elusive Surplus 135

10 Artisans and Entrepreneurs: the Industrial Dilemma 152

11 The Aid Machine 168

12 The Prospects for Progress 188

Notes 203

Glossary 213

Index 215

List of Maps

Map 1   Bantu expansion   15

Map 2   Empires of gold   38

Map 3   Ghana, Sokoto and other West African
        states, 1600–1900 AD   43

Map 4   Kingdoms of East, Central and
        Southern Africa, 1600–1900 AD   53

Map 5   Africa today and African peoples   98

To Shamshad
who has contributed so much to the
writing of this book, and to my life

Preface

I first went to work in Africa in January 1962 at the age of eighteen as a volunteer before going up to Cambridge University. Nigeria, the country I went to work in, was then one year into independence, although some media coverage at the time gave the impression that this made the country also one year old. Within two hours of my arrival, however, I found myself standing outside the enormous mosque of central Kano – a firm reminder of the centuries-old history of Islam in that part of the country. During my year there I was to receive daily witness of the strength and depth of Nigeria's long history, and of the brevity of the colonial occupation.

I have spent some time in Africa in almost each of the subsequent twenty-eight years. For six of them I worked for the Governments of, first, Zambia and then, Tanzania. My wife comes from Zanzibar and we are regular visitors to that part of Africa's long coastline, which is rich in the history of contact between Africa and the rest of the world.

The quarter of a century following 1962 should have been a period of achievement; the majority of Africans believed it would be, and many well-informed and objective westerners shared their view. The climate in the early 1980s was optimistic, and to work in newly independent

African states was to share in a great adventure of 'nation building' which seemed to be part of a long march away from the ills of the colonial period. The disaster of independence in Zaire appeared at the time to be one of only a small number of setbacks. Majority government in the Portuguese territories, in Zimbabwe and in South Africa itself seemed to be a question only of time. Living and teaching at the school for southern African refugees in Dar es salaam in 1964, I believed that the students would be running their countries by 1970 at the latest. In the event, independence for Angola and Mozambique was ten years away, for Zimbabwe fifteen years, and in both cases only following massive guerrilla wars in which many of the students of the refugee school were killed.

The costs of these guerrilla wars, and of the unresolved conflicts which have replaced them, were very high. But equally high prices have been paid elsewhere in Africa: of civil strife, of decade-long drought, of mis-allocation of money on a grand scale, and of frequently unwanted and counter-productive intervention by the 'great powers'. Observed from inside Africa, leaders who once seemed attractive democrats have too often become unresponsive autocrats. For the man on the small farm waiting for a bag of fertiliser, or in the shanty town waiting for a water pump, resigned submission has replaced the 'glad confident morning' of *uhuru* (freedom). By the early 1970s, a small farmer on Mount Kilimanjaro could ask a Tanzanian cabinet minister, 'When will this *uhuru* business be over?' In Zimbabwe, a late-comer to freedom, ministers are popularly dubbed *chefs*, a term with connotations of the more negative aspects of the pre-colonial chiefs – though several of them were leaders in a guerrilla struggle that was generally deemed radical.

Observed from outside Africa, the litany of near and absolute disaster has become so familiar it has ceased to have much meaning. Only physical disaster involving tens of thousands stricken by drought or war is worthy of attention. Africa is indeed 'in doubt', and these doubts are are as prevalent inside Africa as outside it.

I am convinced that the difficulty in interpreting events in contemporary Africa is at least in part the consequence of a general lack of knowledge of what was happening in Africa before the colonial powers took over the continent in the late nineteenth century. The full blown colonial period was extraordinarily brief – for most of Africa it lasted only about seventy years, although contact with the East and Europe had been flourishing for at least 2,000 years. The patterns established in African social structures during the centuries before the colonial period – from politics to agriculture – were not destroyed but survived to influence the present in one form or another.

I have set out in this book to trace some of the ways in which this long standing 'weight' of Africa's history affects the present, how to some extent it explains her many political and economic problems, and how it is likely to shape her future. Understanding that 'weight' is as important as analyzing price trends, land availability, and market opportunities, – which are my own principal preoccupations as an economist, and the limits of which I understand only too well.

I have sought to marry my own working knowledge to that of some of the novelists, historians, anthropologists, agriculturalists and economists, from both inside and outside Africa, who have written so much in recent decades. Among the most influential of the historians have been John Iliffe (*African Capitalism* and *A Modern History of Tanganyika*), Basil Davidson (*The Africans: an Entry into Cultural History*), and Ali Mazrui (*Nationalism and the New States in Africa*); among the anthropologists, Jomo Kenyatta (*Facing Mt Kenya* – still a classic), John Mbiti (*African Religions and Philosophy*), and Monica Wilson (*For Men and Elders* – unique in its treatment of change over time); among the agriculturalists, W.H. Allan (*The African Husbandman* – the best book on African agriculture so far written); and among the economists, Colin Leys (*Underdevelopment in Kenya*) and Roger Riddell (*Foreign Aid Reconsidered*). Bridging these disciplines, and in a class of its own, is the splendid *Afrique Noire: Ruptures et*

Permanences by Catherine Coquery Vidrovitch, definitely
the finest book on Africa to be published in the 1980s.
Detailed references to these and many others appear in the
footnotes; the library of the School of Oriental and African
Studies in London has them all and I remain in its debt.

I am particularly grateful to a number of friends and
colleagues from both Africa and Europe who have read and
commented on the draft of this text, and to my interlocu-
tors in innumerable conversations in villages, shanty
towns, buses, bars and landrovers across the continent
without whom I would have nothing to add to what others
have already written. Finally my debt to my wife,
Shamshad, knows no bounds since without her this project
would never have been completed.

Laurence Cockcroft
October 1989

1
Introduction

Returning from a meeting of African Heads of State convened by the Organization of African Unity in 1966, Julius Nyerere of Tanzania commented, 'Africa is in a mess. There is a devil somewhere in Africa. I am a good superstitious African, and I believe in devils.'[1] He was thinking of an external, malevolent devil, and particularly of the ex-colonial and neo-colonial powers whose grip over Africa has sometimes appeared so strong. Over twenty years later Africa is in a greater mess, but it is increasingly difficult to ascribe her current problems to external, malevolent forces – although volatile commodity prices and regional conflicts abetted by the superpowers and their proxies have certainly contributed to creating them.

In purely economic terms, recovery from the mess is bound to take more than a decade. Low levels of income and of food production per head, a debt mountain of over $120 billion, and an insignificant share of world trade in manufactured goods all militate against a rapid recovery. Nonetheless, aid donors continue to pump over $10 billion a year into Africa, a large part of which is given in support of institutional reforms designed to overcome those very problems whose origins lie in the adjustment of African

1

cultures to the contemporary world. This political adjustment will take much longer than the economic adjustment
which is now at the top of the aid donors' agenda.

This book examines the ingredients of that older culture,
plots its course of change during the colonial period, and
shows how in spite of internal transformation it has shaped
the last quarter of a century of post-independence African
history. It examines the political structure of pre-colonial
societies and shows that, in spite of their differences, most
of them shared three characteristics: first, they were
authoritarian; second, they concentrated loyalties within
kinship groups; and third, they had seldom evolved a
conflict-free system of succession. These factors continue to
be the chief determinants of African political systems
today. The tendency towards an authoritarian, centralizing
state has also been critical to the development strategies –
whether stated explicitly or not – pursued by African
governments. Until the economic crisis of the early 1980s,
most African governments pursued policies in which the
role of the state was dominant. This was more than a
sympathetic response to the prevailing wisdom in left and
liberal circles in the West. It fitted in well with traditional
systems in which kings and chiefs had played a role in
economic accumulation and regulation. It also set the stage
on which aid donors have operated over the last thirty
years, with conspicuous lack of success.

This interpretation of Africa's past and present does not
neglect the fact that the colonial period caused enormous,
disruptive shocks to African society, preventing any kind of
continuity in its development. The re-direction of economies
towards European markets, and the creation of modern
businesses within them, undermined those traders and
artisans who had previously supplied local and international markets on a modest basis. The economic institutions which Africa inherited were not of her making, and
for most countries were only fifty years old at independence. This inheritance was fundamentally different from
that of Latin America, where the European immigrants

had themselves developed institutions which they 'nationalized' from Spain and Portugal in the 1820s. It was also different from India where trade and production on a considerable scale had drawn the colonial powers to the sub-continent from the fifteenth century onwards, and where major modern manufacturing businesses were owned by Indian magnates from the late nineteenth century.

However, the economic and political institutions which Africa inherited in the early 1960s were then *managed* on a pattern which owed much to earlier social patterns, with their roots in pre-colonial society. This scarcely makes the African experience unique, as many societies in both South America and Asia were authoritarian in their pre-colonial phase. Other parts of the developing world also share Africa's consciousness of lineage lines and its consequent tribal orientation. In the late 1980s, the key to Pakistan's numerous political factions is increasingly seen as tribal; even prosperous Malaysia's kingdoms can be seen in these terms. The succession question, though particularly difficult for African societies historically, can also hardly be described as a uniquely African problem.

It is the *conjunction* of these three characteristics, and their prevalence throughout most of sub-Saharan Africa, which gives them greater significance than in societies where only one or two of them are in evidence. Latin America, if periodically authoritarian, has been experimenting with changing leaders by ballot since the 1820s. Its Indian population was either made subject to European immigrants, or exterminated by them. Thus in Latin America the lineage line question has always been confined to a group without political power.

This heritage, and the problems it creates, is obviously not equally significant in all African countries, but everywhere it has set limits to the potential for nation building. This book will argue that those countries which have, at least sporadically, put the priority of production on an equal footing with the priority of politics – such as Kenya, Cameroun and Botswana – have managed to

overcome some of the more negative aspects of the
heritage, and achieve growth rates well above the average.
However, the relative success of these countries was based
on conditions existing in the 1960s. For most of their
neighbours, and for at least Cameroun of the three, the
situation is now very different. A run-down physical
infrastructure, a collapsing structure of social services and
productive machinery and equipment which is heavily
depreciated would make it difficult for most countries to
build an efficient 'modern' sector. However, as the drift of
population to the towns is maintained, an urban market,
with a mass of low income consumers, is constantly
expanding and re-shaping social and economic priorities. A
rapid acceleration in the growth of the towns is gradually
changing the basis of society with far reaching economic
and political implications, which provide some indication of
the Africa of the future.

In exploring these themes, this book first describes the
essential nature of most African societies in pre-colonial
times. Chapter 2 explores the way in which most of the
land, and particularly the land south of the Equator, was
settled. Migrant groups participating in the Bantu expansion, beginning over two thousand years ago, were the key
to this process. Moving south and east from a focal point in
present-day Cameroun, they pushed the frontier outwards,
absorbing earlier settlers and moving on whenever the
ecology of the local environment, or conflict with similar
groups, demanded it. While this process was ostensibly
complete by the seventeenth century, a great deal of
secondary movement occurred as rival migrants jockeyed
for position. Thus the Kikuyu, moving in from the north,
occupied the land around Mount Kenya only from the late
eighteenth century. Whereas the ethnic composition of
west Africa was determined at an earlier period, the same
pattern of secondary settlement could be seen well into the
seventeenth century in what is now Ghana.

This pattern of physical pioneering required small
groups which were socially coherent and able to work, and
when necessary fight, together in exploiting and retaining

newly conquered territory. Chapter 3 shows how the social character of the clans which combine to form Africa's tribes reflected this priority: they were conformist and authoritarian, and obsessed with the role of the divine in determining their success or failure. The avoidance of giving offence, either to the gods or to those in authority, was therefore a key concern of individuals. Where conflict proved unavoidable in any other way it was often possible to move on to the next available area of fertile ground. When such moves were made, loyalties still remained within the framework of the extended family and clan.

Yet nascent states did arise, from the tenth-century empire of Ghana to the nineteenth-century Ndebele kingdom of present-day Zimbabwe. Chapter 4 discusses whether these states succeeded in building loyalties which transcended those of the clan and in fusing lineage lines into more homogeneous societies. It concludes that they did not, though several came close to it and would certainly have taken the process much further if the colonial powers had not intervened in Africa. The leading societies in this process were the Kingdoms of Asante (in present-day Ghana) and Buganda. But the most determined and explicit efforts to build a nation at the expense of the clan were those of the Zulu leaders, Shaka and Mzilikazi, at the beginning of the nineteenth century, and it was Mzilikazi who came closest to it in founding the Ndebele kingdom. A more subtle route, and one with perhaps more relevance to the present, was that adopted within the Sokoto Caliphate throughout the nineteenth century, which brought together the Emirates of northern Nigeria in a confederation under the influential, but hardly dictatorial control of the Sultan of Sokoto. The conclusion is that even within these innovative and at times powerful societies clan loyalties retained their predominance.

At first sight, the value system of the clan was not likely to survive the colonial period. The innovations introduced by the colonial powers included modes of thinking (Christianity and western education), modes of production (cash crops), and modes of living (rapid urbanization). These processes are described in Chapter 5. In many ways they undercut the cohesion of the extended family, leaving women particularly exposed. The burden of food production and of keeping the family together fell increasingly on them, as more and more men left for the towns in the years between the two World Wars. The need for new value systems created by this enlargement in the scale of economic activity is explored in Chapter 6. Important strands of the old system continued to coexist with the new; sometimes the coexistence was formalized – as in the institutions of colonial government in northern Nigeria – and sometimes it simply evolved – as in the pattern by which entire extended families came to depend on individual wage-paid miners on the Zambian copperbelt. More dramatically, the coexistence could be seen in the millenarian movements of leaders such as Alice Lenshina in Zambia, and in the nationalist guerrilla campaign of Mau Mau in Kenya. Both of these owed much to traditional forms of superstition and to magic, as well as to the colonial experience of mission station and army. In the new value systems the individual faced decisions which might cut across allegiances to, among others, tribe, class or church.

The regimes which have come to power in post-independence Africa have reflected this coexistence of values derived from both the new and the old, with an uncertain tension existing between the two. Chapter 7 looks at how such regimes have not only been authoritarian but have also frequently failed to overcome the strength of localist loyalties, and have nearly always failed to arrange for a peaceful presidential transition within the lifetime of one head of state. However, the Chapter also shows how in different ways Presidents Senghor of Senegal, Kenyatta of Kenya and Nyerere of Tanzania succeeded in overcoming at least one of these three weaknesses – examples upon which their own and other states may now build.

The theme of the centralizing tendency of the state, linked to a network of very local loyalties, has also defined much economic decision-making. Chapter 8 shows that, behind the facade of national planning, the major political objectives have been to take a major chunk of economic activity into government's own hands (through state-owned companies and marketing boards); to curtail the role of companies owned by overseas operators; and to cir- cumscribe the activities of particular social groups, includ- ing some of Africa's most talented people such as the Ibo and Bamilike, and of non-African citizen entrepreneurs such as the Indians and Lebanese. This pattern of priorities has seldom been consistent with securing a real increase in productive investment in the rural areas, nowhere more so than in those countries such as Tanzania and Mozambique which have talked most about it. The fostering of broad- based economic growth has been as elusive as the development of coherent political systems.

Regardless of the successes or failures of national economic decision-making, small farmers have continued to produce increasing quantities of food, though usually at an insufficient rate to meet a growing urban demand. Chapter 9 argues that their performance has been held back by inefficient pricing and marketing arrangements, and by the channelling of government resources into big projects designed, unsuccessfully, to transform agriculture. Given appropriate support and access to land, which is certainly available, they may well be able to feed the future urban population, but are unlikely to generate an increase in exports at the same time.

In their attempts to reduce dependency on international capital, governments might have been expected to create opportunities for local entrepreneurs. Chapter 10 shows how traders and early manufacturers, who had been successful in the nineteenth century, were first under- mined by the colonial regime and then later often seen (as Nkrumah explicitly stated) as a potential countervailing power to government. However, in spite of government policy tens of thousands of self-employed 'informal' artisans have taken advantage of growing urban and rural markets to produce a range of products from grass roots tech- nologies. Although they represent the major growth point in African economies they are unlikely to develop larger-scale, modern enterprises. In those cases where large-scale entrepreneurs have emerged from these or from foreign-owned 'big company' backgrounds, they have not generally been successful in building self-sustaining, large-scale businesses. Too often older values of status and power have eroded the pursuit of marginal returns. Consequently, a lo͐ ͐wned efficient industrial sector remains a goal, but nͫͭ ͫ ͙ͣality.

Given an inefficient but centralizing state, a half-hearted commitment to overcoming the difficulties of agricultural development, and a weak or neglected group of local entrepreneurs, aid donors have had to fit into the interstices of the system while endeavouring to move national economies into self-sustaining growth. Chapter 11 shows how this process has taken aid further and further away from its original objective of an injection of investment funds on soft terms, which within a generation could be replaced by capital from financial markets. Caught between recipient governments' deep ambivalence towards the aid relationship, their own self-interest and a myriad of technical problems, aid has become a kind of economic 'drip feed' which supports incomes but does too little to raise the level of productive investment.

Chapter 12 outlines some of the ways in which social and political values are likely to evolve in Africa over the next generation and suggests some of the likely implications for individuals, for the nature of governments, for external donors and for private sector investors. It suggests that, as the urban economy develops, we shall see many 'counter-countervailing' sources of social and economic power to government from which a very different political system will eventually emerge. A new African identity, carrying the continent beyond the twenty-first century, will only be forged in the course of that process.

2
The Peopling of Africa

In 1969, five and a half years after Kenya achieved independence and Jomo Kenyatta emerged as its head under a constitutional government, two of the principal 'heirs apparent' were brutally removed from the political scene. Tom Mboya, only 38 years old, a young and visionary Minister of Economic Affairs, was shot in public; and Oginga Odinga, the former Vice-President and veteran of the independence struggle, was jailed, while his new party, the Kenya People's Union, was banned. Both these leaders were from the Luo people of western Kenya whom the Kikuyu, who dominated Kenyatta's Government, believed had played a subsidiary role in the fight for independence. The tension between Luo and Kikuyu, now intensified by these events, reflected a long running stand-off between the two which has prevailed ever since the Luo immigration into western Kenya in the eighteenth century. It was made more intense by the fact that the languages of the two peoples are as different as Gaelic is from English, and a lone Kikuyu in Luo areas will find it very difficult to make himself understood without the aid of kiSwahili as a *lingua franca*.

Although Kikuyu and Luo are among the best known tribal names in Kenya, the situation repeats itself many times over as there are ninety distinct tribal languages

9

falling into three of the four main language families of Africa, each of which has a completely different structure. The effort required to learn a language from a different family can be compared to the effort required by a Spaniard to learn Basque or an American to learn Cherokee.

If Kenya provides a dramatic example of a mixture of language families, other countries provide equally dramatic examples of a mixture of languages within the same family. In Cameroun there are several hundred languages within the same Congo-Kordofanian language family, of which Bantu is a subdivision. In contrast to the lack of comprehension between speakers of different language families, within the same language family there can be a high degree of comprehension and cultural affinity.

How did this complex structure of peoples and languages come about? In spite of many gaps in our knowledge, especially about west Africa, this question can be answered much more fully now than even twenty years ago. In this time there has been a great advance in piecing together archaeological and linguistic evidence on the movement of people within Africa, and in building up a picture of the growth of technology and of cultivation.

THE BEGINNINGS

It is useful to begin the story 10,000 years ago. Our present knowledge of different racial types in Africa at that time still does not allow much precision in describing the continent's ethnic mix. It seems, however, that a common ancestral type had differentiated sufficiently for there to be peoples in Ethiopia, northern Kenya and parts of the west African Sahel who would be recognizably close to present day highland Ethiopians, or Tuareg and Fulani. They would be lighter skinned than the negroid peoples who inhabited most of the rest of Africa. As a result of a process of differentiation the latter peoples had subdivided into a present day negroid type, and a type much closer to the contemporary Khoisan people of the Kalahari in Botswana.

However, evidence from skeletal remains suggests that dwarfing changes have occurred amongst the Khoisan over the intervening millenia and explain the small stature of the latter. Similar changes occurred amongst the ancestors of the present day pygmies of the rain forest whose origin may lie with either negroid, or Khoisan peoples – or their common ancestral stock.[1]

These types, no doubt generally unaware of each other, coexisted until 6–7,000 years ago, each maintaining its own form of hunting and gathering economy. Indications of the storage and consumption of cereals have been found at sites of early stone tool 'industries' such as those of the central Sahara (9,000 years old), Ghana (Bosumpra, 7,000 years old), Khartoum (6,000 years old) and Ethiopia (between 7,000 and 5,000 years old).[2] Each of these sites was associated with the initial cultivation of millets, sorghums and barleys. The first hard evidence of cereal production comes from neolithic villages in southern Mauritania. Several hundred such settlements have been identified beside a site which was once a lake. Radio-carbon techniques applied to several grain species show these as being from 3,400 to 2,400 years old. Around the same time, the Nok people of the Jos Plateau of northern Nigeria had become settled agriculturalists growing millet and sorghum as well as being pioneers of iron smelting and pottery.

The techniques developed by these early farmers gave them the means to mix hunting and gathering with cultivation, the latter becoming an increasingly important means of subsistence. Eventually, it gave them the strength to pioneer stable communities no longer dependent on the seasonal movements of animals, but which had to move every few years to virgin land as the fertility of cultivated soils became exhausted. Consequently, once cultivation became a widely established practice there was constant pressure for outward migration, and the pioneers were constantly pushing back the 'frontier' of cultivation. As their techniques improved over several centuries their greater resources enabled them both to destroy and absorb

the hunter-gathers who had previously dominated the
continent.

Folklore in Africa is still full of stories which recall such
pioneering. The following story from north-west Ghana
tells how one village, Eremon, came to be established:

> In the time of our great grandfathers the land around
> Tie became overpopulated. There were so many people
> that they could not find enough land on which to grow
> food. One day a man called Toola said to his brother
> Katon Toola, 'My brother, I can no longer live in Tie;
> my farm is too small to feed my children and there is
> no land for my sons when they grow up. I have made
> up my mind to go away with my wives and children
> and find a new country.'
>
> So at dawn the next day, the families of Toola and
> Katon Toola set out. First, went the men with spears
> in their hands ready to fight any wild beasts who
> attacked them. Then came the women and children
> with loads on their heads. Even the small children
> carried little pots or bundles of sticks. They walked on
> to the south west for about twenty miles, then Toola
> said 'Let us stop here.' There were few trees and the
> place looked very bare. The women grumbled and said,
> 'This place is no good. Where shall we find fruit to
> pick? Where can we grow our peppers?' But Toola
> would not listen.

In this barren land the community nearly came to grief,
but was saved by the intervention of an apparition, 'a
strange looking creature covered all over with hair', who
gave them the command, 'Bring your loads and follow me.'

> The fairy led them to a land where there was waving
> grass and tall trees, herds of antelope and bush cows
> [buffalo], wild fruits in abundance, and much good
> land for cultivation. There they settled and built the
> village of Eremon; but the fairy, having done its good
> deed, disappeared and was never seen again.[3]

THE BANTU EXPANSION

The most dramatic example of the constantly moving frontier of cultivation is provided by the expansion of the Bantu people from a point which probably lies in present-day Cameroun. This began between 3,500 and 2,500 years ago, culminating in the arrival of Bantu-speaking peoples in the Transvaal 1,600 years ago. It was the critical factor in spreading the technique of cultivation through central, eastern and southern Africa, and in ultimately reducing the hunter-gatherers to a small minority.

The first Bantu migrants moved initially into the equatorial forest and subsequently emerged into the eastern savannah about 2,000 years ago. This move

> forced them to change from a predominantly fishing and root crop economy to one which focused on grain cultivation and stock herding. Cognate words widely distributed in Bantu languages today, words that must therefore derive from proto Bantu vocabulary, indicate proto Bantu speakers hunted with bow and arrow and traps; collected honey and wax; fished with hook, line, nets and baskets; paddled canoes; kept goats; molded pottery water and storage pots; cultivated root crops and palms; and ground or pounded their food – activities that were all closely associated with the forest environment in which they lived.[4]

In the course of this migration many Bantu peoples acquired the skill of working iron, probably as originators of the iron-age sites around Lake Victoria (specifically at Urewe in present-day south-west Kenya) which are about 2,500 years old.[5] In this instance the conjunction of linguistic and archaeological evidence is remarkable. The Bantu languages of eastern (and southern) Africa have an extensive vocabulary for grain cultivation, iron-working and stock-keeping that are absent from the proto Bantu languages of the point of origin.

The migration pushed rapidly eastwards and southwards after the early development of iron-working in the Lake Victoria region. Thus evidence of Bantu iron-working techniques have been found in the Transvaal dating back 1,600 years, indicating that more than 2,000km were covered in 200 years. The southward migration stopped abruptly at the Transvaal and Natal, where the unfamiliar climate and ecology may have presented problems which the migrants found daunting. In southern Africa the Bantu undoubtedly co-existed for much of the last 1,600 years with the hunter-gatherers who had previously peopled the area and whose forebears had developed the relatively advanced 'stone tool' industries identified by sites in Zambia and South Africa.

Other groups of Bantu-speakers moved eastwards from the Lake Victoria area to the east African coast and established settlements which became the nuclei of the Swahili peoples along 1,200 miles of the coast. As they moved eastward, they borrowed many words from the Cushites (originating in southern Ethiopia) who at that time peopled many parts of inland east Africa, and from 1,000 years ago came to borrow words and culture (notably Islam) from the Arab traders who frequented the coast.

The vast areas of central and southern Africa which the Bantu migrants came to dominate, however, continued to contain minorities who spoke either Khoisan or Nilo-Saharan languages. The overlap with the latter was very strong in present-day Ruanda, Burundi, Uganda and Kenya. In these countries, oral tradition (ostensibly covering the last 900 years) suggests the 'immigrant' status of, for instance, the Tutsi, traditional overlords of Ruanda and Burundi, of the Bacwezi, overlords of western Uganda and north-west Tanzania from about AD 1300 to 1500 and of the Luo in north-eastern Uganda and western Kenya. These stories of invasion or immigration occur more than 1,000 years after, and in the case of the Luo in Kenya 1,800 years after the earlier Bantu migration into this part of Africa.

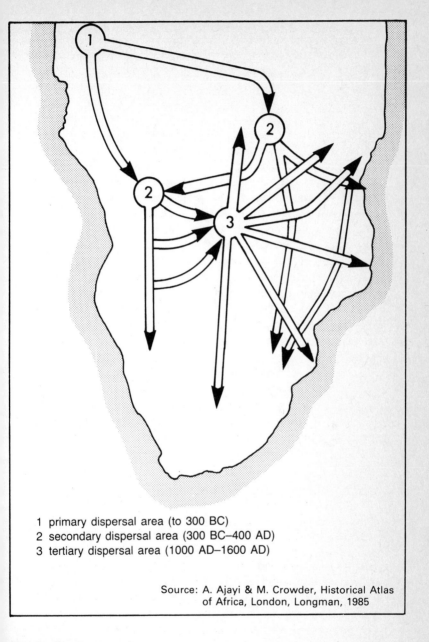

1 primary dispersal area (to 300 BC)
2 secondary dispersal area (300 BC–400 AD)
3 tertiary dispersal area (1000 AD–1600 AD)

Source: A. Ajayi & M. Crowder, Historical Atlas
of Africa, London, Longman, 1985

Map 1   Bantu expansion

MOVEMENT OF SEED AND CROPS

The Bantu expansion was sustained by a continuous adoption of new crops, notably those introduced to the African continent by the Indonesians who settled Madagascar 1,500 years ago. These crops included bananas, Asian yams, cocoyam, and sugar cane. In a few areas the planting of combinations of these introduced crops was to be the key to the areas of high population density such as Ruanda, Kilimanjaro, the Zambezi Valley and possibly Ibo-land in southern Nigeria where farming systems had developed capable of sustaining 2–300 people per square mile, but which were not typical of Africa as a whole.

A subsequent addition to the possible combination of crops was the introduction from South America by the Portuguese of cassava and maize in the fifteenth and sixteenth centuries. These crops spread fairly rapidly, although their major impact was not to be until the late nineteenth and early twentieth century when both crops expanded very rapidly in the savannah zones of eastern and southern Africa, and the forest zones of western Africa respectively.

The folklore of Bantu-speaking people is full of stories of migration which confirm the archaeological and linguistic record. The Chewa are a people of eastern Zambia, but according to their traditions they came from a country called Urua somewhere to the west or north-west of Lake Tanganyika. Their legends say:

When the land for cultivation became too small for the people they used to find other gardens nearby. Therefore there was not enough good and fertile soil for all the different tribes. Because of that, Karonga and Undi, leaders of the Mulavi tribe, led their people out to the east and arrived at Nyanja Ya Malawi [the 'Lake of Flames', Lake Tanganyika].

They formed a new focus of settlement by the Lake of Flames, and then, when all the fertile land in the neighborhood had been occupied, the ancestors of the

Chewa and Senga moved out and travelled southward along the shores of Lake Nyasa to their present homes in the Eastern Province of [Zambia]. There, according to the story, they took the land from a small people – presumably of bushman or pygmoid stock – who were living entirely by hunting and collecting wild produce.[6]

But such folklore tells not only of the movement of people, as the availability of land necessitated, but also of the movement of the seeds of new crops.

The Lamba who live near the copperbelt of Northern Rhodesia have such a legend. Long ago they say there were few Lamba and they had no proper food; they ate mostly wild fruits, leaves, and roots, and whatever else they could gather in the bush. Then a stranger came to live among the Lamba 'a superior man' called Chipimbi, who brought with him seeds of maize, sorghum, groundnuts, and other crops unknown in Lambaland. Chipimbi did not come alone; his household came with him and his sister Kawanda Shimanjemanje and her household. The crops they brought to the Lamba were not known in Chipimbi's own country, which lay somewhere to the west of Lambaland. Kawanda Shimanjemanje was something of a traveller; she and her son had been to Lubaland on the Lualuba River where they had seen the great variety of crops grown by the Luba people, and by a stratagem obtained seeds of all of them. With this seed Chipimbi and his household planted gardens in Lambaland and gave food to the people. This, says the legend – or, rather, one version of it – was the beginning of Lamba agriculture and also of the institution of chieftaincy; for Chipimbi, the giver of food, became the first of their chiefs.[7]

MOVEMENT OF PEOPLES IN WEST AFRICA

One of the few identifiable factors underlying the move-

ment of people in west Africa has been the fluctuating
aridity of the Sahara and the Sahel. The last geological
phase in which the Sahara could be occupied as a result of
higher levels of moisture was between 12,000 and 8,000
years ago;[8] the reversion to a very dry climate in the
Sahara increased the pressure for some southward migration of those peoples who had been occupying parts of its
centre and south. However, this was not a determining
factor in the subsequent peopling of west Africa. In fact,
while historians have in the past sought to assign northern
and eastern origins to, for instance, the Yoruba (in their
case even specifically to the Yemen) current linguistic
findings indicate that the groups of people in southern
Nigeria who lie between the Yoruba and the Ibo have been
close to their present habitat for at least 6,000 years.

> These findings seem to indicate a process of slow,
> steady population expansion and cultural differenti-
> ation, beginning some thousands of years ago in the
> area of the Niger/Benue confluence, and continuing
> with little external interruption right down to the
> nineteenth century. They also suggest that, if current
> dates given for the foundation of the great dynasties of
> Yoruba, Benin and Igala are anything like correct,
> population expansion and cultural differentiation were
> largely completed by the time these dynasties arrived
> on the scene.[9]

An exception to this general uncertainty about the origins
of west African peoples are the Fulani or Fulbe peoples.
While their ethnic origins are almost certainly the result of
mixing between Berber peoples from the Sahara and the
negro inhabitants of the Sene-Gambia, their language is
part of the Congo-Kordofanian language family with its
roots firmly in black Africa. However the Fulani were not
absorbed by any of the political systems which grew up in
the western *sudan* (such as the 'states' of Ghana, Mali and
Songhay) but retained their identity as semi-nomadic
pastoralists living from their large herds of livestock. By

this means they were able to expand throughout the savannah zone of west Africa between the twelfth and nineteenth centuries spreading as far west as present-day Cameroun. In the course of this expansion many Fulani adopted a settled way of life, became strong adherents of Islam and through *jihad* (obligatory holy war) established reformist Islamic states. In spite of this extensive migration, and of social and political miscegenation, the Fulani remain very conscious of their own identity accentuated both by close association with cattle, and by the racial (i.e. caucasoid) appearance of their truly nomadic members.

THE LEGACY

The key characteristic of the pattern of human settlement in Africa is the constant splitting off of small groups of families from an extended family or clan to found units in new, if adjacent, geographical areas. The process was accentuated where the migrant group had access to improved agricultural technology which enabled its members to compete effectively with the existing inhabitants, if any. Once the 'carrying capacity' of the new environment had been met, the offspring of the migrants would be obliged to move on and repeat the establishment of a new social nucleus. Whether or not the migrants inter-married with the inhabitants of the area into which they moved, social loyalties developed within a relatively small group, and the consequence of this constant pattern of outward migration was to reinforce rather than reduce clan loyalties. Further, this process occurred within each of the major language families and their sub-divisions, generating a complex web of clan loyalties and antagonisms which remain very much alive today.

The Bantu expansion was the seminal event in the history of eastern and southern Africa until the colonial period of the late nineteenth century. It explains why there is such a strong common cultural heritage between many apparently distant African peoples within this language family, which is expressed in common forms of religion and in a common understanding of the supernatural.

As a result the composition today of the people of Africa can perhaps best be seen as a series of geological strata in which the bottom layers consist of the earliest migrants, and the higher strata consist of the various subsequent migrants. In some cases living evidence of the composition of the earliest layers (for instance, the hunter-gatherers who pre-dated the Bantu in eastern Africa) is almost non-existent. But nearly everywhere the pattern exists of a complex series of strata of people whose internal tensions and conflicts arise partly from the history of their individual migrations, which were sometimes simultaneous, more often sequential and usually competitive. This pattern is perhaps not so different to eleventh-century Britain, with Celt, Viking, Anglo-Saxon and Norman ethnic interests to reconcile, but such reconciliations do not admit of easy political solutions. Thus the death of Mboya and the imprisonment of Oginga Odinga, both outsiders to the dominant Kikuyu clans in Kenya, illustrate the price which Africa is paying in finding such solutions.

3
Patterns of Allegiance

The migration of peoples from west Africa was under-pinned, as we have seen, by kinship loyalties, which were exemplified by the clan. It now needs to be examined how such kinship loyalties expressed themselves, how they were reinforced, and how they grew outwards from the immediate family to the clan, or in some cases, to a chief or even a tribe. Clans led by chiefs were the earliest manifestation of incipient 'political' systems in Africa, and it is therefore instructive to see how loyalty from one chief was transferred on his death to another. This 'problem' of succession, as we shall see in later chapters, dogs the political systems of most, if not all, of African states today.

THE FAMILY AND CLAN: PAST, PRESENT AND FUTURE

The family was more than its contemporary members: people identified themselves first of all with their living relatives, secondly with their dead ancestors, and thirdly with their unborn children. This association with the past, present and future family widened into the clan as a result of the physical subdivision of families. Such separate lines then became the principal objects of individual loyalty, and 'tribes' were comprised of groups of lineage lines. The term 'tribe', however was introduced by the colonial powers, mainly as a term of convenience which frequently gave greater definition to a group of clans than the clan members actually experienced. Tribes were in reality groups of clans who might be gaining the adhesion of one clan, just as they were losing another.

Countervailing lines of loyalty were often fostered within and between different lineage lines: for instance, amongst the Asanti an individual joined his mother's clan but nonetheless belonged to his father's spirit (ntoro) group. Amongst the Kikuyu and many other east African tribes individuals were initiated at puberty into age sets that cut across family groups. The Nyakyusa of southern Tanzania developed a system whereby young boys at ten to eleven years established the nuclei of completely new villages which were physically separate to those of their fathers, and which might include children from adjacent 'mature' villages. Once every generation, power was handed from mature to junior villages and land was completely redistributed.

The clan system was thus the ideal vehicle for fostering loyalties within a social group laying claim to an area of land which was new to them. 'I am because we are; and since we are, therefore I am'[1] is an adage which had reality in a situation where survival on a frontier was an individual's overriding objective. Once frontiers had been conquered, and where populations became more dense, clan loyalties were retained but became intertwined with other, balancing, loyalties to other clans in the same area.

In African societies today, the clan loyalties which are the result of this long history of 'pioneering' are very much alive, albeit balanced by loyalties to God (Christian, Islamic and ancestral), to lineage lines which intersect with those of the immediate clan, to the modern state and to self-interest. Where states were created in African history, such as those of Ghana or Songhay, they did not create loyalties which were stronger than clan loyalties, but used them to build the state. Superficially, clan loyalties were conformist and depended heavily on ritual as a means of ensuring loyalty. In practice the pioneering dimension of African history has always been vitally important, and it has given African society the ability both to exploit continually new areas for cultivation and to be open to new forms of culture, such as Islam and Christianity. So clan loyalties were crucial but seldom so conservative as to prevent change when it was necessary (when land was exhausted), or opportune (when in the interest of trade).

The clan, then, was the lodestar to most past generations in Africa. While it was far from being a unique African institution it has survived more intact in Africa than in other parts of the world. It went hand in hand with a system of power which encouraged conformity and maintained a high regard for hierarchy, but was also characterized by ambivalence rooted in 'superstition', and was dogged by an inability to transfer power smoothly from one leader to another. It was flexible enough to allow individuals constantly to hive off and found the nuclei of new clans, and sometimes to allow the formation of the intricate coalitions of clans which became the great states of pre-colonial Africa.

RITUAL AND RELIGION

Most African peoples had a view of God as the Supreme Being and creator of the universe, and as the source of a life force which permeated the natural world. This force could work for good or ill and could be embodied in both animate and inanimate objects. Men could tap into it through intermediaries such as magicians and sorcerers, and through direct or indirect contact with ancestors. After creating the universe, God had shown the ancestors how to live in it: under his direction they had successfully devised

a farming system which enabled the community to sustain
life. The maintenance of the system depended on the God-
given rules being followed, so that life could be sustained
for the unborn as well as the born. Breaking the rules
disrupted the system and offended the ancestors.

This awareness of the ancestors, especially of those who
could still be remembered, as guardians of the clan's
welfare, was one of the clan's links with God. They were
directly relevant to everyday life and the co-operation of
their spirits was necessary to the material and social
welfare of the family. Following a quarrel within the
family, a traditional Kikuyu prayer ran, 'Spirit of our
ancestors, do not be angry, we give you back the words we
spoke'.[2] The wish of the ancestors, as living entities, was
sufficient reason for a certain course of action to be
justified.

There was, therefore, a very close relationship between
people's religious beliefs and everyday practical affairs,
including farming practice. The problems faced by African
communities in developing the systems which would
enable them to survive as they pushed back the frontier of
cultivation were complex. Systems were only developed by
trial and error. Once a new system had been developed it
became the 'received wisdom', was given the stamp of
ancestral approval, and was duly ritualized.

While lines of loyalty always included the dead, the
living and the unborn, they were often drawn in addition
towards a chief of the clan or tribe or state. There was a
major division between those communities which allowed
such a centralizing force to control them, and those which
remained essentially segmentary. The chief provided a
point of convergence and reinforcement of people's beliefs
rather than a new point of departure for them. 'Kith and
kin', past, present and future, remained the key to
individuals' loyalties, although the office of chief acquired
mystical power and great political authority.

Traditional ritual thus often integrated the role of the
chief with behaviour sanctioned by ancestors and thereby
with the practices necessary to sustain life. In societies

without unifying chiefs, the ancestors themselves served as the guardians of traditional practices. Deviation from them alienated the individual from his community, his chief, and his ancestors and might cause the life force emanating from God to work to his disadvantage and potentially to the disadvantage of the whole community.

In its most dramatic form such ritualization could (and can) be seen in the *kuomboka* ceremony of the Lozi of western Zambia. The agricultural system of the Lozi depends on the sequential grazing of the flood plain of the Zambezi with the higher ground which is still available when the river is in flood. Every year in February or March, at the time of the rising flood, the *litunga* (paramount chief) leads his people in a long procession of canoes from his main palace in the flood plain at Lealui to his summer palace on the higher ground at Mongu ten miles away. This *kuomboka* ceremony is the symbolic high point of the Lozi year. It attributes to the *litunga* the folk wisdom derived from the long process of communal experimentation which enabled the Lozi farming system, which when fully intact was very sophisticated, to be developed.

In his survey of traditional African beliefs, John Mbiti describes the role of the chiefs as follows:

> Where these rulers are found they are not simply political heads: they are the mystical and religious heads, the divine symbol of their people's health and welfare. The individuals as such may not have outstanding talents or abilities, but their office is the link between human rule and spiritual government. They are therefore divine or sacral rulers, the shadow or reflection of God's rule in the Universe . . .
>
> People consider kings to be holy, mainly in a ritual rather than a spiritual sense, and they must therefore speak well of them, respect them, bow or kneel before them, let them have sexual rights over their wives, pay them taxes and dues, obey them, refrain from copying their clothes or coming into direct contact with

them, and even render them acts of reverence and obeisance.[3]

The connection between the office of chief and the values of the community was often represented by a physical symbol such as the royal stool of the Asante or the magical drum of the Kingdom of Ankole. The latter was believed to link the contemporary Banyankole to the founders of the kingdom, and to represent the values embodied in the royal office. The drum acquired a parallel mystique and attacted similar loyalty to the monarchy itself.

Concern with ancestral spirits manifested itself on the one hand in a very practical view of personal morality, and on the other hand in an intensive practice of ritual, designed to achieve practical results. The former assumed that an individual's morality could only be judged by its impact on the community by what he did or did not do. There was, for instance, no place for the sin of *coveting* another's wife or property, so long as this remained in the mind. Social education was geared largely to teaching children the right behaviour in relation to other individuals within the hierarchy of the family and clan. 'Correct' behaviour would preserve harmony within the community and secure the approval of the ancestral spirits. In ancestor-based religions there was no sense of the search for personal spiritual uplift central, for instance, to Christianity and Islam, although such a search became a major facet of Islamic movements in west Africa, particularly from the eighteenth century onwards.

Ritual is important because it gives individuals a sense of belonging. it reached its high point in many African societies in the initiation ceremonies associated with puberty. In the case of boys this usually involved circumcision, and in the case of girls it often involved clitoridectomy, an operation which later received a major assault from Christian missionaries (but was accepted by Islam). These ceremonies were the most profound experience for adolescents and their completion a source of joy to the whole community. Camara Laye, in the autobiography of his early years in northern Guinea in the late 1930s, 'L'Enfant Noir', describes the atmosphere of celebration:

> As soon as the operation was over, the guns were fired. Our mothers, our relatives in the compounds heard the reports. And while we were being made to sit on the stone in front of us, messengers rushed away, tore through the bush to announce the happy news, arriving bathed in sweat and gasping for breath, so much so that they could hardly deliver their message to the family that came running to meet them.[4]

Each repetition of the ceremony served to renew society's sense of itself and of its own worth.

While ritual could be both mystical and joyful, its effect was believed to be to attract towards the object of the ritual some of the supernatural power prevalent in the universe. Thus in the course of his investiture, a new chief would be raised from the status of an ordinary individual to one having divine powers, an effect particularly achieved by identifying him very closely with the ancestors. The paradox of this ritualism, however, was that its goal remained very mundane: that society should continue to satisfy its basic needs. The Asante used to pray to one of their gods:

> Drobo, the edges of the year have met. The chief has given you yams, he has given you a sheep, he has given you eggs, and now he has brought this drink. Let the tribe prosper; may the women bear children; do not let our children die; those who have gone to trade, may they get money; may there be peace during the present chief's reign.[5]

Thus the deities played a very practical role in the life of the community, and their assistance had to be sought by practical means, so that a kind of 'practical mysticism' characterized everyday life.

WITCHCRAFT AND MAGIC

Operating on a different level to chiefly power, but with equally important consequences for the individual, was the process of reasoning itself and the attribution of responsibility. Almost any event was thought to have a secondary or tertiary cause. A simple example of this would be the conclusion that rain fell because God willed it to fall, because the rainmakers had prayed in the approved manner. It was believed that a physical fact had an ulterior explanation, and consequently nothing happened by accident. The ulterior explanation usually lay in the view that some of the life force at work in the universe had been channelled into the community through the aid of a local priest, healer, or sorcerer. As a consequence, almost any human fortune or misfortune, even where it could be clearly attributed to strength or weakness of character, was in fact attributed to the intervention of wizardry. Such sorcerers might well not be full time practitioners; the offended party in a personal dispute, especially where community practice supported him or her, might well invoke sorcery to redress the case, and might be considered justified in doing so.

The importance of this approach to causation is particularly clear from its application to death, which has been very clearly described by John Mbiti as follows:

> every human death is thought to have external causes. By far the commonest cause is thought to be magic, sorcery and witchcraft. This is found in every African society, though with varying degrees of emphasis; and someone is often blamed for using this method to cause the death of another. . . The curse is something greatly feared in many societies, and a powerful curse is believed to bring death to the person concerned. Even when God may be seen as the ultimate cause of death, other intermediary agents may be brought into the picture to satisfy people's suspicions and provide a scapegoat . . . This means that, although death is

acknowledged as having come into the world and remained there ever since, it is unnatural and preventable on the personal level because it is always caused by another agent. If that individual did not cause it, then the individual would not die.[6]

This approach to causative explanation is complex, and had an internal logic of its own which is very different to the processes of European thought, at least since the eighteenth century. It is also based on a high degree of exposure to observed phenomena which contemporary Africans find it difficult to explain, not least in the controversial area of extra-sensory perception. However, the fact that this approach assumed a high degree of supernatural intervention should not be used to suggest that its processes were in any way less complex than those of western logic. The number of variables it assumed as relevant to a particular problem might be quite as numerous as in a western explanation, and the level of 'intelligence' required for problem solving was no less great. Its consequence, however, was to create within communities an atmosphere of suspicion and intrigue, abetted by the effective absence of a formal judicial system. Thus the very closeness of the ties of obligation and duty which bound people to each other made it extremely difficult to redress perceived wrongs, and provided a fertile ground for wizardry as a means of redressing them. Further, because communities were largely closed societies, any individual who believed himself to be the object of wizardry could lay the blame at the door only of one of his neighbours. Thus a vicious circle was created which might demand permanent defensive tactics. Amongst the waChagga, for example:

> ways of harming people secretly included depositing witchcraft substance in or near their homesteads. Precautions against such attacks included planting boundary fences of 'dracaena' which because of the connection between the plant and the dead ancestors afforded some supernatural protection.[7]

The net effect of the tradition of mutual obligation, linked to the atmosphere of intrigue and suspicion, created a sense of ambivalence in which many things were not quite what they seemed to be. This sense of ambivalence continues to inform African political and social life today.

Within traditional society it was reflected in the complexity of lineage loyalties, in the prevalence of overlapping secret societies, and in the approach to the problem of the succession to chieftainships. Lineage loyalties, as we have seen, could be as complex in segmentary, as in centralized, societies. For instance, the Nuer of southern Sudan:

> have contrived to find ways of integrating descent lines so that relatively large numbers of Nuer can if necessary act together. They have got round the difficulty caused by exogamous marriage rules – which suppose rivalry to the point of warfare between major descent lines – by mixing up their major lines or 'segments'. A Nuer village or group of villages never contains only one descent line . . . but is dominated by a single descent line living in amity with members of other lines. So that while large groupings of Nuer may be in 'chartered opposition' to each other, the area of peaceful cohabitation has become steadily enlarged.[8]

Thus in many societies it was common to find that loyalty to the clan in which one lived was balanced by a countervailing loyalty to a different clan.

Clan loyalty could also be balanced by loyalty to an age set (as with the Kikuyu) or a paternal spirit group (as with the Asante). It might, in addition, be balanced by loyalty to one of the secret societies which were particularly prevalent in west Africa. Such societies had different characteristics and different functions. For the most part, however, they were concerned with the enforcement of custom and promotion of the welfare of the community. Mary Kingsley, a diligent observer of west Africa in the early 1890s, wrote in 1897 that:

every tribe has its secret society. The Poorah of Sierra Leone, the Oru of Lagos, the Egbo of Calabar, the Yasi of the Igalwa, the Ukuku of the M'pongwe, the Ikun of the Bakele, and the Lukuku of the Bachilangi, are some of the most powerful secret societies of the West African Coast. These secret societies are not essentially religious, their action is mainly judicial, and their particular presiding spirit is not a god or devil in our sense of the word.

However, Kingsley went on to say that many men (and there were societies for women too) joined more than one society including the 'leopard' societies. Some of these societies she described as:

> practically murder societies, and their practices usually include cannibalism, which is not an essential part of the rites of the great tribal societies, Yasi or Egbo. In the Calabar district I was informed by natives that there was a society of which the last entered member has to provide for the entertainment of the other members, the body of a relative of his own, and sacrificial cannibalism is always breaking out, or perhaps I should say being discovered, by the white authorities in the Niger Delta.[9]

Such organizations clearly exerted a major pull on their members' loyalties, notwithstanding the fact that those loyalties were divided.

This division of loyalties, and the associated spirit of ambivalence, frequently resulted in a strategy of 'trading-off' competing loyalties, and a recognition that while a certain course of action may be consistent with one set of loyalties it may be inconsistent with others. This ambivalence is then a form of risk insurance, the psychological roots of which lie in a recognition of the competing influences within the spirit world, and a deep rooted sense that any one course of action may be subverted by hostile forces outside the immediate physical world.

THE HIERARCHY IN PRACTICE

What was it like to live in communities like this? The best evidence from oral history and from earlier accounts is that it was intolerant of the individual, strictly hierarchical, obsessed with the supernatural, and very conscious of the proximity of death.

'Go the way that many people go; if you go alone you will have reason to lament,' say the Lozi, and they speak for many other societies. The individual's relationship to the community was defined primarily by obligations and not by rights; he existed to fulfil a defined social role. Farming was for the most part an activity in which families were interdependent and the principal activities were carried out on a timetable which was followed for the whole community. Society was structured on a hierarchical basis in a number of different ways: among age groups, within marriage, and in relation to chiefs. The authority system derived from this was complex and left almost no scope for individuality in the western sense. It gave great power, often unlimited, to those in senior positions in relation to those in junior positions:

> Never, or rarely, does a person or being of a higher status do what constitutes an offence against a person of a lower status. What is considered evil or offensive functions from a lower level to a higher level ... something is considered to be evil not because of its intrinsic nature, but by virtue of who does it to whom and from which level of status.[10]

Of course a higher level of status was attributed to husbands than to wives, and it was a social imperative for wives to obey their husbands in all respects, and to accept beatings, 'justified' or otherwise. The maintenance of this subordinate, wifely position was reinforced, rather than subverted, both by the fear of sterility and sickly children and by the pressure of peer groups as the following anecdote from the Nyakyusa illustrates:

It is said that when a wife has sworn at her husband in secret her child grows thin. Or perhaps if she has sworn at him openly, or at her mother-in-law, or her husband's father's sister, then when her own mothers come to see her they are shocked.
They say: 'Why is this child so thin?'
She replies: 'I don't know'.
Mothers: 'You have sworn at your husband'.
'No'.
They beat her and tell her to admit it.
At length she confesses: 'Indeed, I did swear at my husband'.
They take the child to a doctor to get medicine.[11]

Polygamous marriage was common, and within such marriages a strict order of seniority among wives was followed: the senior wife and the 'favourite' might achieve a rewarding relationship with the husband but for the others this was unlikely as another Nyakyusa comment, from the 1930s, illustrates:

One is the favourite, and another also loved, but the others are just rubbish, they are beaten much and can do nothing about it.[12]

In addition to the extreme subordination of that half of the population which entered marriage as wives, there was often the additional subordination to chiefs and kings. Following the rituals which made them the conduit of divine power, such chiefs commonly set themselves apart and did not appear in public as ordinary men. Their consequent powers were indeed great. For example, among the Bemba of northern Zambia the *chitumukulu* (paramount chief) possessed rights over his people's labour; rights to certain monopolies in trade with the Arabs such as ivory tusks, gum and cloth; the right to enslave some of his own people; and the right to inflict savage mutilation on those who had offended him. It was said amongst the Bemba in the 1930s, and with reference to previous generations, that the royal family had been named after the crocodile because 'they are like crocodiles that seize hold of the common people and tear them to bits with their teeth'.[13] These formidable rights were nonetheless maintained with a great deal of mysticism and secrecy. The advisory council of the *chitumukulu* always met in secret and until the early twentieth century spoke an arcane language distinct from that spoken by the Bemba common man.

THE PROBLEM OF SUCCESSION

Chiefly succession provided a problem for traditional society which it solved in many different ways often reflecting its widespread spirit of ambivalence.

Examples from two societies of present-day Zambia, the Lozi and the Bemba, reflect this. The Lozi 'are apparently terrified of giving away power and always think of the dual pressures and the ambivalence of power on an individual'.[14] For this reason the senior minister of the *litunga* was designated the *ngambela* and his chief responsibility was to restrain the *litunga* from the misuse of power. Remarkably, a second *ngambela* was appointed to monitor the first to ensure that he, too, did not misuse his power. Such a system applied to all positions involving responsibility in Lozi life. In the case of the Bemba the evidence comes from a remark of great significance recorded by the pioneering student of the Bemba, Audrey Richards, in 1935. She reports the *chitumukulu* as saying:

> I am not afraid of my 'bakabilo' (senior council) now because I know the bwanas listen to me and not to them.[15]

Apparently fear of his own counsellors had been as much a part of the world view of the *chitumukulu*, as fear of the *chitumukulu* was for his own people.

The question of the succession itself was dramatized by the need to end the life of a chief when his powers were failing. Such intervention was necessary since the chief's most important role was to intervene with the ancestors, or directly with God, to ensure the prosperity of his community. A chief failing in his powers would be unable to do this. Thus in the Kingdom of Ankole when sickness or age brought on debility the *mugabe* (the senior chief, effectively king) took poison prepared by his own magicians. Amongst the Nyakyusa it was held that the chief must die 'with the breath in his body' and an ailing chief was accordingly smothered or 'snuffed out' by his senior headmen and priests. The last such recorded smothering was in 1924.

In other societies succession was determined by violence even if approved by unwritten constitutional practice. Among the Ankole, once the *mugabe* had taken poison, or died from some other cause, the succession was determined by a period of fighting between his sons which might last as long as a year. During this period, in order to maintain continuity in the office of kingship, an *ekyihumba* (temporary king) was appointed. Having succeeded in slaying his brother contestants for the throne, the *mugabe*-elect then slew the *ekyihumba* and took over the office of kingship. Consequently, the key figures at court were the king's mother and sister since there were no brothers left, and they had the power to veto his judicial decisions. His mother also had the important duty of making offerings to the ghosts of the princes whom the king had killed, a practice which confirmed a sense of the precariousness of power and the continuing possibility of the invasion into this life of the spirits of the recently dead.

The succession question remained an issue which African societies found it difficult to resolve, and which was most successfully tackled in the Islamic states of west Africa. Outside these states, although the approach to the succession differed widely, it nearly always involved intrigue and violence, albeit of a licensed form.

4
States Beyond the Clan

For many centuries Africa has had its own political
systems which have not only emerged from the framework
of clan allegiances, but have moreover been expanded and
consolidated. These systems cannot be labelled 'states' in
any modern sense of the term, but they certainly shared
some of the characteristics of states as we know them
today. They have variously included: a central authority,
definable frontiers, a bureaucracy, a subject people, a
common culture, and, albeit more rarely, a recognized
system for passing power from one leader to another.

However, even at their height these 'states' were
basically the product of dominant groups within dominant
clans, who by one method or another succeeded in forming
an amalgamation of like-minded clans, frequently linked
by family relationships. The position of the dominant group
was built on and reinforced by its ability to control long
distance trade, and in the west African savannah to use
Islam both as a resource (in facilitating trade with the
Mediterranean) and as a unifying ideology. This underlying structure implied certain key weaknesses which go
some way to explaining the fact that not one of the major
states was able to maintain its most extended frontier for

more than a century and a half – although we cannot assess to what extent Asante and Sokoto would have consolidated their position in the absence of the British invasion.

The 'states' of eastern, central and southern Africa were smaller in area than those of West Africa and were not directly influenced by Islam. However, they were to a greater or lesser degree influenced by their connections with the east African coast where the culture of the Swahili trading ports was predominantly Muslim. The dominant fact in the peopling of these parts of Africa was the Bantu expansion, and this ensured that a clan system was at the base of the social structure in this part of the continent.

In examining how close African societies came to substituting a wider loyalty system for the narrower one of the clan, we shall look at some of the more important 'states' to emerge from these African political systems.

EMPIRES OF GOLD

The empires of the western *sudan*, Ghana, Mali and Songhay, flourished between AD 900 and 1600: in the case of Ghana between AD 900 and 1170; in Mali from AD 1250 to 1400; and in Songhay from AD 1460 to 1590. Ghana, strung between the Senegal and Niger Rivers, encompassed an area of about half a million square kilometres; Mali commanded a larger area of about 2 million square kilometres from the Atlantic Coast to the northern bend of the Niger at Gao. Songhay controlled the same area but extended it further west towards, but not including, the Hausa states of Nigeria.

A good deal is known about these states through the writing of contemporary Islamic scholars such as the Andalusian al-Bakri (writing on Ghana in 1067), and the peripatetic Ibn Battuta who visited Mali at the height of its power. Their accounts and other evidence suggest that at their base the empires comprised scattered village communities, each largely of one lineage line or clan. Such

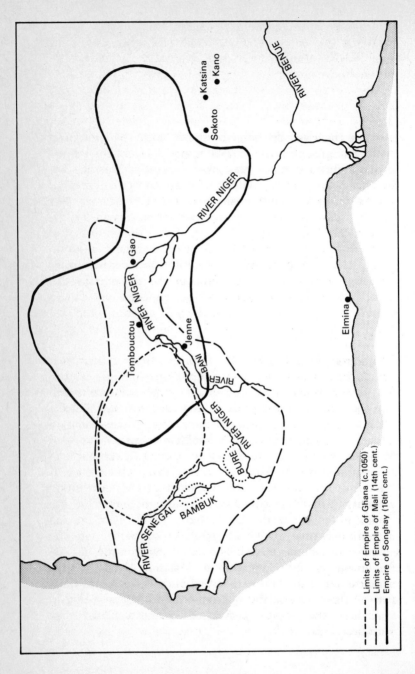

Map 2 Empires of Gold

- - - - - Limits of Empire of Ghana (c.1050)
- - - Limits of Empire of Mali (14th cent.)
———— Empire of Songhay (16th cent.)

communities were initially grouped in a federation of clans speaking the same language and practising the same religion. Eventually one clan was able to assert its authority over others, and establish a right to tribute.

Ghana

Because the rise of Ghana coincided with the growth of the trans-Saharan trade in gold, mined south of the empire on the higher reaches of the River Senegal, it was possible for the Soninke rulers of Ghana to extract substantial wealth from the gold trade and so to reinforce their material position. This was further strengthened by the presence of Muslim traders and scholars in the state capital (probably at Kumbi Saleh, close to the border of contemporary Mauritania and Mali), some of whom also acted as interpreters, treasurers and ministers to the empire.[1] In spite of this Muslim influence, a king such as Tunka Menin, ruling at the time of Al Bakri's account, practised the Soninke people's pagan faith sustained by a group of palace sorcerers.

Ghana benefited for most of its existence from direct contact with Islam and hence with the dominant culture both of the Middle East and much of the Mediterranean. However, during the period of its strength it remained a 'state' of the Soninke people dependent upon the common culture of its constituent clans. While its position at one of the southern extremes of the Islamic world was a source of material and political strength for most of its existence, it was also the source of its downfall. The Almoravid movement, an off-shoot of the dominant force in the expansion of Islam in the Mahgreb and Spain in the eleventh century, was ultimately responsible for the conquest of Ghana (probably in 1077) and for the forcible conversion of its leadership to Islam. Although this conquest was short-lived (the Almoravid leader Abu Bakr died in 1087) Ghana did not regain its historic strength, which had always depended on one group of clans – the Soninke themselves.

Mali

By the time the empire of Mali (so named after the
Malinke people) filled the vacuum left by the fall of Ghana
and other, smaller, successor states, the trade network of
the Islamic world was even stronger. From the eleventh
century onwards gold from west Africa was essential to the
coinage of the European and Islamic states. Mali was even
more effective at taking advantage of this than had been
Ghana, as the major gold field of Bure on the upper Niger
came to replace that of Bambuk on the Senegal, and Bure
was an integral part of the empire of Mali. Furthermore,
through control of the port of Jenne on the River Bani, a
tributary of the Niger, Mali controlled the trade route to
the Akan goldfields in the forests further south. The kings
and those close to the court in Mali embraced Islam, which
had the important characteristic of being an integrating
religion, capable of overcoming the cultural divides between the peoples over whom they ruled. However, Islam
frequently coexisted with many local cults, and the empire
of Mali is also best seen as a confederation of clans whose
allegiance was partly to the centre but largely to traditional lineage lines.

A state organized on this geographical scale, twice the
area of Spain, could not fail to impress those who observed
it. Both Timbuktu and Gao, key points on the trans-
Saharan trade routes and centres of learning, were
incorporated within the empire. The visit of Mali's greatest
king, Mansa Musa, to Cairo *en route* to the pilgrimage at
Mecca in 1324 was noted as a major event of the year by
contemporary writers in Cairo – particularly because of his
largesse in the distribution of gold.

The detailed history of Mali indicates that while at its
peak it controlled many non-Malinke peoples the monarchy
passed from one branch of the founding Keyta dynasty to
another, and the core of the empire remained firmly
Malinke – so much so that the sons of vassal kings, both
Malinke and non-Malinke, were held at court as hostages.
Mali held together as an entity only during the fourteenth

century and eventually fell apart through the weakness of its later monarchs, allowing local affiliations to resume their basic strength.

Songhay

One of the constituent peoples of the empire of Ghana had been the Songhay from Gao on the northern bend of the River Niger, who were to form the nucleus of the most powerful of the three western-*sudan*ic empires. Songhay's power dates from the 1450s and the campaigns of the founder of the empire – Sunni Sulayman – who pushed the boundaries of the state westwards. These campaigns, and those of his immediate successor, Sunni Ali Ber, created a state in which the majority of people were non-Songhay, and which, like Ghana, maintained close and formal relations with the Islamic world.

However, all the *askias* or kings of Songhay after Sulayman and Ali Ber, for the subsequent 200 years, were the descendants of Alhaj Muhamed I, a general who usurped power from Sulayman's founding dynasty.

> Many of the most important offices of state were held by the Askia's family, and when a new Askia came to power he would often re-distribute the key offices to favour those brothers he was closest to and trusted.[2]

At its apex Songhay was a family oligarchy, and a highly effective one.

Its close links with the Islamic world proved to be its undoing when, following a long standing disagreement centering on the salt mine of Taghaza (much closer to Morocco than Songhay), it was invaded by the Moroccans in 1590. The invading force of 4,000 men, through its possession of muskets and gunpowder, beat the Songhay force of 30–40,000 cavalry decisively. The *Askia* Ishaq II fled, and the Moroccans established a series of puppet *askias*, but the empire dissolved in their hands over the next seventy years. By 1660, the Friday prayer in the mosque at Timbuktu was said not for the Moroccan sovereign but for the local 'Basha'.

POLITICS AND THE PROPHET

The most sophisticated political achievement of the followers of Islam in west Africa was the alliance of Hausa and Fulani states in northern Nigeria, welded together and controlled throughout the nineteenth century by the Caliphate of Sokoto, situated about 150 miles west of Kano. The Hausa states of northern Nigeria have their origins in the kingdoms established by the Mbau peoples who were the earliest occupants of the Nigerian savannah. To the west, the Mbau people had as their dominant neighbour the empire of Songhay and to the east the state of Kanem, superseded in the fourteenth century by Bornu.

From the fifteenth century onwards the Mbau kingdoms were increasingly drawn into west African trade since the area had significant deposits of gold, silver, iron and tin. Control of trade enabled the kings to acquire greater surpluses and so to increase the size of the area they ruled over, and the range of peoples under them.

As in other societies of the west African savannah, the introduction of Islam into the Mbau kingdoms was closely tied to the growth of trade with the Mediterranean. The traders promoted not only their wares but also their faith, and those rulers whose position depended on trade frequently found Islam attractive. The first of the major Mbau rulers to adopt Islam was that of Kano, probably in the late fourteenth century, followed by Katsina in the late fifteenth century. From this time until the eighteenth century, the Islam adopted by the ruling houses coexisted with variants of the older traditional cults, to which the majority of country people continued to belong. Consequently, and no doubt in order to bridge the gap between the faiths, the older pagan rites were frequently practised at court.

However, *realpolitik* was not the only motivation of those rulers who were the first to adopt Islam: Sarki Umar, Emir

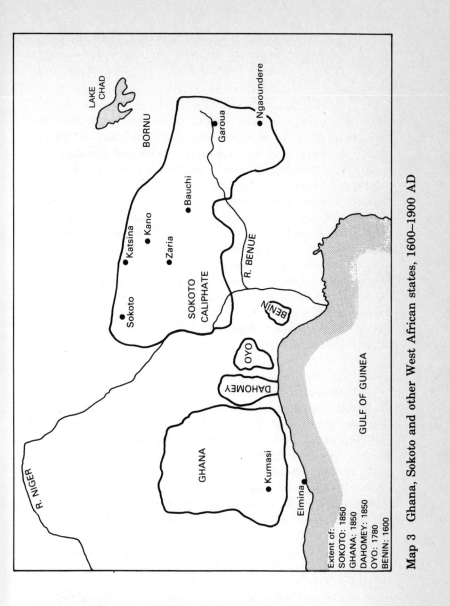

Map 3　Ghana, Sokoto and other West African states, 1600–1900 AD

of Kano from AD 1410 to 1421, is reported to have abdicated from a sense of piety.[3] The asceticism which inspired such a decision was fuelled by the evangelism of itinerant Muslim scholars, Arab, Berber, and Fulani, who had direct contact with the centres of Islamic learning at Timbuktu and Gao. They were to be a constant influence in the next three and half centuries, operating both at court and from bases in the countryside which were centres of debate and reflection, and provided the formative influence on many evangelists. By the seventeenth and eighteenth centuries major centres such as that at Birnin Gazargamo (100 miles west of Lake Chad) and hundreds of smaller ones maintained a steady output of books of both a discursive and propagandist kind, which had the effect of greatly increasing popular awareness of Islamic teachings.

As such awareness grew, tension also grew between those who wished to see Islam govern everyday life, and the supporters of the status quo represented by most of the ruling houses. The reformists called for the introduction and strict enforcement of sharia law and in particular for the ending of illegal taxation and usury. The conviction grew that it was impossible to be a true Muslim while subjected to non-Muslim laws – a familiar position in the late twentieth century.

The Fulani played a particular role in this context. Although they had been present in the Mbau and Hausa states since the fifteenth century, and individual Fulani had played an important role in most of the state governments, they retained a separate identity with their base in the countryside rather than in the towns. They were well placed in every sense to serve as the shock troops of reform.

The Sokoto Caliphate

Uthman dan Fudiye, born in 1754 in the Sultanate of Gobir about 200 miles north-west of Kano, provided the charismatic leadership which carried the cry for reform to open revolt. Dan Fudiye had spent most of his young adulthood in several of the rural centres of Islamic learning found in Gobir and neighbouring states. By the time he was forty, he had established his own centre both for his large extended family and numerous Islamic scholars. From this base he consistently criticized the ruling Sultan of Gobir, calling for reform of government to correspond with the sharia.

The clash was eventually so severe that Dan Fudiye (now 'the Shaikh') became committed in 1804 to military action or *jihad* against the Sultan. In this campaign, as in later ones, he was supported by numerous local Emirs as well as those Fulani clans to whom he, and his closest associates, were connected by marriage. The early phases of the campaign were not decisive and the Shaikh and his followers were obliged to embark on a *hijira* (flight) which in the course of 1804–5 took them through Gobir and neighbouring territory. The final battle with the Sultan was on a considerable scale. In the course of it, the Shaikh lost 2,000 men, of whom 200 knew the Koran by heart.[4]

Following this decisive victory, Dan Fudiye established an Islamic society at Sokoto, on the borders of Gobir, which at that time was sparsely populated. This society was established on the basis of an interpretation of the earliest Islamic community in eighth- and ninth-century Arabia. Dan Fudiye became its first Caliph and he was succeeded in 1817 by his eldest son and military commander, Muhammed Bello. The regime was able to maintain its authority throughout the nineteenth century, until the British invasion of 1902. In order to ensure the security of the state, Bello specifically promoted the settlement of previously migrant Fulani clans, not least on the grounds that it was easier to maintain sharia law in a semi-urban community, and established frontier forts manned by young men brought up in the scholastic atmosphere of the Shaikh's camps.

However, the greatest achievement of the Sokoto Caliphate was in its impact on the other Hausa and Hausa-Fulani states which came to accept the suzerainty of Sokoto to a greater or lesser degree. This was manifest in the fact that the Sokoto Caliph established the right to approve the Emirs of other states and to depose them. For instance, two Emirs of Zaria, Sambo and Abdullah, were held at different times on the estate of the Caliph's vizier (effectively prime minister) in Sokoto, the first having been held in chains. Even more significantly, the Emirs accepted the call by Sokoto to an annual *jihad*, the justification of which was an expansion of the boundaries of the Islamic states, or the curbing of a local rebellion within Sokoto. An additional, and perhaps even more important objective, was the taking of large numbers of pagan slaves who were put to work on the farms of the ruling elite in the Emirates, a key source of revenue since most forms of taxation had been outlawed. The first four caliphs after Dan Fudiye sent out eight major military expeditions from 1817–66. Hugh Clapperton, the earliest European observer of Hausaland, recorded accompanying an army on *jihad* in 1829 which was 50,000 strong.[5]

Yet this commitment to religious warfare was matched by a continuing insistence on piety and humility, maintained until the end of the century and beyond. The traveller, W. Wallace, when he first saw the Caliph's vizier Muhamed Bukhari, found him

seated on a mat placed on the mud floor of the small house he occupied in Kano, quietly studying, through a pair of large horn rimmed spectacles, an Arabic manuscript. It struck me as a curious contrast to see him sitting in the darkened house without kingly garments or the least sign of state, while within a few hundred yards the Emir of the province of Kano was seated on embroidered robes on a gaudy throne, and was surrounded by a courtly retinue dressed in all the tawdry imitation of eastern courts.[6]

In fact, the leaders of the Caliphate, their associated scholars and several of their wives maintained a steady output of books on religious practice, of histories and of

poetry, written in any of the three current languages
(Arabic, Fulani and Hausa), on Italian paper imported
across the Sahara. The poems of the early leaders of the
Caliphate are today learned by children by rote, and are
regular features on the radio.

The success of Dan Fudiye's interpretation of Islam
permeating the Hausa states is testament to the extent of
the tension between reformists and supporters of the status
quo in the later part of the eighteenth century, and to the
preparedness of people for a stronger interpretation of the
faith. The leading historian of the Caliphate, Dr Murray
Last, has written that:

> the universal nature of the Law, having an existence
> and validity separate from the Caliphate gave Sokoto
> the power it did not have militarily. Emirs outside
> Sokoto respected this Law, and obeyed Sokoto as
> established under it. Thus the armies of the subor-
> dinate Emirs could be relied upon to fight the wars of
> Sokoto against anyone who could justifiably be called a
> rebel. Clearly it was in the interests of the subordinate
> Emirs to maintain the status quo – it gave their
> position the same universal legality which the cali-
> phate possessed.[7]

However, it needs to be examined whether the Sokoto
Caliphate, notwithstanding its brilliant political and religious achievement, really established a loyalty system
which transcended lineage and clan. Since the majority of
people in the Caliphate were Hausa, the non-Fulani
obviously played a major role within it. However, at its
inception the Caliphate was a Fulani achievement, and in
1812 of a list of eight key Emirs named by Muhammed
Bello, seven were Fulani. In Sokoto itself, as the controlling centre of the Caliphate, Fulani power depended on
four Fulani clans – Konni, Kebbi, Sullebawa, and Alikawa.
A few individuals, such as the first vizier Gidado, had links
by marriage with several or all of the clans; more

commonly marriages were within clans. Although the Caliphate did not pass from father to son, but was determined by agreement within a ruling council, a prime consideration for succession was closeness of descent from the Shaikh. Key functions, such as political relations with the major Emirates, tended to be kept within specific families on a hereditary basis.

Once established, the Caliphate was essentially an authoritarian regime whose objective was to improve the observance of Islam, including that practised by the nomadic Fulani, and to eliminate the pagan traditions which had been handed down from the earlier Mbau cults. In slave raiding expeditions, pagan men were frequently put to death and women and children carried off as slaves, so that the next generation could be brought up in the faith. Slavery was partly justified on the grounds that it facilitated the urban settlement of the nomadic Fulani by providing a pool of agricultural slave labour, thus freeing the Fulani to spend more time on religious observance. The Caliphate was, then, a highly structured theocratic society with the norms of correct behaviour interpreted by a relatively small group of informed Islamic scholars and men of government, most of whom were closely related.

The power of the Caliphate collapsed in 1902 when the British army fought with the Caliph's troops outside the walls of Sokoto. The infinitely superior fire power of the British ensured that the battle was quickly won. Although the Caliph Attahiru 1 immediately fled the city, his vizier and other senior members of the government remained. Ultimately they accepted British suzerainty on the grounds that they had lost to a military power of much greater strength, and that the freedom to observe Islam had been guaranteed, though not the right to *jihad*.

RECONCILING CLAN AND KING

There are several instances in both west and east Africa where a centralized kingdom was instituted despite the strength of competing clans. The power invested in the king varied according to the political culture of each clan system. In Asante we can see the successful reconciliation of strong allegiance to particular lineage lines with an underpinning loyalty to a central authority. In Benin and Dahomey we see a succession of dynamic leaders using a despotic power to subdue subordinate clans. In Buganda, in contrast, the power invested in the king was developed by careful consensus and supported by the beginnings of a bureaucracy.

The Asante

In contrast with the orientation of Sokoto to the Arab world, the Kingdom of Asante, gaining strength throughout the eighteenth century, looked primarily to the markets of the Ghanaian coast and thus to the rising economic powers of northern Europe. Furthermore, its military confrontation with Britain had been recurrent from 1823 to 1896 and the Asante leadership was more aware than Sokoto of the threat of military subjugation, although there were major differences within the leadership about the appropriate reaction to the threat.[8]

The Asante kingdom grew as a result of the movement northwards of Kwamaan people in the seventeenth century and earlier, from an area about 100 kilometres south of the future Asante capital of Kumase. Its formal inception in 1701 followed a series of battles against the original inhabitants, the Dyenkira, with whom the Kwamaan immigrants had originally co-existed. From the start, Asante was in formal communication with the European powers: the Dutch on the Gold Coast attached an Ambassador in 1701 to the first king or *Asantehene*, Osei Tutu. The Asante kingdom quickly became a state built on commerce as it had within its territory, which steadily expanded through the eighteenth century, sufficient gold to employ several thousand prospectors. Some of these were Asante farmers and some were slaves. The latter were critical to the Asante economy since a large number of the prisoners of war captured in territorial expansion were

exported as slaves to the slaving centres at Elmina, and
Accra; and other 'tied' labour was imported from further
north. In return, the Asante merchants purchased guns
and gunpowder, commodities not available in quantity to
the Hausa states. In 1748, the Danes at Christiansbourg
Castle in Accra reported that 2,000 Asante merchants had
in that year come to buy weapons in return for slaves and
ivory.[9]

The combination of military and commercial strength
enabled the Asante state to control an area which
corresponds to most of present-day Ghana and included
parts of neighbouring Ivory Coast and Togo. In the second
part of the eighteenth century the *asantehene*, in a series of
administrative and military reforms, adapted government
to these new and wide-ranging responsibilities, though not
without the resistance of those Kwamaan pioneers who had
helped to overwhelm the indigenous Dyenkira, and who
had nominally been granted autonomous status by the first
asantehene. The state's economic strength was derived both
from tribute sent by the conquered districts (although this
was frequently irregular, depending upon whether pro- or
anti-Asante factions were in power), and from attracting a
part of the surplus generated by the gold and slave
trades.[10]

Although the strategy of the *asantehene* and their closest
advisers from the late eighteenth century was to build a
centralized state, the underlying bonds of loyalty within
Asante society remained those of kinship. K.A. Busia has
described each lineage line as a political unit which had
(and indeed still has) its own headman who represented it
on what became the governing body of the clan. A district
chief was drawn from a particular lineage by the heads of
the other lineages, a system which in theory enabled
lineage lines to live together without abandoning the prior
claims of kinship. The commemoration of ancestors,
common to several lineages, linked them together. Consequently, the installation of a chief, and particularly the
asantehene, was designed to identify him closely with the
ancestors. In policing the state his authority:

took cognisance only of offences which endangered the good relations between the community and the ancestors and gods, for the maintenance of those relations was deemed essential for the well being of the community.[11]

The loyalty system implied by the paramountcy of lineage lines in a range of African societies, including Asante, was discussed in Chapter 3. The concern here is to confirm that the major political, military and commercial achievement that the Asante kingdom comprised was consistent with the primacy of lineage. The genius of Asante was to develop a political system which enabled an integration of potentially conflicting loyalties in the personality of the *asantehene*. But the spirit underlying this genius remained strictly among the lineages of Asante people and, by definition, could hardly have extended to a majority of the three to four million people – including the many slaves – who were ultimately embraced by the kingdom.

Benin and Dahomey

The principles on which the Asante kingdom was established had parallels in other states between the Volta and the Niger Delta, and in particular in the kingdoms of Dahomey and the Yoruba. The original nucleus of states which formed the basic units of the Yoruba kingdoms, including the largest, Oyo, were

based on an association of patrilineages to one or other of which the individual's allegiance lay. At the same time there was an elaborate system of institutions which cut across lineage boundaries and provided for the conduct of the affairs of the whole community. At the head of the system there was a figure whose office we may call that of 'king' provided we recognise that he was more a symbol of community unity than the holder of real power.[12]

The welding together of such small societies into the larger political entities of Ife, Oyo, Ijeba and Benin, which was more or less complete by 1400, was achieved by a dynamic leader from one group of clans subduing groups of others. In the resulting states of the Yoruba heartland, succession to the leadership was passed fairly regularly between the various related lineages, and constrained by an influential council. However, in the case of Benin, the king was able to assume despotic power with all the chief offices of state in his personal gift, and with primogeniture established as the principle determinant of the succession. Similarly, in Dahomey the king achieved or acquired comparable despotic status. In these two cases, at the apex of the system, an individual despotism came to replace a power that was dependent on the balance between lineages, but it did not replace the strength of kinship loyalties at the local level.

Bunyoro and Buganda

Our knowledge of the kingdoms between Lakes Albert and Victoria is derived almost entirely from oral tradition and archaeology since there are no written accounts until the nineteenth century. However, the oral history of this area is not only abundant but is considered reliable over a period covering the past 500 years. It is also considered to provide a reasonable sketch of events beyond that period. The history revealed by these traditions is one in which the Bantu peoples settled in the area from about 2,000 years ago, and were in turn the subject of several waves of invasion.

These were initially of unknown origin: the first wave of cattle-keeping invaders (the Batumbezi) achieved dominance from about AD 1000 to 1200, and the second (the Bacwezi) from about AD 1350 to 1500. Oral history attaches considerable mystique to the Bacwezi in particular ('You could not look them in the face, because their eyes were so bright that it hurt your own eyes to look at them, for it was like looking at the sun').[13] However, their

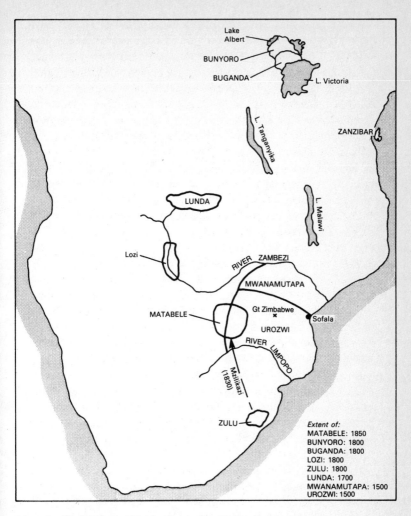

Map 4   Kingdoms of East, Central and Southern Africa, 1600–1900 AD

hegemony lasted only 100–150 years, after which they mysteriously departed under the leadership of their last king, Wamara, apparently suffering conditions of major political or ecological misfortune.[14] Their dominant position in Bunyoro was taken by a group of Luo peoples (the Babito), speakers of a Nilotic language from southern Sudan, who had first reached the area of what is now northern Uganda in AD 1300 and some of whom went on to colonize western Kenya in the sixteenth century.

The hegemony established by the Babito peoples lasted until well into the twentieth century, their kingdom evolving into the Bunyoro of the colonial period. However, in the course of that three-hundred-year period, profound changes occurred in the state, as the Bunyoro of AD 1900 was only about one-third of the size it had been at the height of its power. Initially the Babito were simply another group of immigrants, who as both farmers and cattle keepers, were able to find a niche within the local economy. Later, and while retaining their identity, they were able to set up a dynasty which remained purely Luo until the late eighteenth century. Subsequently, the Babito elite and the indigenous Bahuma intermarried, and by this time a system of agricultural tribute had been established which facilitated the emergence of a governing class, although this remained Babito-dominated. The process underlying this development included more competition for land, a series of disastrous droughts, and more or less continuous frontier fighting.

From the fifteenth century onwards the nucleus of the state of Buganda, at one time incorporated in the Bunyoro empire, established its autonomy and came to absorb most of the land which Bunyoro lost. The major expansion took place from the 1650s, accelerating in the eighteenth century. Although Buganda never comprised more than about 60,000 square kilometres – about one-tenth of the Asante kingdom – it had an effective political structure. Until the late sixteenth century the king, or *kabaka*, had been no more than the head of one of the Muganda clans who, like the *asantehene*, was the focus of his clan's

political and religious allegiance. From the time of the
Kabaka Katerega, from 1584–1614, the *kabakas* came to
appoint district rulers from among those who had served
them well in expanding Buganda's frontiers, rather than
from among recognized clan leaders.[15] Furthermore, the
principle of a royal clan was effectively abandoned, as each
clan became eligible to present the *kabakah* with suitable
girls, and the successor *kabakah* was chosen from among
the offspring. As a result, most clans had a vested interest
in a strong *kabaka*-ship, and in the welfare of Buganda as
an entity. On the other hand, competition between the
princes for the succession was frequently intense and
violent, and the outcome was inevitably linked to the
strength of the clan of the mother of a particular prince.

The fact that district rulers were appointed directly by
the *kabakas* caused an increasing concentration of power
within their court, and in the course of the eighteenth
century the *kabakas* became increasingly despotic. At that
time the incessant border wars, and the successful
expansion of Buganda's frontiers (notably at the expense of
Bunyoro), enabled the *kabakas* to reward their people with
generous booty – in both slaves and goods. However as this
rate of expansion slowed down in the nineteenth century,
and as the kingdom from the 1850s, was increasingly
influenced by its contacts with Arabs and Europeans, these
constitutional arrangements proved unstable. In the last
two decades of the century the clan chiefs re-asserted their
powers at the expense of the three *kabakas* (Mwanga II,
Kiwewa, and Kalema) who ruled from 1879–1906. The
leading muGanda historian of Buganda has written that,
until this time:

It would have been a most unusual development if the
Buganda took up arms against the king to promote
democratic government for they did not normally
promote sedition. Before the 1880s there is no record
. . . of either a popular uprising to mark the advance of
political enthusiasm, or the consciousness of social
injustice. All evidence suggests that if the Buganda

wanted to get rid of an unpopular ruler their only weapon was to support a rival candidate for the throne.[16]

The political system developed by the Buganda had similarities to that of Asante: the clan system continued to be the key to people's immediate allegiance, but it was reconciled with a broader allegiance to a king who was king of many clans. By abandoning the principle of a 'royal clan', from which kings must be chosen, Buganda established a means by which the king could be the king of all of the Buganda people, if not of their subject peoples. Further, by developing a system of appointees as district or 'county' rulers the *kabakas* pioneered a form of centralized, or bureaucratic, government which was far removed from that which was common within the clan system.

POWER-HOUSES OF THE SOUTH

Great Zimbabwe: a merchant priesthood

Further south, the greatest achievement in state building was in the inter-related states of Urozwi and Mwana-mutapa, both of which have their origins in the Bantu-speaking Shona people. The migration of the Shona into present-day southern Zimbabwe occurred between AD 1100 and 1300. By the fifteenth century one of the Shona clans, the Rozwi, whose leaders were surrounded by a strong religious mystique, was able to mobilize the Karanga group of Shona clans to secure dominance over an area from Sofala on the coast to a point about 400 miles up the Zambezi River.

The gold and copper mines of Great Zimbabwe had been worked since before AD 1000. There are over a thousand ancient tunnels and shafts into gold-bearing deposits[17] which are associated with this period. In addition, over the same period there has been a developed trade in ivory, some of which originated amongst the San people of the Kalahari desert. The trading system which handled these products was well developed by the late tenth century: its products were carried to the coast by herders, and then shipped by the Swahili coastal peoples from centres such as Sofala and Kilwa to entrepôt ports in the Middle East. The Shona in its heyday succeeded in gaining control of this trade.

The greatest achievement of the Urozwi kingdom was the construction of the series of stone buildings at Great Zimbabwe. Their design and construction evolved over time, and resulted from a wider tradition of building in stone practised elsewhere in Zimbabwe by the Shona. The first examples of Great Zimbabwe itself are from the eleventh century; the most elaborate examples are from the fourteenth and early fifteenth centuries.[18] The later buildings are clearly a much more sophisticated version of the first. Their thirty-foot-high exterior wall is a monument to the skills of Urozwi's builders, and to the ability of Urozwi society to mobilize an economic surplus. The design of the buildings, and Shona oral tradition, strongly suggest that a major part of their function was religious, as well as defensive. Archaeological finds at the site also confirm its importance as a centre of trade, of exports in gold and copper, of imports of beads and of glass from the Near East, and of Chinese and Persian pottery. It is very likely that at Great Zimbabwe the Bantu tradition, combining religious and political power, was linked much more strongly than in other communities of the Bantu diaspora to control of a trading network.

Around AD 1500 a dynastic struggle caused the Rozwi kingdom to split into two parts, the northern part of which became Mwanamutapa. In the course of the sixteenth century the Portuguese eventually wrested control of the trade in Mwanamutapa from the Shona and, at the coast, from the Swahili, reversing the flow of gold from the Middle East to Europe via the Cape of Good Hope. In pursuance of this trade the Portuguese continuously harried the state of Mwanamutapa, eventually reducing it in the nineteenth century to little more than a slaving estate, and a key source of slaves destined for Brazil.

To the south, Urozwi retained autonomy under its king, the *changamire*, who continued to rule from Great Zimbabwe. This kingdom held together until the Ngoni invasions of the 1820s. While the detailed organization of the Urozi state is not fully known, oral traditions confirm that its organization fell into the general pattern of a closely-related small ruling group, maintaining the loyalty of other karanga clans by a combination of religious mystique and self-interest. This coalition of clans exercised effective control over non-Shona indigenous peoples widely known as Tonga, and usually regarded with contempt; some non-Shona people were incorporated into a system of domestic slavery.

The scale of these kingdoms, and of others in the region such as that of Kongo in present-day Angola and of Lunda in present-day Zaire, was small in absolute terms and in comparison to those of west Africa. In comparison to Buganda's maximum of 60,000 sq km, Urozwi's suzerainty extended over about 100,000 sq km, or an area with a diameter of about 320 km. While Buganda and Urozwi may have had the internal strength to expand further they were both destroyed by outside powers: in the case of Buganda by the British occupation in the 1890s; and Urozwi by the fighting Nguni armies which swarmed over the country from the 1820s onwards, triggered by the campaigns of Shaka Zulu further south.

Nation-building in Zululand

Shaka was a dynamic, almost possessed leader of the Zulu, whose campaigns and institutional innovations had a domino effect far outside the Zulu heartland in Natal. It stretched as far to the north-east as Tanganyika, and as far to the north-west as the Zambezi floodplain in western Zambia.

At the time of Shaka's birth, in the late eighteenth century, the Zulu were a relatively minor clan amongst the Nguni, a Bantu people who had arrived in Natal several generations previously. By the 1790s, acute pressure on land had created a situation of endemic conflict between Nguni clans, in the course of which there had been substantial changes in their social structure. Among these was a modification of initiation rites. It had become necessary to incorporate teenage boys in military age sets before the process of initiation had run its course in order to have the maximum complement of fighting men on hand.[19]

One of those involved in the struggle for paramountcy between the three major factions of the Nguni was Dingiswayo, to whom Shaka's clan owed allegiance. Around 1815 Shaka, the son of a Zulu chief who had been brought up mainly by his mother, established his claim to the chieftainship of his clan by killing the heir apparent, and pledging stronger support to Dingiswayo. In order to make this effective he reinforced the changes which had already occurred in the formation of age sets, by transferring their command to himself, and to his immediate military leaders or *indunas*, thereby taking them away from the traditional clan leaders.

The resulting military command structure proved highly effective and Shaka became Dingiswayo's key ally. Following the latter's death in a battle in 1818, Shaka took over his position of leadership, and was then so successful that he extended the kingdom to embrace many other clans. From these, the young men were integrated into the age sets under central command, and allocated to the royal households, each detailed to a military settlement. In a scheme of social engineering reminiscent of Alexander the Great, girls were also allocated to parallel age sets, and were married *en masse* to an age set of boys when the latter had completed their military service.

By 1826 this military machine had proved so effective that Shaka had overcome all significant rivals within the Nguni, and dominated an area of about 150,000 sq km – about one quarter of the Asante empire at its peak. However, following the death of his mother in 1828, Shaka indulged in a stream of apparent madnesses which were

both self-indulgent and cruel, many of which were witnessed first-hand by the British traders resident at the
royal kraal. In response, he was murdered in 1830 by two
of his brothers, and his most trusted *induna* Mbopha. This
triumvirate was, however, short-lived, and one of the
brothers, Dingane, succeeded in killing the other two
conspirators and taking the throne.

Dingane was not successful in maintaining the boundaries of Shaka's empire, which in the course of the
previous twenty years of warfare had seen several groups
of Nguni, under experienced military leaders, take large
fighting columns of men out of Natal and into Mozambique,
Tanganyika and Zimbabwe. The most significant of these
leaders was Mzilikazi, whose Ndebele warriors occupied
Matabeleland in south-western Zimbabwe in the late 1830s.
Developing his own variant of Shaka's model, Mzilikazi
used the system of regiments of age sets to merge his own
people with the Sotho, also immigrants from the south,
and with the indigenous Shona. Military age sets comprised
young men from all three groups, and the new state came
to be organized around their settlements.

The Ndebele experience, and its antecedent in Zululand,
was a rare and successful example of a deliberate blending
of peoples. However, Mzilikazi was not able to complete the
process, and many of the indigenous Shona were never
integrated in the military settlements. Neither did he
succeed in establishing a system of succession since his own
successor, Lobengula, was accepted as chief only at the cost
of civil war. Nonetheless the experience of the Ndebele,
and of the other pioneering Nguni groups, might have
proved the start of a genuine nation building tradition,
escaping the limitations of lineage, if government by the
European colonial powers had not been established throughout the area of settlement within another two generations.

THE PARAMOUNTCY OF LINEAGE

At the base, then, of the great states of pre-colonial Africa
was a system of loyalties which centred on the clans of the

dominant peoples within each of the states. These clans were held together in coalitions either by common consent, or by force, with an ill-defined border line between the two. Such coalitions nearly always existed as a group which dominated other peoples within the state.

The 'empires of gold' – Ghana, Mali and Songhay – owed their strength to the fact that they were indispensable to the supply of gold to the Mediterranean world. But the Soninke, Malinke and Songhay peoples who created them kept control firmly within the grasp of a small number of leading clans, even though the Songhay state embraced a majority of non-Songhay people. The Sokoto Caliphate came close to building a federal system of states of equal strength, acknowledging the 'moral sway' of Sokoto and accepting its leadership. However, within Sokoto itself power was never devolved outside four Fulani clans; everywhere the Caliphate depended on a subdued class of non-Fulani, and on a large underclass of slaves, who would never be accepted into full citizenship.

The kingdom of Asante was bound together more tightly than the Caliphate, and its intricate political arrangements succeeded in reconciling loyalty to the clan with a loyalty to the *asantehene*, which transcended clan. However the wealth which sustained the state was derived from subject peoples throughout much of present-day Ghana, and it is doubtful if the state had the will to absorb non-Ashanti other than as subject peoples. The restraints which existed on the *asantehene* did not constrain the rulers of Benin and Dahomey, where primogeniture was established as the principle of succession, but within the framework of individual lineage lines.

Bunyoro, as one example of the former 'kingdoms' of Uganda, was the product of an elite of immigrants who were successful in both dominating the original indigenous population, and in ensuring its loyalty through intermarriage. However, power was retained by the dominant immigrants, whose prime allegiance remained to lineage lines. Buganda, as a second case from Uganda, was very different, and by the eighteenth century the *kabaka* had acquired powers which enabled him to appoint district chiefs and maintain a standing royal household. This was an embryonic bureaucratic government, and one in which the court 'was intimately linked by bonds of matrimony or office with every single clan in the country'.[20]

Further south, in present-day Zimbabwe and Mozambique, the Urozwi kingdom integrated trade, religion and political authority in a way which was unusual within the Bantu diaspora. However, real power within the Karanga group of Shona clans rested with the Rozwi clan from whom the *changamire* was selected. But even loyalty within the Karangas was limited, and breakaway kingdoms were a frequent occurrence. It was in the Nguni wars of the late eighteenth and early nineteenth centuries that a deliberate effort was made to develop viable alternatives to the clan system, specifically by Shaka and Mzilikazi. But, as with the Sokoto Caliphate, the European occupation prevented the full development of these early experiences in nation building. As a result, when the colonial states were turned into independent states after eighty years of European rule, the focus of loyalty for most African peoples remained that of the clan.

5
The Colonial Impact

Africa did not fall to the colonialists without a struggle and some of the early wars of resistance from the 1880s onwards were bloody for both sides. The French conquest of Senegal and Mali was brutal and evoked a sometimes heroic response from leaders such as Samori Turay. The destruction of the Asante Kingdom required a number of British campaigns – Sir Garnet Wolsey's campaign of 1884 met a deserted capital of Kumasi which was shortly reoccupied by the *asantehene*. The Germans faced major resistance in south-west Africa and the gruelling 'Maji Maji' war in central Tanzania from 1905–7. In southern Rhodesia the British South Africa Company, having dispossessed Africans of land and cattle throughout Matebeleland from 1893 to 1895 faced an effective revolt by combined Matebele and Shona forces from 1896 to 1898.

By the First World War, however, nearly all Africa was under not only the nominal but also the effective control of the colonial powers. The experience of such bloody resistance as occurred was to emphasize the apparent invincibility of the European powers, an effect achieved primarily through access to vastly superior firearms, and to a lesser extent through the fascination of consumer goods and the mystique of the written word. Confronted with this reality, the rapid establishment from the 1920s onwards of key western institutions in the fields of law, education and agriculture created great conflicts within African society, the legacy of which suffuses Africa today. These conflicts were triggered by the European administrators and missionaries who in the first decades of the colonial period adopted a stance of rejection of the social and cultural values which they confronted. In the case of the British, this is largely in contrast to their attitude in, say, India. Consequently, to 'progress' within the colonial state, younger Africans had to accept the new values, or face the prospect of rural stagnation.

THE RELIGIONS DIVIDE

Few of the early European missionaries and administrators accepted the existence of a consistent African philosophy or set of philosophies (such as that described in Chapter 3). Practices which appeared savage, such as human sacrifice, or the abandonment and effective murder of twin babies, were allowed completely to obscure the possibility of an underlying idea. Mary Kingsley was particularly conscious of this problem and wrote in 1897:

> The bad effects that have arisen from their |i.e. the Protestant English missionaries| teaching have come primarily from the failure of the missionary to recognise the difference between the African and themselves as being a difference not of degree but of kind.[1]

Writing forty years later and with reference to the Kikuyu, half a continent away, Jomo Kenyatta, expressed this even more strongly:

> While a European can learn something of the externals of African life, its system of kinship and

classification, its peculiar art and picturesque ceremonial, he may still not have reached the heart of the
problem . . . he fails to understand the African with his
instinctive tendencies (no doubt very like his own), but
trained from his earliest days to habitual ideas,
inhibitions and forms of self expression which have
been handed down from one generation to another and
which are foreign, if not absurd, to the European in
Africa.[2]

The primary message of Christianity in Africa, as elsewhere, was one of individual 'becoming', rather than
collective 'belonging', and it could not fail to take its new
adherents a considerable and very disruptive distance from
their spiritual roots.

By contrast, in both west and east Africa, Islam
demonstrated a remarkable ability to coexist with traditional religion including its taboos and spirit worship.
African Islamic societies retain many elements of tribal
religion such as divination, witchcraft, spirits, and an
awareness of the ancestors. Thus both Islam and the Coptic
Christianity of Ethiopia, which also drew heavily on earlier
traditions, had a very different effect to the Christianity
which was introduced into Africa from the late nineteenth
century. After the initial 'forced' conversion of Ghana to
Islam by the Almoravids, Islam and the Coptic faith were
introduced at the discretion of the leaders of the time,
rather than at the instigation of outsiders.

The crucial factor in the introduction of Christianity was
its synchronization first with trade activities and then with
colonization. Those Africans who believed that their best
strategy was to co-operate with the traders and colonizers
found it politic to convert to Christianity and to receive the
educational benefits associated with the missions. The
consequent dilemma for them as individuals lay in their
relationship with the traditional power structure of society,
which was spiritually ordained, blessed by the ancestors
and held the keys to society's agricultural success or
failure. This was also a dilemma for the colonizing powers,

particularly the British and the French, who frequently sought to promote the principle of indirect rule and so to rule through traditional chiefs.

This is well illustrated by an official report on the Asante area in Ghana in 1905 which indicates that the chiefs resented the alienation of Christian converts from their community, and their refusal to perform ordinary services to their chief. In 1912 a committee consisting of the Governor of the Gold Coast, the Chief Commissioner, three other colonial officials and representatives of the missions then working in Asante attempted to resolve the conflict by ruling:

> No Christian shall be called upon to perform any fetish rites or service, but shall be bound to render customary service to his chief on ceremonial occasions when no element of fetish practice is involved.[3]

This was an attempt to bridge the unbridgeable: to hold a mass without the eucharist. The whole point of such ceremonial occasions was the symbolism which invoked the assistance of supernatural powers; no colonial mandate could turn them into purely secular occasions. Writing forty-one years later in 1953 Kofi Busia could comment:

> many Ashanti Christians join in the Adae celebrations and . . . share a sense of dependence on the ancestors . . . for the Ashanti to a large extent still retain their own interpretation of the universe and of the nature of men and society; and the difference between this and the European interpretation of the same phenomena constitutes the fundamental conflict between the Ashanti and the European way of life.[4]

From 1900 to 1930 and later the same processes were at work in many parts of non Islamic Africa, manifesting themselves in many different ways. We have seen that Nyakyusa and Ngonde society renewed itself by forming

new villages built up from nuclei of young men set apart
from mature society. Eventually the latter ceded most of its
ground to the former, and its chief was eventually 'snuffed
out'. By the 1930s, such cell-like division and renewal by
age sets had been buffeted by a number of different factors,
but particularly by the preference of Christians for living
together as a community *within* villages. The implication
of this was much more than a decision to pray together to
the Christian God: it cut across the whole basis of
traditional land usage and mutual responsibility.

Among the Kikuyu, as previously noted, clitoridectomy
was a central part of the ritual which confirmed girls at
puberty in their role within society, 'the *sine qua non* of the
whole teaching of tribal law, religion and morality'.[5] In the
1920s the Church of Scotland sought to ban it altogether
among its members. This was too great a departure for the
Kikuyu from everything they held sacred and it coincided
with increasing appropriation of land for white settlement.
Consequently, in 1929, some Christian Kikuyu established
the Independent Kikuyu and Karenga schools, the families
of whose members were specifically allowed to maintain
the practice of clitoridectomy. The combined effect of the
forced annexation of land, the conversion of significant
numbers to Christianity, and the introduction of many new
rules by the colonial Government was:

> a welter of disturbing influences, rules and sanctions,
> whose net result is only that a Gikuyu does not know
> what he may or may not, ought or ought not, to do or
> believe, but which leaves him in no doubt at all about
> having broken the original morality of his people.[6]

THE NEW COMMERCE

Of course these changes in men's minds were being shaped
not only by the impact of missionary education and colonial
authority but also by fundamental changes in the productive system. These were a by-product of changes in the
international trading system shaped largely by the

economic hegemony of the colonial powers. Apart from
the appropriation of land in Kenya, Rhodesia, the Congo,
Mozambique, Angola and South Africa the two key
innovations in the early colonial period were cash crops
and mining, with the consequent development of labour
migration. Exchange and barter trade had, as is implied by
the trade in slaves and gold, existed for many centuries,
but the introduction of the minted coins of the colonial
powers implied a radical change to a completely different
order. This was a reality brought home to people even in
the years before the First World War when the principle of
a poll tax was introduced by many colonial governments.
Chiefs, specially created in the segmentary societies where
none had previously existed, became the main means of
collecting such taxes.

The demands of the new situation have been very
effectively summarized by William Allan, once a Director
of Agriculture in Northern Rhodesia:

> Money was necessary to pay the tax imposed on every
> able bodied man, and rigorously collected against
> threat of fine or imprisonment; and, later, more money
> was needed for the satisfaction of new wants. It had to
> be earned by wage labour where work was available,
> or by the sale of subsistence food production where
> markets offered, or by growing industrial cash crops
> where these were introduced by the new masters.
> These changes did not come easily and were at first
> resisted. In many cases volunteer labour for the new
> economies had to be supplemented by arbitrary con-
> scription, not only for public works but for mines,
> plantations and farms, and there are few areas in
> Africa where industrial cash crops have been estab-
> lished without some measure of coercion, open or
> disguised. The ultimate acceptance of this money
> economy and new standard of values, grafted on to the
> old forms of social organisation and land rights, was to
> create unforeseen agrarian problems which have been
> intensified and rendered almost despairingly difficult

[by the 1960s] by the comparatively recent upward surge of populations.[7]

In some states, such as Uganda, Sudan, and Ghana, new cash crops were spectacularly successful in an economic sense by about the late 1930s and in each of these colonies the local leadership (the chiefs of Buganda, and the merchant class of Khartoum in Sudan and Cape Coast in Ghana) had played a key role in encouraging the introduction of cotton or cocoa. In other colonies cash crops were much more difficult to introduce since they could only be planted in the same short time interval available for the planting of food crops, and so led to a reduction in the availability of subsistence foodstuffs. Whether their introduction was easy or difficult the cash crops caused a revolution in family and clan relationships.

The role of land in the life of the community changed from the means by which, in association with the ancestors and the gods, the welfare of the community was assured and for which cultivation systems were laid down in communal ritual, to the means by which individuals could feed their family, pay their taxes to the colonial state and acquire the first tranche of manufactured consumer goods. Older Nyakyusa men, reflecting in the 1930s on the rapidly disappearing traditional system of cultivation remembered it in the following way:

Great stress was laid on keeping in step in cultivation, no man starting to burn his rubbish in a millet field ahead of his neighbours, no women planting before her neighbours or lagging behind them.[8]

Such a co-operative approach to production became increasingly rare from the 1930s as the pressures and opportunities created by cash crops were realized. Monica Wilson observed developments amongst the Nyakyusa and Ngonde at periodic intervals from the 1930s to the 1970s, creating a fascinating and perhaps unique record of change

in a particular community over such a long period. In her
work 'Of Men and Elders', she concludes that the amount of
food available per person fell from the 1930s to the 1950s
partly for the following reasons:

> by 1934 the Nyakyusa population had begun to
> increase fast and cash crops were established. Up to
> 1938 land was plentiful and cattle were normally in
> excellent condition as photographs at that date show.
> By 1955 the population had increased, and the demand
> for land for cash crops had grown even faster. There
> was still unoccupied bush land in the middle region,
> but pastures in Selya and Bukubwe were visibly
> shrinking and what in 1938 had been all pasture grass
> was reduced to stubble.[9]

By the 1960s land was even scarcer and it had become
family rather than village property; by this time, too, a
landless class had emerged, and immigrants into the area
were no longer welcome.

But cash crop farming was not the only major innovation
among the Nyakyusa and many other comparable communities. The demands of the international trading system
also ensured from the first years of this century, especially
in central and southern Africa, that the development of
mining was a major colonial objective. Labour migration to
meet the needs of this new market, and to pay taxes, added
a further major change to the structure of village life. The
gold mines of South Africa, and the copper mines of
northern Rhodesia drew able-bodied men from northern
Malawi and south-western Tanzania at a very fast rate. In
a sample of twenty-four villages taken in 1937 within 5
miles of Karonga on the Lake Malawi plain, an area from
which many men worked as labour migrants, the proportion of men to women was 80:100. In Rungwe District
(home of the Nyakyusa) in 1954 14,000 men, or 25 per cent
of the total, were absent. A similar situation prevailed, for
instance, amongst the Bemba of northern Rhodesia, the
Lunda of southern Zaire and Angola, and of course

amongst many of the tribes of South Africa itself. Although for the most part migrant miners returned to their village areas, often much richer than when they left, the effect of this system was to undermine completely the cohesive structure of village life and earlier value systems.

THE DESTRUCTION OF AUTHORITY

The separation between production and belief, with the implied dichotomy between secular and religious life, had a further directly associated consequence: the destruction of traditional authority. This was manifested in the weakened legitimacy of chiefly authority and the associated power of the ancestral spirits, in the greater freedom acquired by some women, and in the increased power of the young in relation to the old.

In the case of chiefly power there was an important paradox. For the colonial powers almost universally sought to build up the secular power of existing chiefs, even to appoint them where they had not existed before, and yet the very fact of their support undermined the spiritual or magical basis on which those powers had traditionally rested. Thus while there often was an increase in their apparent power it was often at the expense of their traditional mystique.

The effect was clear from early colonial days. Before the German occupation of Tanganyika in 1886 the senior chief of the waChagga of Kilimanjaro had obtained revenue to sustain his position from a share of war booty, and from exchanging ivory with Swahili traders for imported goods. Following colonisation the German government in Tanganyika sought to create revenue by decreeing that the senior chief of the waChagga could collect local poll taxes on its behalf, and enforce a contribution of labour 'in kind', keeping some of the revenue for himself. Labour 'in kind' was then arranged by the chief from among local wrong-doers who were supposed to have been tried by local custom. In fact those supplied to work on German-administered 'chain gangs' were simply those who had offended the chief in a variety of different ways. As this practice was maintained over the thirty years to 1916, the waChagga during this period came increasingly to see their senior chief (who had only recently established some kind of hegemony by force of arms) as an authoritarian colonial puppet.

Unlike the Germans, Belgians and Portuguese, the British and French did not generally rely on forced labour. The objective in British and French territories was to reduce or eliminate those aspects of chiefly power which were no longer acceptable in the light of western civil law. For instance, in 1916 the British South Africa Company (BSA) sought to remove from the *chitumukulu* of the Bemba such rights as slavery (prevalent in many chiefly courts up to 1914), the power of mutilation and the power to administer tests of 'innocence' such as the 'poison test'. Yet initiatives such as this were taken in parallel with initiatives designed to increase their secular power in that they could in turn deliver support for the colonial government. In 1929 the Government of Northern Rhodesia (which by that time had taken over responsibility from the BSA) actively sought to revive the chieftainship, but by this time, with large numbers of Bemba menfolk working on the copperbelt, there was no means of reviving traditional systems of tribute, and the government was only prepared to allocate derisory sums to paying the *bakabilo* (advisory council). As a result, there was no significant revival in the power of the Bemba chieftainship.

Most colonial attempts to revive chiefly power were similarly unsuccessful, and were particularly inappropriate in the segmentary societies, for whom there was no precedent of a centralizing force. Such power as remained with the chiefs was in any case being assailed in more subtle ways. New institutions developed which not only embraced all the clans of the tribe, but also linked them to the wider world. Among these were the Church and co-operative societies, both for the most part independent of chiefly patronage. The Church, as the prime source of western education in the early colonial years, added important secular responsibilities to its religious ones, and its influence was therefore bound to undermine chiefly power. Co-operative societies were initially formed in the inter-war years at the instigation of colonial administrators, notably in Tanzania and Uganda, and quickly gained a momentum of their own. The more successful ones were associated with cash crops like coffee, such as the Kilimanjaro Native Co-operative Union of the waChagga. In the inter-war years they acquired a responsibility for providing services some of which were well outside the agricultural sphere, and created a completely new kind of link amongst its members independent of the chiefs.

As a result of these social changes, and as a result of exposure to western education, some chiefs, such as Peter, the Kyungu of the Ngonde in Malawi, formally abrogated their divine powers and ability to communicate with the ancestral spirits.[10] This trend culminated in the mid 1950s and later, when in the face of the growing strength of the nationalist movements, the chiefs' position became increasingly exposed. As functionaries in the system of indirect rule, and often responsible in the British Territories for the Native Authorities, the chiefs could see that their position would be further diminished under an African government controlled by nationalists. For this reason the *asantehene* in Ghana opposed 'total' independence under Nkrumah's Convention People's Party in 1957 and at the eleventh hour organized the National Liberation Movement, a party committed to the introduction of federal government. Under such an arrangement the *asantehene* and other Asante chiefs would continue to play a dominant role in Asante. This move, and most similar initiatives elsewhere, proved unsuccessful.

The most conspicuous exception was Nigeria, where the northern leadership organized a political party (the Northern People's Congress) to fight the 1952 local elections. In the General Election of 1959, which determined power in the first independent government, it was so successful that the Sardauna of Sokoto, chief adviser to the Sultan and a direct descendant of Uthman dan Fudiye (see Chapter 4) was elected Prime Minister of the North, and his protégé, Tafawa Belewa, was elected Prime Minister of Nigeria. However, this regime survived for only six years and no subsequent regime in Nigeria, either civilian or military, has had such direct links to the traditional chiefs.

WOMEN: NEW CHAINS FOR OLD

The massive changes which gathered speed in the inter-war years, and which ultimately undermined the content of older systems of belief, could hardly fail to effect the position of women within the family, and particularly their relationship with their husbands.

In many traditional societies a few women had played an important ritualized role which gave them great influence. This was the case for the mother and sister of the *mugabe* of the Banyankole; it was also true of the Queen Mother at the court of the Swazi king, whose institutions were well developed by the eighteenth century; and it was even true of some Islamic societies in west Africa. This is clear from written accounts of the Hausa kingdom of Maradi, near Katsina, in the 1820s and 1830s, at a time when it had temporarily escaped the influence of the Fulani *jihad* described in Chapter 4. At this court the 'Iya', or Queen Mother, was selected by the council of nobles from among the senior royal kinswomen and

presided over all marriages and kinship ceremonials involving girls and women of the royal lineage. She was usually single, though previously married, and was the official head and patron of local prostitutes and devotees of the pre-Islamic cult of spirit worship [bori] whom she led in to greet the [king] on the Muslim sabbath. She was consulted in all [bori] initiations and public ceremonies, such as market renewal rites. Through her slaves 'Iya' levied grain from market vendors, and annual taxes from prostitutes and cult specialists. Her compound was an official sanctuary. She had her own clients, horsemen and attendants attached to the office, whom she equipped with war gear and from whose booty she received a portion.[11]

Such ritualized positions, however, could never be of much relevance to the position of the majority of women which can best be described as one of servitude to their husbands, made worse in societies where polygamy was prevalent. In many societies the position of the husband was symbolized by the axe, and that of the wife by the hoe.

The first changes in rural society were initiated by the mission stations who urged new attitudes towards marriage and family. They campaigned for the rejection of polygamy, and customs such as the killing of twins, sometimes with their mother.[12] In many societies in which mission influence was strong, women came to play an important part in church life. For instance, amongst the Nyakyusa and Ngonde, the Moravian Church appointed women as church elders in the inter-war years. The formalized legal system introduced by the new colonial governments also tended to support women who refused to enter a distasteful marriage. Not surprisingly, however, the abrupt change in domestic mores initiated by mission teaching actually led to a sharp increase in instability in marriage relationships which continues to the present time.

Monica Wilson reported that

In the Nyakyusa view the increase in divorce began when European rule was established in 1893. Without statistics it was impossible to demonstrate what change, if any has taken place. What is certain is that in the 1934–8 period elderly chiefs who regularly sat in court were convinced that divorce had increased since they were young. It is also certain that both young and old thought marriage ought to be stable, and the increase in adultery fines in 1935 was agreed upon in the hope that adultery and divorce would diminish.[13]

As we might expect, the most common grounds for friction between husband and wife were over the changing division of work, over the sharing of food and other property, and over adultery. If such friction was really on the increase so was the countermanding facility of easier divorce, whereas in the past:

> At betrothal the groom thrust a spear in the ground in the courtyard of the bride's home. She plucked it out and handed it to her father in token of her consent to the marriage. It meant: 'With this spear you may slay me if I run away from my husband.'[14]

However an increasing problem for women during this period was not their daily subjugation to men but the latter's long absence as migrant miners and estate workers. Men were often absent for contract periods of three years, sometimes renewing their contracts for additional periods, and sometimes becoming permanent residents of the mining towns leaving their wives and families stranded in the village. The workload of wives thus became heavier for, although they would be living in extended family compounds, they necessarily had to take on a greater role in providing food and shelter. Such communities could become very depressed, in spite of sporadic remittances from their menfolk, as the more demanding aspects of agricultural labour were neglected.

World War Two absorbed yet more manpower, but its long-term effect was through the returning servicemen's insistence that their wives should wear cotton dresses, like the women throughout the world whom they had seen for the first time. The bark cloth which people had used to dress themselves in much of east and central Africa was rapidly discarded. This increase in self-reliance, and in westernized forms of dress among non-Islamic women, did not, however, go very far in reducing men's authority over women, and key social resources such as education continued to be available mainly to men.

Was it different in the towns? On the coast of west Africa women had always played a key trading role: the market women of Freetown as described by Mary Kingsley in 1897 are much the same today. As with many black American families, among these coastal people the women were and are the focal point of the family and the menfolk come and go, a social fact reinforced by the presence of the descendants of thousands of returned slaves in Sierra Leone and Liberia whose influence spread up and down the coast.

In the rapidly expanding inland towns, so often the product of mining development, two distinct patterns emerged among women which were recognizable as far afield as the tin mining town of Jos in northern Nigeria to the copper-mining towns of Katanga and Northern Rhodesia and further south to the goldfields of the Rand. On the one hand, there was the battered but still extant urban version of traditional marriage, now usually nominally monogamous. On the other, there was the life of the *femmes libres* of these new communities who often retained close links with rural parents and family. The first was usually retrogressive from the women's point of view, the second was precarious, but certainly liberating. For women caught up in either of these patterns the change of role was very great, for they were living in an environment which was entirely the result of European influence. From having been part of a communal female group with a ritualized role they were now part of an urban way of life which in essence was similar to urban life throughout the industrialized world.

The first pattern of traditional marriage, was particularly clearly represented by the copperbelt of Northern Rhodesia. Here women were totally dependent on their husbands' wage packets. An account from the 1950s[15] shows that although they were quite unaware of the amount their husbands earned, they had to use their allocation of it to buy the food from the company store

which would previously have been grown at home. However, this reduction in the work-load was generally
welcomed. One woman is reported as saying:

> I am sometimes afraid of going back to the hard work
> in the village. You do more work in the bush, and most
> of it very hard. We have work here too, but it is all
> done at home, and not in the bush, so that when you
> feel tired you can relax comfortably in a chair or lie
> down on a sack. Not so in the village. You work hard
> in the garden, you return home and still have to do
> domestic duties, such as drawing water from a far
> distant well, cooking and pounding.[16]

Hortense Powdermaker, the author of this study, concludes
that

> Although women had less hard work and an easier life,
> which they liked, yet men were more their masters
> than in the past. In the new economic system only a
> small proportion of the women were employed outside
> the home, and they had an economic dependence on
> their husbands unknown in the past.[17]

This situation of continued subjugation was not a passing
phase, and as we shall see has certainly not been
eliminated in the post-independence years.

The situation with the second group, the *femmes libres*
was rather different. In the 1950s it was estimated by a
Belgian administrator in Elisabethville (Lubumbashi) that
a quarter of the town's women were single girls who
survived mainly by prostitution. In Leopoldville (Kinshasa)
Baladier described these girls as

> More or less brilliantly dressed and made up, with bold
> eyes and lacquered fingernails, audacious, determined,
> frivolous, fickle, seizing life with both hands they
> dominate the city life of Congo Africans: on that

everyone agrees. They flock to the bars laugh the innocents out of their fears, initiate the village boys new to the city, corrupt the stolidly married husband, organise in their own defence, fleece the lascivious European, and generally carry on in gross defiance of Morality and Family Order.[18]

In Brazzaville the girls were grouped together in associations which 'curiously mingle mutual aid (to each other and to their parents) with amusement and with prostitution'.[19] These girls did achieve, and continue to achieve, a real personal freedom which, when all goes well, takes them a vast distance from the marital subjugation of village life. However, they can hardly escape the age-old penalties paid by girls pursuing such a profession. The successful use their funds to set up a shop or trading business, and with luck set up house with children and occasional men. The unsuccessful sink back into the poverty of the African city, no more cared for than the poor of big cities elsewhere, no nearer to finding a life pattern which gives support without subjugation.

NEW FORMS OF EXPRESSION

The fundamental changes in traditional societies experienced in the first half of the twentieth century led to the development of completely new forms of religious and political expression. A manifestation of this which is very much alive in the second half of the twentieth century is the strength of the free churches which grew up in the shadow of the established church, observe much of conventional Christian teaching but preserve forms of religious expression which owe more to the African past than to missionary teaching. In 1969 it was estimated that there were 5,000 such separatist independent churches in Africa, ranging from the Church of the Cherubim and Seraphim in Nigeria to the African Watchtower Movement in central Africa. John Mbiti has summarized their attraction as follows:

> Beneath the umbrella of independent Churches,
> African Christians can freely shed their tears, voice
> their woes, present their spiritual and physical needs,
> respond to the world in which they live and empty
> themselves before God.[20]

These churches represent one of the arteries of modern
Africa through which its lifeblood flows.

They are the current manifestation of a tradition which
in central Africa can be traced to the Watchtower
Movement which originated in the United States and was
carried to Nyasaland by missionaries in the late nineteenth
century. It was taken up at that time by Kenan Kamwana
who preached the message of a new age which would arrive
in 1914, giving it a particularly anti-colonial twist: one of
its principal features would be the disappearance of the
colonial officials, and the arrival of a self-sufficient
economy in which 'we shall build our own ships, make our
own power, and make or import our own guns'.[21]
Watchtower has remained a major force in Malawi, Zambia
and Zimbabwe continuing to preach a millenarian message, promising a new dawn, whose 'levelling' content is
scarcely less relevant today than in the colonial period.

One of the most dramatic expressions of this tradition
was the strength acquired by the Lumpa Church led by
Alice Lenshina in Zambia from 1957 to 1964. Alice became
convinced at the age of twenty-nine that she had died, been
received by God, and at His will returned to earth. She
acquired a massive following, leading at one time to the
encampment of 60,000 supporters at her Church of New
Zion at Kasomo in northern Zambia. The movement was
obsessed with the need to divine and eradicate witchcraft
and ultimately it clashed both with the Roman Catholic
Church and with the transitional Government of northern
Rhodesia (in which Kenneth Kaunda was already a
Minister) causing the death of 700 of Alice's supporters in
struggles with the police and the army. Their courage had
been greatly strengthened by Alice's statement that the
army bullets would turn to water. Her ability to steel their

hearts was remarkably similar to that of Joan of Arc. The depth of the experience for members of the Lumpa Church was indicated by the fact that in 1978 (two years after Alice was released from a twelve-year detention) 4,000 Lumpa supporters decamped from Zambia into Zaire, there to rebuild 'New Zion'.

The continuing vitality of this tradition is indicated today by the surprising success of the priestess Alice Lakwena, the daughter of an Anglican deacon from northern Uganda, in opposing the Government of President Yoreveni Museveni of Uganda in 1987. Convinced of her own divine inspiration she was at the centre of the 'Holy Ghost' movement, which was in effective armed opposition to the Museveni government long after other rebel groups had collapsed. Using ritual fetishes as a standard, and promising that shea butter oil would ward off army bullets, she rallied 2,000 bush fighters (including an ex-minister of education) and evaded capture until giving herself up to the Kenyan authorities across the border. She was released back into Uganda in mid 1989 and her followers continue to put up a sporadic resistance.

In the period after World War Two, in which the world-view of many African servicemen who fought outside Africa had been completely changed, nationalist political parties sometimes developed forms of expression which continued to reflect both Christian and more traditional forms of religion. Mau Mau was the clearest example, although in the 1960s there were to be several comparable movements in eastern Zaire.

Mau Mau was the creation of a number of Kenyans who had been in the British army during World War Two (the 'Group of Forty') who seized control of the Kenya African Union in 1952, and steered it in the direction of encouraging and supporting the hit-and-run raiders who eventually became the Kenya Land and Freedom Army. These men and women, who at their peak numbered 15,000, formed a group of forest fighters who were bound together not only by the objective of ridding Kenya of the British, but also by a mixture of traditional Kikuyu religion, Christian ritual and African nationalism. The loyalty of individuals was assured by the administration of oaths which depended for their effect on the traditional use of animal intestines, blood and the sanctity of 'facing Mount Kenya'.

The physical and verbal symbolism of oath-taking was pursued by the Mau Mau leadership as the most effective means of ensuring the passive or active support of the Kikuyu people. This reliance on magic and superstition encouraged the recurring phenomenon of the supposed ability to counter-act bullets. A very successful raid on a police post at Naivasha in 1953 (during which 173 prisoners were set free) was led by a mute who had only recently learned to speak, and of whom it was said his Kikuyu knife could turn all bullets into water.

Whether we look at the strength of the free churches, at the experience of Watchtower and of Lenshina's Lumpa Church, or at the ritualistic aspects of Mau Mau, there is a consistent thread in the rejection of forms of worship imposed by Europeans, and a search for forms of expression which are closer to the pre-colonial forms. In the case of Watchtower, the Lumpa Church, and Mau Mau this extended to an emphasis on the supernatural and magic, transposing these elements from traditional belief into a new context. The search for new forms of religious expression was and is intense and has certainly not yet run its course.

SHIFTING SANDS

The disruption of colonial rule created the shifting sands upon which the emerging independent nations had to build. The new ambivalence towards traditional forms of religion, of commerce, of authority and even of family ties, was a direct consequence of the profound mis-match between Africa's traditional values and those promoted by the European powers during their period of formal control. These factors were the critical ingredients in African society between the wars, the formative period for the leaders who took power at independence. For the most part these leaders were the children of individuals who had accurately identified both the opportunities and demands of the new situation while only half-understanding its content or its implications, and who ensured that at least one of their off-spring would acquire the new learning. As a result there were few among the new leaders (Kenyatta being a notable exception) who understood that in gaining part or all of a western education, they had sacrificed a traditional knowledge, or who understood the extent to which the societies they were to lead would be torn between two worlds.

6
Torn Between Two Worlds

As we saw in the previous chapter the first missionaries and educationalists failed for the most part to perceive that, in the words of Mary Kingsley, there was an 'underlying African idea'. Instead, they were so appalled by the outward manifestation of traditional culture that they felt their duty was to obliterate it, and remake the young Africans who came through their schools in their own mold. It would be wrong to suggest that there was not an important minority of Africans who agreed with this view but their motives almost certainly had as much to do with material and political advancement as with genuine acceptance of a culture considered to be superior. This clash of cultures was least significant in the Sudan and in the Islamic parts of west Africa where the fact that the local culture was clearly an outgrowth of a major world religion, and one with which the British and French were familiar, allowed a much stronger spirit of respect to be adopted.

This dichotomy of values was further exacerbated, albeit indirectly, by the steady increase in Africa's involvement in the world economy. This led to the planting of cash crops for sale to the market, and made work in the mines or on estates a necessity for many young men. The rapid development of a money economy made a nonsense of the old links between the economic welfare of the community, the chief, the ancestors and God. The individual had an unprecedented opportunity to acquire effective, if not formal, ownership of land and to shake off traditional community obligations. Chiefs experienced a rapid decline in their powers of influence and control. Women, who as mothers were the traditional pillar of life in the family compound, also saw their position greatly changed. On the one hand, they found support from missionaries to withdraw from distasteful marriages; on the other, whatever superficial advantage this gained them was lost in the new confines of the need to survive in a partly monetized economy. The keys to 'progress' in this new world – western education and money – remained primarily in the hands of men.

MWATA KAPULU: A HISTORY

Mwata Kapulu, the son of a traditional chief, was born in 1914 near Balovale, a small settlement on the eastern bank of the Zambia River, 500 miles upstream from the Victoria Falls. A Lovale by tribe, his people had for several centuries lived in the shadow of the Lunda Kingdoms of southern Zaire and the Lozi Kingdom of western Zambia. In the year of his birth the British South Africa Company had only just persuaded the *litunga* of the Lozi to cede to them the mineral rights which embraced the whole of the Zambian copperbelt. But the Company's writ did not run in Balovale, and it was the first Christian missionaries, the American Plymouth Brethren, who brought a new set of values to the Lovale. They also provided a haven for Kapalu's mother when she left her husband, a polygamous chief.

As a young man in his twenties, Kapulu perceived the opportunities and demands of the new situation, thrown up by the conjunction of the missionary presence and the development of the copperbelt 300 miles to the east. He was a firm convert to the Plymouth Brethren's code of behaviour, and rejected the traditional custom of paying tribute to chiefs, as well as their arbitrary selection of young teenage girls as additional wives. His mother's experience taught him that although such marriages were often opposed by both the girl and her parents it was difficult if not impossible to oppose a chief. For these reasons, although he was twice offered the Lovale chieftainship between 1940 and 1960 he refused it. In the 1930s he agreed to set up a mission school west of the Zambezi. In the late 1940s, while working as headmaster of the school, he established a trading post on the border with Angola selling consumer goods which he had walked to the copperbelt to purchase. In the 1950s this became his full time activity.

His six children attended the Mission School and in the 1940s the family's life revolved to a large extent around Mission activities. Under the loose umbrella of the colonial government village life came to be deeply influenced by the Missionary Church and its practices. A decade later these influences had usurped older practices and beliefs to the extent that the early visiting campaigners for the nationalist movement found a responsive audience. Kapulu was particularly receptive to this message. As one who had abandoned many aspects of traditional culture he was looking for a new source of self-respect for his people and was resolutely opposed to the authoritarian nature of the colonial regime, whether expressed through restrictions on movement or through levying of the poll tax regardless of ability to pay. He became a warm supporter of Kenneth Kaunda's nationalist party – UNIP – and was appointed its chairman in the area, against the wishes of the missionaries. His two elder children, both girls, became active participants in UNIP in the build-up to independence in 1964.

When independence came, the family was well-placed to take advantage of the opportunities it created. Pezo, the eldest, was appointed a Member of Parliament by President Kaunda, one of only six women MPs in the new Parliament. She quickly became an outspoken campaigner on

political issues ranging from the proportion of the population that was likely to remain in subsistence farming, to
the absolute need for family planning, to the mistreatment
of wives by drunken husbands. The hostile reaction she
provoked from her fellow male UNIP MPs proved to be so
difficult for her to manage that within three years she
asked the President to relieve her of her post. This he did,
although a small group of both male and female MPs
privately encouraged her to maintain her struggle, without
being prepared to speak out themselves.

The experience of campaigning on such issues persuaded
Pezo that she should expend her energies elsewhere and
she has adamantly avoided politics ever since. Her family's
story serves to show how those who had been most
profoundly influenced by the early missionaries were
frequently those who were the most committed to the
nationalist movement; but also the extent to which
ingrained attitudes, in this case male chauvinism, frequently prevented that nationalism from embracing
progressive social causes. By the time Mwata Kapulu died
in 1974 he had not only witnessed, and welcomed, the
demise of 'traditional' society, but he had also seen the
inadequacies of both missionary paternalism and of the
new nationalism. Few individuals, at any time in history,
can have participated in such rapid rates of social change,
or to have had to make decisions in such a shifting
framework.

REALIGNMENT OF INTERESTS

The enlarged scale of society i.e. from village to city and
beyond, has created an entirely new framework in which a
functional morality, maintained by an intimate knowledge
of the interplay between the individual and his immediate
society, is no longer feasible. The right and wrong of an
action in the new urban environment or commercialised
rural environment may not be clear; its effect may in any
case be seen only over a number of years; its impact may be
perceived differently by people from different backgrounds.

Is it, for instance, right for senior civil servants to use public funds to provide medical care in Europe for a sick close relative? Traditional values would say that an individual should do everything in his or her power to ensure the welfare of such relatives, whereas western values would reject as unacceptable the use of public funds for the privileged treatment of relatives. Should single mothers who have moved from the rural areas to a working life in the towns leave their children with their extended family in the village, or try to bring them up in the generally hostile environment of the town? In the West, the breaking up of the extended family has made mothers overridingly responsible for their children, and they rarely leave them for months, or even years, at a time. But in practice, the enveloping family network of the African village may be infinitely more supportive to the child than the harshness of the city, and in most cases that is the solution which single mothers adopt. The drawbacks of that choice do not become clear until much later, when perhaps ten years of separation have made mother and child strangers to each other, and when the prospects of the child eventually caring for the mother have effectively disappeared.

Such dilemmas are experienced to a varying degree and in varying ways by the many different social strata of urban life. One way to look at these is by socio-economic status. Classes that can be identified are: an elite bourgeoisie, occupying the highest levels of the civil service, state-owned companies and some of the higher management levels of foreign-owned businesses; a middle class of lower-level managers and clerical staff; a class of formally employed wage-paid labourers; and a class of informal sector workers, including the self-employed and the unemployed. All but the last are small as a proportion of the total urban population, and the boundaries between this class and those in wage-paid employment are fluid, as the more skilled manual workers frequently move between both categories of work. Furthermore, alignments of interest between classes may occur: members of all classes except the elite bourgeoisie supported Idi Amin's expulsion in 1974 of the 30,000 Asians from Uganda, and in 1983 of the Ghanaian immigrant workers (perhaps numbering a million) from Nigeria.

A more important and basic alignment of interest, however, comes from values which cut across such class allegiances. Thus loyalty to clan and tribe, to church or mosque, and even to political party have frequently proved as strong, or stronger, than loyalty to class. Once in power, political parties, have seldom sought to encourage class conflict. One result has been that trade unions have generally remained weak and have seldom been more than a source of irritation to government. The unions in Nigeria and Zambia have at times proved the exceptions to this. The Nigerian general strike of 1964 played an important part in the build up to the 1966 coup; the trade union leadership on the Zambian copperbelt was able to mobilize successfully its membership and persuade the government to withdraw from its agreement with the IMF in 1987, although in this case with middle class and elite support.

In contrast to the relative weakness of trade union organizations, loyalty to clan and tribe is often maintained by the strong links which members of all urban classes retain with the rural communities from which they came, traditionally motivating them to support several members of their extended family. For middle class townspeople this is increasingly difficult to do, not only because their own incomes are under pressure but also because the new housing estates of Africa's cities make no more provision for a group of aged uncles, or half-educated cousins than do their equivalents in Europe. In the case of low-income townspeople the task is almost impossible since incomes are inadequate for the support of even a nuclear family. For these reasons support to the extended family weakens the longer individuals have been resident in towns, and it is a legacy from traditional society which is slowly receding.

New loyalties are, however, being formed to a host of associations designed to promote the interests of their members in many different ways. Outside Douala, in Cameroun, the fifteen-strong Comité de Dévélopement de Jeunesse de Yabi à Douala meets for at least one day a week to farm a 4-hectare block of yams and bananas, the proceeds of which go towards developing a school in their own hometown. The members draw wages or salaries in addition in the formal sector. In Nairobi, the Kenya Small Traders' Society has recruited 5,000 members from among the self-employed traders and artisans from all of Kenya's major towns. Wilson Mushiri, its chairman, sees it as an organization which can fight for the rights of its members as micro-businessmen who need credit, legitimacy and space. In Zambia, the Planned Parenthood Association, a voluntary organization with a democratic structure and 2,500 members, has in the 1980s succeeded in reversing the extremely hostile attitude of most MPs to family planning and has become the major agency for the distribution of a growing quantity of contraceptive supplies. Such organizations are creating new networks of loyalties, sometimes within and sometimes outside those of the tribe.

THE FAMILY TAKING THE STRAIN

On the other hand the problems faced by women in urban marriages remain formidable. We saw in the account of women on the Zambian copperbelt in the 1950s that the relationship between husband and wife remained hierarchical in the context of the town. In the subsequent thirty years the frustrations of urban life have, if anything, caused a deterioration in the status of many married women exemplified by the frequency of wife beating. The increasing frequency of divorce among the rural Nyakyusa (reported as being close to 30 per cent in 1971)[1] is overshadowed by even higher divorce rates in the towns and cities. In Douala, in Cameroun, divorce cases are nearly always initiated by the wife in response to consistent beating by the husband.[2] The origins of this problem lie in the consent which traditional morality gave to husbands to beat their wives as a matter of punishing supposed inadequacies. A Nyakyusa told Monica Wilson, 'a husband beats his wife even if he loves her'.[3] But the experience of Pezo Kapalu in post-independence Zambia shows how little can be done to expose it publicly.

In Tanzania the need to search for a new basis for relationships within marriage was recognized in the 1971 Marriage Law. The legislative proposals which formed the basis of this, and which were publicized for general discussion, stated that one of the prime objectives was that 'neither the husband, nor the wife would be allowed to inflict corporal punishment on his or her spouse', and that 'if either party has a complaint he or she may go to the appropriate authority'. The law incorporated these elements, and also stated that a girl of over eighteen years could marry without parental consent, and that a transfer of cattle should not be a condition of legal marriage. The legislation was an important attempt to adjust to changing private perceptions, primarily amongst urban women, of the marriage relationship, and to prevent a debasement of traditionally-accepted norms as they were transferred to the modern context. The extent to which male attitudes have yet to change in Tanzania, however, is indicated by *The Wicked Walk*, a novel published six years after the new Marriage Act which depicts the extreme exploitation of women in low income Dar es Salaam, who are trapped in an economic and social environment with no escape.[4] Young rural women also had doubts about the effect of this legislation. In the year after it was passed one commented:

It is better for a woman if her father and mother receive some bride price, even if it is just a little. Because when he says: 'Woman, leave my house, I don't want you, I want to marry another woman!' ... she goes to her father and mother. If her husband hasn't paid anything ... her father will say: 'I don't know you! You left when you were still a child. Now when you are old, you come to bring me trouble! And

your man never paid the bride price. . . . Go back where
you come from.[5]

Bride price was and is attractive not only as a token of
respect but also of security.

REJECTION OF THE PAST

The converse of the adoption of western culture, or norms,
is the rejection, in varying degrees, of black culture. This
was brilliantly expressed by the late Okot p'Bitek, a
Ugandan writer and poet, in his book-length poem *Song of
Lawino* – the song of a traditional wife married to Ocol,
now a highly-educated young man:[6]

> Husband now you despise me
> Now you treat me with spite
> And say I have inherited the stupidity of my aunt;
> Son of the Chief,
> Now you compare me
> With the rubbish in the rubbish pit.
> You say you no longer want me
> Because I am like the things left behind
> In the deserted homestead.
> You insult me . . .
>
> Ocol says he is a modern man,
> a progressive and civilised man,
> He says he has read extensively and widely
> And he can no longer live with a thing like me
> Who cannot distinguish between good and bad . . .
>
> Listen,
> My father comes from Payira,
> My mother is a woman of Koc!
> I am a true Acholi,
> I am not a half caste
> I am not a slave girl,

> My father was not brought home by the spear
> **My mother was not exchanged for a basket of millet.**

But the point about the song, apart from its beauty, is that we know Lawino's cries fall on deaf ears, that she is part of the past. The homes of Africa's new middle class do not reflect links with the village, on the contrary, they reflect strong links with the international culture with which Ocol so strongly identifies. Children brought up in these new homes are part of that international culture, reflected in the books they read, the television programmes they watch, and even the food they eat.

The prospects for a reversal of this rejection of traditional culture are weak. While state machinery in the form of Ministries of Culture are ostensibly established to fight the tide, their effect may be negligible. For instance, in 1982 in Kenya the well-known writer, Ngugi wa Thiongo, wrote and produced a play called *Maitu Njugira* (Mother Sing for Me). It was set in the 1920s and 1930s and, in his words,

> depicts the struggle of Kenyan workers against the very repressive colonial labour laws including the 1915 labour registration act which came into effect in 1919 and which required workers to carry passes in metal containers hanging from their necks.[7]

The government refused to issue a licence for a presentation of this play and actors were prevented from giving a performance in the National Theatre or in Nairobi University. In the same year, however, Kenyan television showed the BBC production of *The Flame Trees of Thika* which showed early colonial history in Kenya exclusively from the white point of view. Kenyan television has not yet dared, for either dramatic or documentary purposes, to delve into the rich material provided by the Mau Mau rebellion; an omission unthinkable in almost any other part of the world. White culture is on the offensive in Africa and black culture on the defensive.

However, a process of rejection of this kind is rarely complete at the sub-conscious level. Men's minds are not a slate from which their forefathers' emotions can be entirely erased, there is always some continuity. John Mbiti has described the tension between the two processes of thought in the following way:

> Modern change tries to plant a form of culture which is shallow, at least on the African soil. Men and women are forced to live in two half cultures which do not unite to form a single culture. Those who bring the foreign culture give it to Africans only in part while withholding the other part. Africans also receive part of that culture and reject the other part; they kick away part of their traditional cultures while retaining the other part . . .
>
> The speed of casting off the scales of traditional life is much greater than the speed of wearing the garments of this future dimension of life. The illusion lies in the fact that these two entirely different processes are made to look identical. This lack of distinction between the two processes remains in all spheres of modern African life, and so long as it remains, the situation will continue to be unstable if not dangerous.
>
> . . . the subconscious of tribal life is only dormant, not dead . . . On the material or economic level, the trend is clearly the cultivation of individual and national prosperity. But on the emotional and psychological level, it is towards tribal solidarity and foundations.[8]

These tribal foundations continue to be important not only at the level of the individual but also at the social and political level. While the content of the old beliefs has gone they continue to give form to the present, and to play a role in shaping the realities of both politics and economics.

It is not only among the citizens of urban Africa that older beliefs may play this residual role. In rural societies deep economic changes have frequently torn the heart from traditional religion, without necessarily eliminating belief in spirits and the ability of witchcraft and sorcery to invoke them.

Sometimes the validity of these forces is recognized by the state. In March, 1968, five rainmakers were jailed in Tanzania for allegedly causing too much rain, which destroyed people's fields. More often, villagers exist in a psychologically enclosed world in which these forces play a major part but cannot be discussed with outsiders. Thus the explanation of events within a village, and not least of farming success or failure, continues to be linked to questions of superstition which have ceased to be part of western thinking, and cannot be accounted for in any development strategy.

Within village society the approach to causation in which every event, particularly death, has a secondary cause, remains very much alive. In one village in northern Burkina Faso in 1985, one farmer who was the subject of a farm survey was alleged to have been killed by a sorceress, the wife of another subject of the survey. She in turn committed suicide, and was therefore deemed to have admitted her guilt. Her husband was subsequently asked to leave the village but refused to do so. He was consequently confined by the other villagers to his hut. He was denied food and died after a few weeks.[9]

THE PUBLIC GOOD

At the heart of the moral dilemma in contemporary Africa is the frequent absence of a sense of the public good, a sense of the welfare of society as a whole. Thus the public good has yet to replace the good of the clan. The clearest example of this is the corruption which in most of urban Africa has become the norm. In some societies, such as Tanzania, this has occurred within the last twenty-five years. Each action and decision based on a corrupt payment is by definition the denial of an objective social good. It is now common in African cities to provide hospital treatment in return for a small bribe, perhaps the

inevitable conclusion of a situation where supply is so far
from meeting demand. Perhaps more surprising instances
would include the demand from a senior civil servant in a
small West African country that a letter requested by an
overseas investor to confirm government policy on imports
should be paid for by a bag of rice. The underlying
assumption in such a case must be that public policy as
such has no validity, it is up for sale in the market place
like everything else.

For young people born in towns, even the sense of
belonging to the same society as rural people may be
eroded. In 1962, one year after independence, young
Nigerians from the coastal cities, when confronted with the
rural 'pagans' in the north could comment, 'These people
are not Nigerians'.[10] At a political level such attitudes can
make it even more difficult for the rural poor than for the
urban poor to find some kind of justice. In 1984 the Kenyan
Government took punitive measures against, and ended by
killing, a number of Boran cattle-owners in north-east
Kenya who were protesting about the inadequate state of
wells in their area. The failure of communication between
bourgeois and peasant can be total, and far in excess of
anything experienced in contemporary, though not in pre-
twentieth century, Europe. It is perhaps least acute in the
Islamic societies of West Africa where the city-based
members of the traditional aristocracy often maintain a
formal role within the rural hierarchy from which they
come.

The confusion of social and moral values inherited by
African societies at independence has effectively intensified
over the last thirty years. Among those who determine
social norms in urban society, the adoption of western
patterns of consumption has created more dilemmas than it
has solved; within rural society the old network of rights
and duties has been disolved but its underpinning of magic
and superstition is frequently very much alive. The two
worlds view each other across a gulf which requires more
than political action to bridge.

7

Chiefs Without a Tribe

In the bright sunshine each September in central Africa, the *ngwazi* (conqueror) Dr Kamuzu Banda, Life President and over eighty years old, has addressed 20,000 members of the women's federation of Malawi for no less than three hours. His words, spoken in English, are translated into Chinyanja. At relevant moments Dr Banda waves his fly whisk. When the oratory is finished the ladies begin dancing on the floor of the arena; after some time the *Ngwazi* descends to join the dancing, fly whisk waving merrily, and for at least an hour joins in the celebration.

Dr Banda, abroad for more than forty years during the colonial period, has a very paternalistic view of the way Malawi should be run. His regime calls for great personal reverence for himself, as Life President and elder and brooks no serious dissent on grounds of personality or policy. An early attempt by ex-ministers to overthrow Banda in 1964 ended in total failure; three high-ranking party members disappeared in a car crash in 1982. An early contestant for the role of heir apparent, Aleke Banda, a minister in the 1960s, was restricted to his village for several years before being partially rehabilitated only to fall in disgrace again in the mid 1980s. Dr Banda is on record as saying:

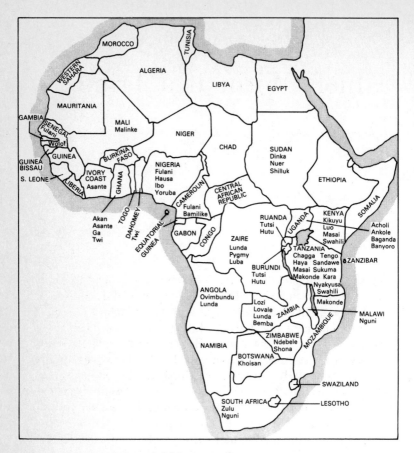

Map 5   Africa today and African peoples

Everything is my business. Everything. The state of education, the state of our economy, the state of our agriculture, the state of our transport, everything is my business.[1]

Dr Banda's approach has had considerable success. Malawi has not been debilitated by localism, and experienced considerable economic growth in the 1960s and 1970s with a strong agricultural performance and an unusually effective civil service. The economic problems experienced in the 1980s are largely due to the destabilizing impact of the civil war in Mozambique.

Nonetheless, the authoritarian nature of the regime has won it many enemies both inside and outside the country, creating an atmosphere of suspicion and intrigue amongst the educated elite. Furthermore, there is no sign that Dr Banda will be able to engineer a smooth and lasting transition to a leader with widespread popular support, and he thus endangers the achievements of his regime.

Malawi's experience illustrates fundamental problems in the complex interweaving of traditional and modern values which coexist in Africa. There are three areas in which the political characteristics of pre-colonial societies can be identified in the contemporary situation. First, that the loyalty of most rural and many urban people is still to tribe rather than nation; second, in the continuous drift towards authoritarian systems of government; and, third, in the failure to resolve peacefully a system of succession of heads of state. We shall examine these in turn, relating them to specific national situations.

NATIONALISM v. LOCALISM

In most African countries the prime loyalty of the majority of people continues to be the extended family and its clan, and ultimately the tribe as the 'widening out of the family'.[2] So localism is a major political reality, and the tendency towards localism has been stronger than the tendency towards a national identity. The contradiction

between the two could be seen in the nationalist movements which paved the way for independence, in which
there was a constant tension between the attempt to build
a genuine nationalist movement and the tendency for
support to be delivered on a tribal basis.

Nigeria

Nigeria provides a striking example of this process at work.
The first party to campaign for independence was the
National Council of Nigeria and the Cameroons (NCNC)
founded by Dr Namdi Azikiwe in 1945. The name of its
newspaper, *The West African Pilot*, clearly indicated the
all-Nigerian and even all-West African nature of its
objectives. In the following six years the NCNC succeeded
in attracting a good deal of support amongst the Yoruba of
western Nigeria. However, by 1951 tension between
Yoruba and Ibo outside the party, Yoruba objections to
Dr Azikiwe's leadership, and the weakness of political
organization within the west, led to the establishment of
the Yoruba-dominated 'Action group' by Chief Obafemi
Awolowo. The Northern People's Congress (NPC) led by a
schoolteacher, Tafawa Balewa, and backed by the northern
Emirates, was also founded at this time, early enough to
fight elections held in 1952. Any attempt to build a truly
all-Nigerian party since the failure of Azikiwe's pioneering
initiative has fallen foul of the rivalry between the major
tribal groups.

This rivalry, reflected in the conflicts between the
successor political parties, and the interest groups they
represent, has continued to be the main engine of Nigerian
politics to the present time. It was not satisfactorily
accommodated by the new constitution introduced for the
1979 election, as indicated by the return to military rule in
1984. It is the key to the attempts of General Babangida,
Nigerian head of state in 1989, to restrict to two the
number of parties allowed to fight the proposed 1991
general election – in theory in order to prevent excessive
faction fighting based on ethnic groups.

Zambia: the KK carousel

In Zambia, although it has a population at least ten times smaller than that of Nigeria, localism has also been the prime concern of domestic politics. The concessions and trade-offs which have come to form the main content of Zambian politics have proved fatally debilitating, even though the skill with which they have been orchestrated by President Kenneth Kaunda (KK) has ensured that Zambia is one of the least oppressive societies in Africa. Nationalist politics in Zambia were initiated in 1951 under the banner of the Northern Rhodesian African National Congress (ANC – but not to be confused with the present-day ANC) led by Harry Nkumbula, from the Ila people of southern Zambia. The ANC at that time had very close links to the African Mine Workers' Union, the largest group of whose members were Bemba, but which included members of tribes from all over Zambia, as well as from Tanganyika and Nyasaland. At this time localism had not yet become a threat.

The ANC led the fight against the formation of the Central African Federation, but failed to prevent its establishment in 1954. Nkumbula's lack of vigour in attacking the Federation, once established, and in supporting participation in the elections for the Legislative Council in 1958 led to the breakaway from the ANC of Kaunda, Simon Kapwepwe and others who set up the United National Independence Party (UNIP) in 1959. It was UNIP which eventually took control of the first independent government winning, in January 1964, fifty-five seats to the ANC's ten. It was clear that the ANC would, from then on, be a minority party relying heavily on local support in the Southern Province.

Kaunda's commitment to a multi- or non-tribal society eventually alienated Kapwepwe whose support base lay much more firmly amongst the Bemba. By 1971, the tension was so great that Kapwepwe broke with Kaunda and formed the United People's Party (UPP) which depended on a flimsy alliance between the Bemba and other tribal groups who at that time felt they were out in the political cold.

In elections held at the end of 1971, the UPP won only one seat, Kapwepwe's own. It was then banned in February 1972, and a one-party state declared. Kapwepwe and 123 supporters were detained, although Kapwepwe himself was released ten months later. In 1974 the remaining ANC MPs were allowed to join UNIP, as was Kapwepwe in September 1978.

Since that time Kaunda has operated an unending game of musical chairs between tribal interest groups. At one level this has enabled him to achieve the considerable feat of maintaining reasonably stable government for more than twenty years. He has, however, paid a very high price for living with the politics of localism. For tensions between regional factions within the party have constantly subordinated a consensus on development policy to the struggle for power. In the UNIP contest for the 1979 presidential nomination, when both Kapwepwe and Nkumbula challenged him, Kaunda showed that he was not prepared to tolerate any real alternative to himself, even when the bid came from the two most experienced politicians in the country. The consequent reactions, both at grass roots level in increasing lawlessness exemplified by the Mushala Gang, a guerilla group in the north-west, and among the elite in a coup attempt organized by Edward Shamwana, a well known Lusaka lawyer, were typical reactions to a regime which was seen as protecting vested interests from below and being inefficient and bureaucratic from above. In 1988 there were no contestants other than Kaunda for the party's presidential nomination, since Nalumino Mundia, a veteran of the independence struggle, withdrew, being unable to secure Bemba support. Living with localism and the drift to an authoritarian system created a dangerous impasse in Zambian society, and left it singularly ill-equipped to deal with its economic collapse in the late 1980s.

Localism has thus continued to be a reality in Nigeria and Zambia and has conflicted with attempts to build a national identity and a national politics. However, there are important cases, particularly Senegal and Tanzania, where the tendency towards a national identity has been more important than localism, which is not to say that the conflict has not existed. In Tanzania, for example, localism among the waChagga and waHaya is potentially as strong as among any of the major tribes of Zambia. It has, however, been contained by an environment in which President Nyerere's political leadership promoted a strong national ideology, and in which, for reasons which lie in Tanzania's nineteenth-century history (including both the replacement of traditional authority by trader barons and the unity achieved among some peoples in resisting German colonialism) localism has been much less strong than among many African peoples. This history gave Tanzania a *lingua franca* (kiSwahili) which was common to most parts of the country, and so the local identity which comes from language runs in parallel with a national identity also based on language.

THE DRIFT TOWARDS AUTHORITARIANISM

The second facet of continuity from pre-colonial times is the authoritarian nature of most African governments. In Chapter 3 it was argued that pre-colonial society was indeed authoritarian, and that this expressed itself in a great stress on the conformity of the individual, and on a hierarchy of relationships between young and old, between chiefs and people and between men and women. In the course of the colonial period, the outward form of these relationships underwent great changes to become, in some cases, almost unrecognizable. The changes did not, however, alter the underlying assumptions about the need for authority, or create a climate in which individual dissent, as in the Anglo-Saxon tradition, was considered necessary to the health of the body politic.

Uganda: kingdoms at war

In some cases there has been a close relationship between the strength of localism and the tendency towards authoritarian government. This is particularly true in Uganda where the British-derived constitution was premised on a uniquely complex attempt to reconcile the interests of the four historic kingdoms, including Bunyoro and Buganda, with the new nation. This attempt was a reaction to the experience of the British in Uganda in the 1950s. Thus the last British Governor, Sir Andrew Cohen, favoured in 1952 the approach which Milton Obote tried to make work after 1966:

> the future of Uganda must lie in a unitary form of central Government on parliamentary lines covering the whole country... The Protectorate is too small to grow into a series of separate units of Government, even if these are federated together.

He looked forward to the development of the country

> by a central Government of the Protectorate as a whole with no part of the country dominating any other part but all working together for the good of the whole Protectorate and the progress of its people.[3]

Cohen, however, found it impossible to make this approach work as a result of a confrontation with the *kabaka* in 1953, and by 1955 Buganda had confirmed its special constitutional status within Uganda, a status which was if anything reinforced in the independence constitution of 1962.

This arrangement was made to work, albeit with increasing tension, between 1962 and 1966. In the first two years of this period President Milton Obote's party, the United People's Congress (UPC) formed a coalition with the Kabaka Yekka (KY) Party whose support was entirely drawn from the Buganda people, and whose ultimate loyalty was to the *kabaka* who was also appointed President of Uganda.

By October 1964 in the complex shifting sands of Ugandan parliamentary politics this alignment changed to one in which Obote felt strong enough to break his alliance with the *kabaka*, with whom he moved into a position of open enmity. In 1966 he instigated a military attack led by Idi Amin on the *kabaka's* palace and made the arrangements to terminate the other three traditional kingships of Uganda.

These events were the culmination of a process which ended the attempt to accommodate localism into the political structure through very complex constitutional arrangements. As the people of Uganda retained strong local loyalties, the arrangements could only be replaced by the type of authoritarian regime which Obote now introduced. Its hallmark was a Machiavellian juggling with army cliques, revolving mainly around the role of Idi Amin and Oyite-Ojok as rival claimants to the position of head of the army.

It was hardly surprising that this should result in the coup of January 1971 in which Amin overthrew Obote while he was absent abroad. Nor was it surprising that after the apparently mindless brutality of the Amin years, Obote's eventual return to power in 1980 was characterized by the continuing dominance of the army as the real force in Ugandan politics, supporting a parliamentary facade of no real legitimacy. In this situation, between 1982 and 1985 the army could pursue a civil war with the Buganda of whom 150,000 were killed in the Luweru Triangle, which forms the heartland of Buganda. These events ultimately led to the second overthrow of Obote by Yoreveni Museveni in 1985.

In Uganda, the apparent impossibility of integrating localism with an effective central government, and the consequent reliance on military authority, has had tragic consequences: civil strife or open war was prevalent from at least 1971 until 1986. The last British government in Uganda, initially seeking an integrated state in recognition of local realities, was forced to contrive a more or less federal one. The tensions involved in trying to make that quasi-federal arrangement work proved too great for Obote. He became increasingly authoritarian and reliant upon the army, which in turn led to the eight years of Amin's rule, the Tanzanian invasion, Obote's second government and ultimately the civil war in which Museveni took power. Today it remains to be seen whether Museveni's essentially centralist approach will be more successful than its predecessors.

Tanzania

Tanzania, in spite of the national rhetoric inspired by President Julius Nyerere, was also essentially authoritarian during Nyerere's presidency. This is true even though the ruling party – initially the Tanganyika African National Union (TANU) and since 1972 the Chama Cha Mapunduzi (CCM) – has always accepted a system of primary elections to select parliamentary candidates. In the four general elections held since independence the turnover of MPs has been as much as 50 per cent.[4] In contrast the authoritarian nature of Tanzanian politics can more usefully be measured by the number of political detainees which exceeded several hundred in the mid 1970s[5] or in terms of the degree of pressure brought to bear on the rural population from 1974 to 1978. It is also true at a more subtle level in that Nyerere, perhaps the finest political debater in Africa (and responsible for the first translation of Shakespeare's Julius Caesar into kiSwahili), left himself with no-one to debate with, at least until he left the presidency to be party chairman in 1985.

His survival over the years since independence in 1961 does not alter the fact that the discussion of real policy choices in a public manner has hardly ever occurred. This is not to say that the National Executive Committee of the ruling party allows Nyerere total control of the party and therefore of government policy; in fact there have always been a number of important policy issues which Nyerere has had to argue through the NEC and which he has not always won. One such issue since the Union of Tanganyika and Zanzibar in 1964 has been the degree of influence of leading Zanzibari politicians in the affairs of the mainland government and party, and the status of Zanzibar in general. Another, in the late 1960s, was the position of the Ruvuma Development Association (RDA), a group of seven villages near Songea in the extreme south-western corner of Tanzania which grouped themselves in an association of mutual support designed to foster their development and which were ultimately compulsorily disbanded in 1969.

However, none of the major stages in Tanzania's development as a centralized socialist state were publicly discussed in any way which made open debate possible. The three major steps were first, the nationalizations which followed the Arusha Declaration in 1967; second, the take-over by government of the wholesale distribution system (largely Indian-owned) in 1971; and thirdly, the compulsory villagization programme of 1974–8, affecting the physical location of the homes of at least 5 million people.

The extent of opposition to the Arusha Declaration and its associated 'leadership code' is indicated by the desertion of Nyerere's closest colleague, Oscar Kambona, who fled Tanzania in 1967. The take-over of the wholesale distribution system was strongly resisted by the responsible minister, A.M. Babu, and was implemented directly by the President's office.[6] On a trumped-up charge of assassinating the first President of Zanzibar, Abeid Karume, Babu was held in detention from 1971 to 1978.

Even more significant at the grass roots level was the reversal of government policy on self-help villages, christened *ujamaa* villages (which in kiSwahili means familihood). Nyerere was arguing right up to, and beyond the date of the dissolution of the RDA that *ujamaa* villages must govern themselves. In a paper entitled 'Freedom and Development' published in October 1968 and adopted by the NEC later that month he said:

> No one can be forced into an ujamaa village, and no official – at any level – can go and tell the members of an ujamaa village what they should do together, and what they should continue to do as individual farmers. No official of the Government or Party can go to an ujamaa village and tell the members what they must grow ... for if these things happen – that is, if an outsider gives such instructions and enforces them – then it will no longer be an ujamaa village![7]

Developments in Tanzania in the mid 1970s were, however, to end in the direct contradiction of this injunction, a contradiction which is at the heart of Tanzania's tendency towards an authoritarian state. By 1972 party leaders and Nyerere himself became disillusioned with the lack of progress in implementing *ujamaa* on a voluntary basis, and in a dramatic switch of policy in 1973 it was decreed that all Tanzanians should live in such a village by 1976. In the course of the next three years over 5 million small farmers moved from individual farms to larger settlements, often including several hundred families. The number of people in *ujamaa* villages by the late 1970s was officially estimated to be 10 million, although many of these were already living in their existing communities which were simply renamed *ujamaa*. Nonetheless, the movement was a vast operation, unparalled in pre- or post-independence Africa. Initially it was assumed that the objective would be for the villages to farm on a communal basis. In practice, by 1975, the resistance to this approach proved so great that settlement was the real objective, with the justification that farming families could be supported in every way – agriculturally, medically and educationally – much more effectively on a group basis.

The important point is not the long-term justification, or lack of it, of the resettlement programme but the very authoritarian manner of its conception and implementation. The experience confirmed Tanzania as a society in which key decisions were made by the president, sometimes in consultation with a few individuals and sometimes not, for implementation by an elite of party workers and civil servants. In the general election of 1970 there had, for instance, been no discussion of the settlement issue; it had been assumed that *ujamaa* would continue to be a voluntary movement. It was as if the president decided to will Tanzania into becoming a socialist community of rural producers living in harmony with themselves and the soil, and was prepared to devote the whole machinery of the state to turning his will into reality. Individuals in the party and the government came to use the situation in whatever way they could to optimize their own position, ranging from exercising the increased power which district and regional officials now had over the citizenry, to carrying out routine tasks perfunctorily while acquiring a significant income from black market activities.

By the late 1980s there were new divisions in Tanzanian society with a clear split between pragmatists and socialists. The former wished to see a revived private sector, the latter wished to preserve the institutional and economic status quo. Beneath these divisions on policy lay deeper divisions based on economic and financial self-interest, with the prestige of Nyerere as party chairman adding weight to the argument for the status quo. In some cases, as in relations between the mainland and Zanzibar, this could be decisive. In other areas Nyerere's influence was more circumspect, but it was successful in maintaining the myth of Tanzania, at least for domestic consumption, as a country committed to building socialism in the long term.

Nyerere's reputation as an individual remains high and was reinforced by his decision to resign as president in late 1985. It has never been doubted by the Tanzanian public that his aims were genuine, nor been considered that he sought to enrich himself. In this sense the very high 'yes' votes he achieved in the four presidential elections since independence have been genuine, but should not be mistaken for support for specific policies, and still less for support for other leaders at either the local or national level.

THE CONTINUING PROBLEM OF SUCCESSION

We have seen that localism and the drift to increasingly authoritarian government have been major problems even for Africa's more successful leaders, and have been disastrous in other cases such as Uganda and Nigeria. Both these factors interrelate with a third major political dilemma: the succession to political leadership. Since 1960, of the 41 sub-Saharan African states there has only been one smooth constitutional transfer of real power from one elected leader to another, i.e. in Senegal in 1981. In 1990 it is not clear whether in late 1987 Julius Nyerere's decision to renew his term as party chairman in Tanzania is compatible with a smooth transition of power from himself to President Mwinyi or to anyone else. There have been three significant cases of the smooth transfer of power from the death of a civilian head of state to his successor. In each case, Liberia in 1971, Kenya in 1979, and Botswana in 1980, the transfer was to existing vice-presidents. In four cases, Ghana in 1976 and 1979, Nigeria in 1980 and Sudan in 1987, military regimes have held elections which have returned civilian governments to power but in all four cases a coup has reinstated a military head of state.

As with the continuing strength of localism and authoritarian government, the roots of the succession problem lie not only in the fragility of the new states, but also in the legacy of pre-colonial societies. Chapter 3 showed for the most part that traditional society had an arbitrary approach to the problem typified by suicide (as with the Banyankole), 'snuffing out' (as with the Nyakyusa and Ngonde) or violent change (as with the Shilluk). Constitutional change through the popular will, or even the long wait for a head of state's death, are not concepts with deep roots in African society.

Kenya after Kenyatta

The acute political problems raised by the succession issue can be seen particularly clearly in the experience of Kenya,

Cameroun and Senegal. In the case of Kenya, Kenyatta's age of almost seventy at the time of independence in 1964 meant that the succession issue was alive from the start. For the Kikuyu the success of the struggle for independence in Kenya lay in the combination of Kenyatta's political activities and in the effectiveness of Mau Mau in eroding settler confidence. But there were other political figures at work in Kenya during the 1950s. These included Tom Mboya and Oginga Odinga, both Luo, albeit from different parts of Luo-land, both having made major contributions to the independence movement (Odinga amongst the Luo and Mboya within and outside the trade union movement), and in 1961 both were founder members of KANU. At independence, the two were relatively young – Mboya in his early thirties, and Odinga in his forties – and could have expected to be considered as candidates for the presidency in the years to come.

In the mid 1960s a dominant group of Kikuyu, who were close to the Kenyatta family, determined that neither Odinga nor Mboya would come close to the presidency. This group included the veteran politician Mbiyu Koinange, who had participated in missions to the British Colonial Secretary in the early 1950s, and Dr Njoroge Mungai, then a minister in the Kenyatta government. In 1966, in the one and only internal KANU election to be held between independence and Kenyatta's death in 1978, Odinga was ousted from the position of vice-president of the party and so from that of the Republic. At the same time maximum uncertainty was built into the party constitution with the introduction of eight vice-presidential posts. The government however continued with just one vice-president and within a few months this post was held by Daniel Arap Moi, a non-Kikuyu who, despite being a member of the Legislative Council, had not been prominent in nationalist politics.

Tom Mboya had supported these moves, not least perhaps because of his long-standing animosity towards Odinga, but in doing so sowed the seeds of his own downfall. He was murdered in 1969 and his assassin did not hesitate to put the blame on the 'big men'. By this time Odinga had formed his own party, the KPU (Kenya People's Union), but following an incident in Kenyatta's presence at Kisumu he was jailed in October 1969 and the KPU banned.

The struggle for the succession now lay more narrowly between Kikuyu claimants and Vice-president Moi. The existing constitution stipulated that in the event of the president's death, the vice-president must act in place of the president for the ninety days which would elapse before an election could be held. In order to ensure that the succession passed to the right Kikuyu clan, an organization by the name of GEMA (Gikuyu, Embu and Meru Association) was formed under the leadership of Njenga Karume:

> Although ostensibly a welfare organisation Gema was in fact a political party within KANU with Kiambu as its nerve centre, but with political retainers through-out the Republic among every tribe.[8]

GEMA organized and led the 'Change the Constitution' movement which had as its objective the prevention of the vice-president taking power in an interim period before an election, and which came to dominate party politics in the mid 1970s. Having failed in its objective, and having incurred the apparent disapproval of Kenyatta in the process, GEMA tried to persuade Kibaki (the technocratic Minister of Finance) to stand as vice-president against Moi in the abortive party elections of 1977. He declined, although a member of GEMA, and stood for the post of national chairman.

The death of Kenyatta in 1978, with no constitutional change accomplished, left the way open for Daniel Arap Moi to take over the presidency and to be confirmed in a national election as president within three months. However, in practice this was only achieved as a result of the very public support of Kibaki and of Charles Njonjo the influential Attorney General (working against the interests of the founders of GEMA), a triumvirate which was itself to break apart with the public humiliation of Njonjo at judicial hearings in 1984.

Although the transition from Kenyatta to Moi was nominally smooth, it was in fact the culmination of a battle for power which had lasted for 12 years. During its course two major contestants had been eliminated, one by assassination and one by detention, and party politics in Kenya had become obsessed with the struggle between personalities and the rival power of different Kikuyu clans. Its side effects, at least in the popular mind, included two other assassinations, those of the popular reformist MP, J.M. Kariuki, and Pia Gama Pinto, an Asian lawyer who frequently wrote radical speeches for Odinga. The problem of succession had by no means been solved, and certainly not in a way that could be used as a precedent for the future.

Subsequently, President Moi has consolidated his position in such a way that it has become difficult, if not impossible, for anyone to challenge his position by constitutional means. In the March 1988 general election, voters were obliged to queue publicly behind their preferred candidates in the nomination process, and after the election the government initiated discussion of the abolition of the secret ballot.

Cameroun: qui gouverne?

Cameroun provides another example of a country whose stability was seriously jeopardized by a major crisis over the succession to the presidency. The conflict between ex-President Ahmadu Ahidjo and President Paul Biya culminated in 1984 in a bloody battle for the presidential palace and the presidency itself.

For twenty years from 1961 Ahidjo had relative success in maintaining stability in Cameroun, and by the late 1970s the country was experiencing high rates of growth. During this period, Ahidjo had a series of prime ministers on the French model. The last was Paul Biya who between 1973 and 1979, as minister responsible for the economy, had been one of the chief architects of Cameroun's successful development strategy. It was his success in this role which made him an obvious choice for prime minister, an essentially 'managerial' post.

Ahidjo decided in 1981 that for reasons of health, he would step down from the presidency but remain chairman of the ruling party, the Union Nationale Camerounaise (UNC). In 1982 the presidency was constitutionally assumed by Biya who continued his drive to 'modernize' the economy. However, by mid 1983 Ahidjo evidently regretted his decision and sought to exercise control, partly from Monaco, over the government from his position as party chairman. The subsequent tension between the two men created an atmosphere in which there were two attempted coups in 1983, both emanating from sections of the army loyal to Ahidjo. By the end of the year, Biya felt strong enough to force a showdown with Ahidjo and the latter lost the position of party chairman while still abroad.

Ahidjo did not subsequently return to Cameroun, and in the presidential election of January 1984 Biya received a 'yes' vote of over 90 per cent, which most Camerounians considered to be a genuine indication of his underlying support. The following month he publicly waived the death sentence hanging over the organizers of the second coup attempt of 1983. This was, however, to be the prelude to an even more serious attempt on his life by members of the Presidential Guard supported by other army units, and working with certain key civilians of the 'systeme Ahidjo'. The attempted coup was eventually suppressed by the loyal Army command.

The retribution for which the army called was uncompromising and included the shooting of hundreds of soldiers and some civilians which only further increased the tension in the country. Paul Biya did not appear in public for over six months, and his position has never fully recovered in spite of winning a new term in the March 1988 presidential election.

While Cameroun's economic activity returned to normal within a few months, the experience of the three attempted coups, and particularly of the last, undermined the sense of renewal which Paul Biya's elevation to the presidency had achieved. Cameroun's tendency towards a secretive, police-dominated state, which had initially been developed in response to a regional rebellion in the 1960s, was strengthened, whereas most Camerounians had hoped to see it reversed. The struggle over the succession between Ahidjo and Biya, in spite of its curious circumstances, had only served to emphasize that the succession problem remained alive and unresolved.

Senegal: the academician at work

The most important conscious attempt to solve the succession problem was made by Leopold Senghor in Senegal, who successfully handed over the presidency to Abdou Diop in 1980 after the re-introduction of a multi-party system in 1977.

Senghor himself had spent much of the 1930s after graduating from university as a teacher and well known poet in France. He was therefore more than at home in French culture, he was an important participant in its development, assimilating it (as he reputedly said) rather than being assimilated by it. As a deputy from Senegal to the French National Assembly from 1945 onwards, he was an experienced participant in multi-party politics, always deeply concerned with the interchange between the French and the African world view. In 1984 he was elected to the very distinguished position of member of the Academie Francaise, bastion of French culture.

When Senegal achieved self-government in 1958, and full independence in 1960, Senghor presided over a one-party state but one in which public debate was more widespread than in most of Africa. His sophisticated perception of the long-term problems of Senegalese politics, however, led him in 1977 to 'invite' the formation of three new parties – liberal democratic, social democratic, and left/Marxist. Party groupings along these lines were indeed formed and fought a general election in 1978. These were respectively, the Parti Democratique Senegalais (PDS), Senghor's own Union Progressiste Senegalais (UPS) renamed Parti Socialiste (PS), and the Parti Africa d'Independence (PAI). The outcome for party politics was healthy: the PS won 82 per cent of the vote; the PDS won 17 per cent; and the PAI won just 1 per cent of the vote.

In this election, Senghor himself was elected to a third seven-year term as president. In fact it must have always been his intention, after this grand restructuring to retire, and in 1980 the PS elected Diop to be party president. Senghor has retired entirely from Senegalese national and party politics and lives partly in France, although disagreements between himself and Diop have subsequently been recorded.

In retrospect, it appears that Senghor's strategy was first to reconfirm that his party and its policies continued to have support from the Senegalese people, by giving them real alternatives, and then to enable a young and clearly competent successor to take over the leadership of both the party and the government. An integral part of this strategy was to establish parties which had support from several or all of Senegal's ethnic groups, by adopting the proportional representation system of election, and avoiding the close identity of an elected delegate with one geographical constituency.

The Senegalese political system has continued to be robust in spite of the country's current grave economic problems, and in spite of secessionist pressures in the Casimance, the area of Senegal south of the Gambia. However, in the February 1988 elections the presidential candidate of the PDS, the main opposition party – Abdoulaye Wade – made public allegations of vote rigging, and was imprisoned before the results were declared. After the official count, he was shown to have won 25 per cent of the vote, and later released though he was not allowed, at least temporarily, to take up his seat in Parliament. Nonetheless, the Senegalese system has dealt with the succession problem impressively, and sustained a multi-party tradition which allows a wide range of opinion to be expressed in public, and in doing so has avoided the most acute problems of localism.

The reasons for this relative success certainly run deeper than Leopold Senghor's personality. There are at least two special features of Senegal's political inheritance which make it unique in Africa. The first of these is the fact that France's contact with Senegal was long and deep. The first French post at St Louis was established as early as 1638. The residents of St Louis and the other three major towns on the coast (Rufisque, Goree and Dakar) were granted full French citizenship in 1916, and from then until independence had full voting rights in French national elections. Two years earlier, on a more limited franchise, the first Senegalese deputy, Blaise Diagne, had been elected to the French National Assembly and had rapidly become a junior minister.

The second special factor has been the role played by the Murid Brotherhood, an Islamic movement founded in the first decade of the twentieth century by Amadu Bamba, which has played a key political role in delivering support first for the French colonial authorities and later for the governments of independent Senegal. The Brotherhood has immense economic power which was at first based on its control of the ground-nut trade but later on a diversified portfolio of business interests, many of them urban. Even in contemporary Senegal the laws of the state are only observed in the territory of the Murid following the assent of its shaikh, Abdoul Khadre. Thus Senghor was able to build a political regime which was not only founded on a democratic tradition two generations old, but also had to accommodate a major countervailing influence to that of the state in the form of the Brotherhood.

TOMORROW'S MEN

The efforts of African leaders to build a new political system within their countries in the last twenty-five years have not for the most part been successful. They have nearly always fallen foul of the three enemies: of localism, of the drift to authoritarian government, and of the failure to deal with the succession issue. Individual leaders have succeeded in dealing with one of the three problems: Nyerere has defeated localism, Kenyatta maintained a relatively liberal state, Senghor managed a peaceful succession. None has yet managed to deal decisively with two, and still less with all three of the problems. Nyerere, if he manages the full handover of not only governmental power but also party power, may achieve the distinction of dealing with two of the problems.

The Ghanaian novelist, Kwasi Armah, gave the title *The Beautyful Ones Are Not Yet Born* to a novel he published in 1969.[9] Its message was that Africa had not yet produced a generation of political leaders capable of providing the leadership it needs. Chinua Achebe's novel, *Anthills of the Savannah* published in 1987 suggested that such leadership had still not emerged almost twenty years later.[10] It seems likely that the 'beautyful ones' will only emerge when and if the second generation of authoritarian leaders are challenged by the growth of countervailing forces to that of the state. The example of Senegal shows the crucial role which such forces can play, and their potential growth elsewhere is discussed further in Chapter 12.

8

The Politics of Development

'Seek ye first the political kingdom'[1] said Kwame
Nkrumah, and nearly all African Heads of State have done
exactly that in the last quarter of a century. Economics has
usually been subordinate to politics, and politics have
generally been dominated by localism and authoritarianism, the latter being reflected in a view that 'big'
government was best. If, as Kamuzu Banda says 'Everything is my business, everything', then the arm of
government has had to stretch far and deep into the
economy. Even in a country such as Ivory Coast, generally
regarded as in the capitalist camp, government has been
the decisive player in the economy not only as policy-
maker but also as holder of equity capital.

Most post-independence governments had, at one level, a
commitment to an economic transformation with several
components. The first was a reduction in their country's
dependence on the export of primary commodities (whether
agricultural or mineral) to an unstable world market. This
was to be achieved partly by diversifying exports, but more
significantly by creating local industries to manufacture
goods that had previously been imported. The second

component was to create educational and health services as rapidly as possible for as many people as possible, and the third was to achieve some fairer distribution of income between expatriate companies and individuals, and the local indigenous population.

PLANS OR LEAPS?

In the 1960s and 1970s most governments set up economic planning organizations which reflected these objectives. The development plans which they produced in the first decade of independence were for the most part competent, well thought out and well presented. They owed something to European social democracy, including the French experience of planning, and something to the planning experience of other parts of the developing world, notably India.

However, the priorities of government manifested on a day-to-day basis frequently ignored the longer-term priorities nominally established in the plans. This was sometimes the result of dramatic political decisions ('great leaps forward') to transform the pattern of economic ownership, sometimes the outcome of political rivalry leading to civil strife or war, and sometimes the result of the attraction of prestige projects. Leading individuals within governments frequently had a different set of objectives to those which their governments nominally espoused. These centred on personal power and wealth and were manifest in Nigeria, for example, by 1966 when the first military coup was staged. General Obasanjo's biography[2] of his friend Chukwuma Nzeogu, the organizer of the coup, makes it very clear that the objective of the coup leaders was to create a government no longer dominated by these values. They had also become evident in Zimbabwe by 1989, when the ten-year-old government was rocked by a series of corruption scandals and five Cabinet members were obliged to resign.

But corruption is only a partial explanation of some of the key strategic decisions taken by the governments.

Chapter 7 discussed the three major changes in economic strategy undertaken in Tanzania from 1967 to 1975. These were far more significant than any item projected in the development plans. In Zambia and Uganda, similar un-planned leaps were carried out between 1968 and 1970, placing a large number of private businesses in the public sector. In Zambia the government took a controlling interest in twenty-six foreign-owned companies in 1968, and acquired a major stake in the two giant copper mining companies in 1969. By 1973 this measure was considered inadequate and the government took total control of the mining companies. In Uganda the nationalizations were to extend to the import and export business, although President Milton Obote in his first presidency was ousted by General Amin before being able to implement the programme.

Inevitably, priorities also shifted as a result of civil strife, which has been of fundamental importance to at least twelve of sub-Saharan Africa's forty-one countries.[3] Major civil conflicts lasting several years – other than the wars of liberation and their aftermath in the former Portuguese territories – have taken place in Nigeria, Chad, Sudan, Ethiopia, Zaire, Uganda, and Somalia. In some cases such strife has proved to be recurrent over twenty years, as in Zaire, Sudan, and Burundi and in others more or less endemic, as in Chad and Uganda and in Ethiopia in its fight to contain Eritrea. In all cases the strife has fundamentally weakened central governments, diverting both energy and money away from development issues to the domestic conflicts which assume overwhelming importance.

Putting aside these cases of major civil strife it is possible to discern some consistency in the pattern of apparently arbitrary economic decisions taken by govern-ments, whether or not in the form of 'great leaps'. The dominant thread has been a key role for the state in both the accumulation and distribution of wealth echoing the role of pre-colonial states such as Asante, Buganda and Urozwi discussed in Chapter 4. This has not extended to the maintenance of capital assets once established, and of infrastructure such as roads, railways, and buildings. Government has gauged its success much more by the number of new investments, than by the efficiency with which existing investments are maintained and serviced. In 1977 Tanzania received thirty-five new diesel engines for the railway system under aid provided by Canada; by 1982 seventeen of these were out of order[4] and by 1988 rolling stock problems had reduced the once-daily service on the Chinese-built railway to Zambia (opened in 1976) to just twice-weekly.

Sudan's greatest economic asset since the 1920s has been the Gezira Scheme, comprising nearly 2 million acres under irrigation, growing a variety of cash crops, notably cotton. By the late 1960s the emphasis of government policy was on the creation of new irrigation complexes, covering an additional million acres[5] at a time when Gezira was experiencing major problems of productivity. Average cotton yields fell by as much as forty per cent in the course of the 1970s.[6] This declining productivity was largely due to salination in the Gezira canals, a by-product of declining standards of management. As a result, the running costs of Gezira became a burden on the Sudanese government budget, while the scheme made a declining contribution to exports. There are countless examples from most African countries of a similar negligence of completed investments, although some of this is a by-product of the nature of development aid, as we shall see in Chapter 11. Hard top roads, built in the 1960s, in countries as different as Tanzania and Cameroun have needed total reconstruction in the 1980s.

PRESTIGE PROJECTS

An equally explicit consequence of the emphasis on the role of the state has been the number of prestige projects associated with the promotion of the individual personality of the head of state. In Chapter 3 pre-colonial chiefs were characterized as 'the mystical and religious heads, the divine symbol of their people's health and welfare'. There can be no doubt that in many African states this status has been consciously sought by leaders who have promoted it through the nature of their public appearances and prestige investments. This has been most dramatic in the case of 'Emperor' Bokassa of the Central African Republic, but equally consistent in the cases of Houphouet Boigny, Banda and Mobutu. The list of prestige projects to which governments committed themselves is long, ranging from magnificent presidential palaces in such countries as Liberia, Cameroun and Gabon, to whole capital cities as in Malawi, Tanzania and Nigeria. Hosting the Organization of African Unity became a prestige project in itself, as several countries (including Ghana and Gabon) built massive facilities to host the annual meeting, or as in the case of Togo, to attract the OAU's permanent secretariat away from Addis Ababa. The latter bid failed. President Houphouet Boigny of Ivory Coast's plan to construct a church larger than St Peter's in Rome at his birthplace at Yameossouko is perhaps the most dramatic of all.

Linked to this persistent emphasis on the head of state as a quasi-mystical individual has been a countervailing disregard for the opinions and practices of village communities, except as the means of export revenue and, where tribal links justify it, as a source of political support. This disregard is reinforced not only by long-standing attitudes to authority, but also by the more recent divide between those with and without formal education. It appears to be even more prevalent in 'socialist' states than in 'capitalist' states: the compulsory movement to *ujamaa* villages in Tanzania in 1975 would have been impossible in a society which genuinely respected peasant opinion. This is equally true for the government of Ethiopia's attempt to move at least one million people, frequently by force, from the northern districts to the west of the country between 1985 and 1987.

It can also be seen in the efforts of the Frelimo government in Mozambique to build a system of communal villages which according to Samora Machel, the first president of independent Mozambique, would:

> constitute the spinal column of the forces of develop-
> ment in the countryside . . . in the collective life the
> immense creative initiative of the people will be
> liberated. Politically [the villages] will be the instru-
> ment for the realisation of worker power in govern-
> ment, defence, production etc . . . we know that
> dispersed and disorganised we [the workers] will never
> exercise power.[7]

By 1978, 1500 such villages had been created incorporating about a million people. The nucleus of each village was for the most part made up of the Frelimo guerillas who had fought in the liberation struggle. By 1980 it was clear that such villages were doing little to improve the lot of their members, whose livelihood now depended on their effective integration into the cash economy. By 1983, although the weaknesses of the programme were increasingly acknow-ledged within the party, the government's response was to resort to more authoritarian methods of 'policing' the villages. Some of the practices of the colonial state were re-introduced, including corporal punishment, and some of those elected to village councils were rejected on the grounds that they had held positions under the previous regime.[8] The villagization programme was an expensive allocation of development resources, as well as a political disaster. It certainly assisted in the development of Renamo in the 1980s as a terrorist group in opposition to government, albeit supported by South Africa.

CENTRALIZING THE ECONOMY

More specific economic policies, which have been widely discussed in recent years, fit within this tendency towards an autocratic state. These include exchange rates, agricul-tural pricing, and attitudes to the local and international private sector. The question of over-valued exchange rates – which minimize the cost of 'imports' but also minimize the value of exports in local currency – has been highly controversial in recent years between African governments and major aid donors such as the World Bank. Most of the structural adjustment programmes (SAP) now in place have involved a significant exchange rate adjustment, which has had the effect of cheapening local currencies in relation to harder international currencies, in a number of cases by a factor of three or four within two to three years.

The over-valuation was, and frequently is, to the advantage of the urban sector in general and the government sector in particular. For a given outlay of local currency it has ensured a higher value of imports than would have been available under a market valuation of the currency. As a consequence, government has been able to expand the sphere of its operations at the expense of the peasant farmers whose primary produce formed the bulk of exports. For instance, under a market valuation of exchange rates Tanzania's coffee producers would have received a significantly higher farmgate price when expressed in local currency, and their capacity to save and invest would have been higher. Yet these coffee producers were primarily waChagga from Kilimanjaro or waHaya from Bukoba, on Lake Victoria. Government was particularly anxious that neither group should retain the relative economic dominance which it had acquired during the colonial period, and exchange rate management was one means by which this dominance could be restrained. In fact, in Tanzania in 1984 farmgate prices for a mix of agricultural products using estimated market exchange rates were only 20 per cent of export prices.[9]

The effect of exchange rate policy has been reinforced by agricultural pricing policy. Marketing Boards have been an instrument favoured by most African governments as a means of ensuring that farmers have an outlet for their crops, and that urban consumers pay for basic foodstuffs at a controlled, often subsidized, price. Consequently, such marketing boards have frequently found themselves in a price squeeze, unable to offer a price high enough to producers, but only able to sell to consumers at a loss. As a result they have also been trapped into importing food, an operation with considerable potential for losses, although ameliorated by exchange rate policy. In many countries this process had a cumulative impact throughout the 1970s so that by the end of that decade the difference between the price paid to farmers for a crop and the price charged to distributors was highly inequitable. In the 1980s there has been an important adjustment in both exchange rates and agricultural pricing policy largely as a result of pressure from international aid agencies. However the extent to which governments are really committed to these policies is an open question, discussed in Chapters 11 and 12.

THE FOREIGN INVESTOR: FRIEND OR FOE?

The attitudes of governments to private foreign investors and to the local private sector have always been complex and varied. With a few exceptions, such as Liberia under Tubman and Tolbert, and Gabon under Bongo, foreign investors have been regarded with feelings of wariness or hositility. Attitudes to local investors from immigrant communities, such as Lebanese and Syrians in west Africa and Indians in east Africa, whether or not they were citizens, have frequently been equally wary. Attitudes to the indigenous African private sector have obviously been more favourable and many indigenous businessmen have prospered, particularly as clients and customers of the government. However, such favoured treatment has often been restricted to individuals from tribes linked to the government of the day.

It is not surprising that at independence most governments identified the international companies from the former colonial power as potential agents of neo-colonialism, who could not be trusted to operate with the interests of African countries at heart. Indeed in cases where such companies had a vital stake, as with the British South Africa (BSA) Company in Zambia, and the

Union Minière in Zaire they were seen to behave badly at the very point at which their host countries became independent. Thus the BSA attempted to extort over £20 million from the new government of Zambia in 1964 in exchange for its mineral rights, but was ultimately forced to accept £4 million. In 1961 Union Minière made a naked bid to split off Katanga from the rest of Zaire. In the early 1970s the cynical and exploitative role of multinational companies appeared to be confirmed as it became clear that Shell and BP, the latter half-owned by the British government, were the principal source of oil supplies to the outlawed Smith regime of Rhodesia.[10]

Such dramatic examples of commercial self-interest were not in reality offset by the more representative efforts of companies such as Unilever, Mitchell Cotts and Booker McConnell in English-speaking Africa, or CFAO in French-speaking Africa who had invested on a long term basis for relatively modest returns. The dominant position these companies occupied in the economy was sufficient for their position to be questioned. A survey of the 1320 companies registered in Nigeria in 1970 indicated that 400 were wholly foreign-owned, including nearly all of the largest.[11] In the same year in Kenya it has been estimated that African citizens and government institutions owned only about 5 per cent of corporate assets.[12]

Consequently, relations between African countries and international companies were for twenty years character-ized by a battle to take some degree of national control. Strategies for control have included the compulsory sale of 51 per cent of the share capital in the businesses nationalized by Tanzania's Arusha Declaration in 1967, the compulsory sale of the majority of share capital by all large companies in Nigeria from 1974 to 1977, and the 'creeping sale' of 20 per cent of issued share capital in the Ivory Coast required from 1975 onwards (achieved by issuing new equity). In Tanzania, Julius Nyerere com-mented, 'Our purpose was primarily a political purpose; it was an extension of the political control which the Tanzanian people secured in 1961.'[13] The objective of the other forms of nationalization was clearly similar and the effect of each of them has been to reduce foreign ownership in the corporate sector to a relatively modest level.

In Ivory Coast the transfer of ownership has been essentially from the foreign private investor to the local private investor: government remains the owner of 50 per cent of corporate capital (as it has been since the 1960s) and the foreign investors' share has been reduced to 30 per cent, with the local private sector taking the remainder. In Nigeria the foreign investors' share is now about 20 per cent, with the bulk of the remainder held in the Nigerian private sector;[14] the localization legislation created over one million individual shareholders.[15] In the aftermath of the Arusha Declaration, the value of corporate assets held by the state in Tanzania increased sevenfold from financial years 1970/1 to 1977/8.[16] The consequences of this creation of a large, government-owned, or parastatal sector, were expensive.

First, in many cases the previous foreign owners of those companies which passed into local ownership, either private or state, were invited to continue as managers for which they received a management fee. As often as not this was fixed and not related to the performance of the company. Thus previous foreign shareholders received not only some (albeit frequently delayed) compensation for the shares sold, but also a reliable annual income. In the 1980s payments of this kind, and for related royalties and patents, have come to equal about 40 per cent of the income in dividends which accrues to foreign investors[17] and they are usually given priority in payment over dividends. In Nigeria they averaged about $200 million per year between 1981 and 1986.[18]

Second, in the cases where the previous management was not invited to stay on, or declined to do so, lower levels of efficiency in management have proved disastrously expensive. Such management has been recruited from a combination of civil servants with little or no commercial experience, individuals with limited commercial experience in, for instance, the co-operative movement, individuals with experience in foreign-owned enterprises but at a low level, or even ex-politicians. Such management has been particularly subject to political pressure in support of localism, both from central government and from regional and district governments.

THE STATE IN BUSINESS

The inadequacies of management in state enterprises have been described in dramatic terms by several Nigerian academic observers, one of whom wrote in 1974 that the reasons for the poor performance of the state-owned sector could be seen in the words of one observer 'in the over centralization of authority ... inspired by sheer love of power'[19] or by another:

> in unwise policy decisions; in day to day ineptness in running the enterprises; in illicit government transfer payments in construction and purchase contracts and through every other imaginable channel; in the use of contractor finance and suppliers' credits to finance the venality of state officials; and in overburdened and unrealistic capital structures.[20]

Such a management style was by no means typical of Nigeria alone. Direct theft from the parastatal system was common in Tanzania by the 1980s. Thus in 1988 the Tanzanian Parliamentary Public Accounts Committee reported that about $5 million had been taken in 1987 in the form of 'outright theft' from parastatal companies.[21]

If there is a prevailing thread in the history of these state-owned enterprises it is the constant under-assessment of risk – of the lack of imported materials to supply a manufacturing process, of failure in the supply of inputs ranging from petrol to fertilizer, of farming communities not producing the cash crops to keep a processing plant in operation, and of failing to find competent management for complex operations. Even when meaningful financial rates of return were calculated, and proved to be low, but just in excess of the cost of borrowing, decisions were taken to implement projects as a result of pressure for action. This risk negligence also affected the choice of technology: projects which appeared to achieve high levels of production rapidly by using advanced technology would be preferred to those which achieved them more slowly by using more appropriate technology.

In fact, government-owned companies, far from providing support to national revenues, became a major drain upon them as is apparent from the following summary from the government's own Economic Survey of 1982 of the state of Tanzania's state-owned textile mills:

The combined output of the five largest textile factories, namely the Friendship Textile Mill, Mwatex, Mutex, Kiltex and Sunguratex was only 67.2 million sq. metres of cloth, compared to their total installed capacity of 152 million square metres. Capacity utilisation for these five factories is thus only 44.2 per cent.

The output of the Mwatex Mill was only 4.8 million sq.metres compared to the existing capacity for the mill of 45 million sq.metres. The mill experienced an acute power problem during the year following the breakdown of its four generators, grinding the mill to a complete halt between October 1982 and March 1983. Even after repair works on the generators had been done, only two of them operated satisfactorily forcing the factory to work on only two shifts instead of the usual three. Mutex also experienced power problems and shortage of spare parts, while shortage of fuel oil used in the boilers affected both Mutex and Mwatex. The Kiltex mill in Dar es salaam closed temporarily due to lack of water and shortage of spare parts, while the Arusha Mill could not operate to full capacity because polyester yarn could not be imported in sufficient quantities. Sunguratex experienced inadequate and intermittent water supplies and shortage of spare parts while Blanket manufacturers was mainly

affected by non-availability of spare parts for its ageing machinery.

This is a description of an industrial disaster seldom
experienced in peacetime conditions. In this situation it is
very difficult to 'rehabilitate' companies since the depreciated assets of these and similar businesses are virtually
worthless.

By the late 1970s the state sector had become not only a
harbour of inefficiency, as in many 'developed' countries,
but also a greenhouse of the hybrid values emerging in
Africa many of which were inimical to efficient methods of
low-cost production.

CITIZEN ENTREPRENEURS

Promotion of the state-owned sector has generally gone
hand in hand with promotion of the indigenous, i.e.
African, private sector, although in 'socialist' countries the
scope of the latter has sometimes been consciously
restricted. In 1966 Nkrumah said that

if he permitted African businessmen to grow [they]
will grow to the extent of becoming a rival power to his
and the party's prestige, and he would do anything to
stop it.[22]

If socialist regimes have been reluctant to promote
indigenous businessmen for this reason, most regimes have
sought to curtail the role of the immigrant groups who had
played a key role in the economy in the colonial period. In
the early 1960s many of these groups had the basic
financial strength and business experience to move into
manufacturing. However, in Kenya the result of these
policies was, for instance, that 'the local Asian bourgeoisie
was really placed in a category of foreign investor.'[23] In
Uganda (a country whose modern sector had been largely

built by Indian entrepreneurs) Milton Obote inserted a clause in the new Republican Constitution in 1966 which restricted the ownership of 'land, property or business' in certain areas to 'citizens of African blood'. Six years later Idi Amin expelled the whole Asian community. In Tanzania the Asians suffered attrition in stages as the combined effects of the Arusha Declaration and the nationalization of both private houses and wholesale trade 'cut them off at the knees' as Nyerere expressed it.[24]

While this attitude of hostility to immigrant groups was less severe in west Africa it certainly played a role in Ghana from Nkrumah's period, and in Nigeria as a result of the 'localization' decree of 1974. It has also been seen in a more subtle form in the moves in Sierra Leone in the 1970s and Liberia in the 1980s by the 'truly indigenous' or tribal population to take economic power away from the creole population which had been active in trading and business for more than a century. This has been the principal objective of President Doe of Liberia, himself of tribal origin. It has been a less serious factor in the French-speaking countries where European traders and shop-keepers continue to operate small businesses, although these could be periodically subject to local political pressures including arbitrary taxation.

In contrast, in countries as distinct as Nigeria and Zambia, governments have supported the indigenous African entrepreneurs who benefited from these restraints on their potential competitors by a range of credit facilities and the judicious allocation of contracts. These allowed many former civil servants to enter business (notably in Zambia) and many of the established traders of west Africa (most dramatically in Nigeria) to move from commerce into production. In theory, each of these has the capacity to grow to be a medium and even large scale business, and to take on the corporate giants in the course of time. In practice, this has very seldom happened except when a local business has accepted a very dependent relationship with an outside investor. These limitations will be discussed in more detail in Chapter 10.

THE PRICE

In spite of the prevalence of economic planning in the 1960s and 1970s, it is doubtful whether a development policy has existed in most of Africa in the last twenty-five years. Rather, the critical determinant of economic policy has been the hidden or not so hidden hand of political priorities. Those priorities have reflected politicians' prime concern: to centralize economic power in the hands of the government in a way which matched the centralization of political power as expressed through the one-party state.

In the agricultural sector, the self-interest of the state has led to policies which have favoured distorted exchange rates, consistently favouring government and the urban population at the expense of the incomes of rural families, and ultimately at the expense of marketed production. Giant and inefficient marketing boards have had the opposite effect of their nominal purpose, and have further squeezed farmers' margins. The voices of rural families have seldom been heard in effective protest, and least of all in socialist states such as Tanzania and Mozambique, each of which have compelled large chunks of their rural population to live in communal villages against their will.

The process of centralization has involved governments in taking a major stake in investments which were previously foreign-owned. While justified in reaction to the dominance of foreign investment at the time of independence, it has proved to be a very expensive strategy. Ownership has sometimes been transferred into local hands (private or state) while the original owners have continued as managers on a financial basis which has frequently been unrelated to their performance. Where ownership has been transferred without continuity of management the levels of inefficiency experienced have often been disastrous, setting up a vicious spiral of under-performance.

While the truly indigenous private sector has been assisted in various ways to play a greater role in the national economy, this has often been at the expense of immigrant communities, who have rights of citizenship based on birth. This process has diminished the role which experienced local skills and capital could have played, and even the allocation of opportunities to the indigenous entrepreneur has seldom been fairhanded, and free of localism and corruption. Four of Africa's most talented peoples – the Ibo, the Bamilike, the waChagga and the Bugunda – have all had their innovative talents circumscribed for many years.

Putting the 'political kingdom' first has been expensive and is now self-evidently an expense which Africa can no longer afford.

9
The Elusive Surplus

The real heroes of agriculture in Africa are the pioneers who down the centuries have brought new crops or cattle to their own or other communities. The story recalled in Chapter 2 of a stranger named Chipimbi who came to live amongst the Lamba of Zambia, and brought them seeds of maize, sorghum and groundnuts, was one such hero. His fellows include those who brought bananas from the Indian Ocean coast to the highlands of east Africa, those who brought cassava from the Atlantic coast of Angola to the forests of Zaire, and those who first trekked the hump-backed Zebu cattle down the valley of the Nile. In every case where such innovations proved lasting, it was because they adapted well to the specific environment of the farmers. Frequently, they were the key to the constant moving frontier of the Bantu expansion.

However, for every successful adoption of a new crop or new variety of crop it is certain that there were many more failed attempts at innovation, for the African physical environment places many difficulties in the path of farmers. Rainfall is uncertain and varied – drought years may be as many as one in five; many soils are eroded and soil quality may vary within as little space as a hectare; even small-scale irrigation may be ineffective as high levels of 'run-off'

prevent the efficient use of water. The first cultivators in
Africa, as in all parts of the world, would farm a field for a
few years and then, when its fertility began to drop, move
on to an adjacent, or occasionally distant, area where high
yields could be maintained for a similar period. When land
became scarce farmers could move back to land that they,
or their fathers had already cultivated. The length of the
period of cultivation in this bush/fallow cycle depended on
the quality of the soils, the requirement of the crops for
nutrients, and on whether fertility was supplemented by
cattle manure from the farmers' own livestock. As a result,
it could vary from one to four or five years, with fallow
periods of four to twenty years, the greater periods being
common in the equatorial forests.

FEEDING THE PEOPLE

In some cases new crops and local innovation made quite
high levels of population density possible, and reduced the
necessary fallow period to only one or two years. These
cases included the waChagga on Kilimanjaro, the Ibo in
eastern Nigeria, the Bamilike of western Cameroun, as
well as smaller groups such as the waKara who inhabit an
island on Lake Victoria and the waTengo in hill country in
south-west Tanzania. One of the first written descriptions
of the waChagga system is that of Sir Harry Johnston in
1894:

> They mostly excel in their industry – the skill with
> which they irrigate their terraced hillsides with tiny
> runnels of water shows a considerable advancement in
> agriculture. Their time is constantly spent in tilling
> the soil, manuring it with ashes, rakeing and hoeing it
> with wooden hoes.[1]

This system was probably capable of supporting about 400
people per square mile. The similarly complex system

developed by the waTengo was based on a pattern in which grass, weeds and crop refuse were composted in pits which were retained in both cropping and fallow periods. This very effectively conserved run-off and avoided water logging. Both these mountainside systems had been developed as a response to communities being forced by hostile forces (the Masai in the case of the waChagga, and the Nguni in the case of the waTengo) to live in a restricted area.

The experience of the waKara is rather different. Here, the pressure of population growth within the confines of a small island of only 29 square miles led to the development of an innovatory, intensive system based on very effective soil conservation techniques – including the integration of fodder and arable crops and livestock. The waKara farmed on the basis of a three-year rotation of bullrush millet, groundbeans and sorghum. During this three-year period they applied two dressings of farmyard manure and in the intervening year they applied an indigenous legume crop as green manure. This system enabled them to maintain an exceptionally dense population, on the best principles of fertility conservation.

The waKara were not exceptional in combining the ownership of livestock with crop production, but they were exceptional in integrating the two. Other African communities, such as the Lozi on the Barotse floodplain in western Zambia, and, on a smaller scale the Yoruba in western Nigeria, maintained livestock herds which were essentially secondary to their crop production, providing manure for crops on an *ad hoc* basis. The true pastoralists, such as the Fulani, the Dinka of southern Sudan and the Masai of the east African plains were in a different category. They were primarily dependent on their cattle for subsistence – particularly from milk and blood – though in some cases also planted short-season sorghum or millet as a supplement. They might make an incidental contribution to crop production by agreeing to graze their herds over settled farmers' land once it had been harvested. Further, the size of their herds could rise and fall dramatically depending upon the incidence of livestock diseases such as foot-and-mouth and rinderpest. In the 1880s, the large herds of the kingdom of Karagwe in western Tanzania were severely depleted by rinderpest, and did not recover for several decades.

Thus the agricultural systems of pre-colonial Africa were in a delicate balance with the environment, and sometimes with each other. They supported a total population estimated at about 100 million, which remained more or less static from 1600 to 1850[2] – or about 5 people per square mile of cultivable land.[3] Although innovation in particular cases had fostered very high population densities, it was the absence of population growth resulting from both the slave trade and the incidence of disease that provided little general incentive to intensify systems which were an adequate response to the difficulties of the environment.

IMPERIAL INTERVENTION

Before the First World War the impact of the new colonial governments on this pattern of agriculture was extremely limited. Their primary emphasis was on the development of large-scale commercial agriculture – either through large, corporate-owned estates (as with oil palm in Zaire, coffee, and bananas in Cameroun, and cotton in Sudan), through individual settlers (as in Kenya, Zimbabwe and Zambia), or through both (as in Tanzania and Cameroun). Sometimes this went hand in hand with the development of small-scale agriculture, although the circumstances in which this occurred varied greatly. Sometimes, as with cotton in Zaire, Chad and Tanzania such planting was compulsory; sometimes, as with cocoa in Ghana, coffee in Cameroun and cotton in Uganda and Sudan it was voluntary. However in these years the total area of land devoted to such cash crops by smallholders was miniscule in relation to the total area in production, and had little impact on the bush/fallow system as it had been traditionally practised.

In the 1920s and 1930s there was a change of policy within the colonial powers which placed greater importance on the need for African colonies to be financially self-supporting. A much stronger emphasis on all forms of export agriculture, particularly through smallholder production, was one way of achieving this. Production of cotton in Uganda grew from 20,000 bales in 1920 to 400,000 in 1935; exports of palm oil from Zaire grew from 40,000 tonnes in 1915 to 150,000 tonnes in 1935.[4] These dramatic increases in production intensified during or after World War Two: in Nigeria groundnut production tripled between 1938 and 1948; in Uganda coffee production also tripled in the 1950s; in Zaire there were 800,000 cotton growers by 1950.

As the total area allocated to these crops increased, so the amount of time and land which a family could devote to food crop production for its own consumption often diminished. Yet, from the inter-war years, as medical services spread, the total population of Africa began to rise sharply. Between 1921 and 1944 the population of Kenya grew from 2.3 million to 3.8 million, and annual rates of growth of more than 2 per cent became the norm across most of the continent. Average population densities doubled between 1900 and 1960.[5] The introduction of cash crops and an increasing population acted together to increase pressure on the land significantly, in specific cases even to critical levels, such as in Ruanda and in the 'reserves' of Kenya and Zimbabwe. By 1970, about 20 per cent of the land in cultivation was down to export crops.[6] Where large numbers of livestock existed, the introduction of modern veterinary services also reduced the mortality rate of cattle. The response of cattle owners was to increase the total numbers in their herd, rather than to maintain a smaller herd with lower mortality levels. Where such cattle were owned by cultivators, as in Sukumaland in Tanzania, this also increased pressure on the land available for farming.

W.H. Allan, once director of agriculture in Northern Rhodesia and the author of a definitive work on change in smallholder African agriculture, summarized the consequent situation in the late 1950s as follows:

> By the end of the first fifty years of agricultural effort, the standard of land use showed a general decline and fertility was falling. An advanced state of decay, with increasing soil loss by erosion, had been reached in the overcrowded regions where the traditional systems had collapsed and had been replaced by continuous cultivation.
>
> Elsewhere a slower rate of degeneration had been set in train by labour migration and withdrawal of the most active section of the labour force from rural areas, the weakening of traditional restraints on harmful land use, and a general loss of self reliance and sense of responsibility for the land under European domination.[7]

Colonial governments responded to this worsening situation with various approaches: first, an attempt to impose a code of conservation practice on existing farms; second, an attempt to produce a group of 'master farmers'; and third, an attempt to transform the practices of whole communities by re-settlement.

One of the most dramatic examples of the first case was in Ruanda, where as early as the 1930s

> under the strict Belgian administration, every adult male has one and a quarter acres a year under cultivation *all the time* and at least a third of this must be under cassava and sweet potatoes. They must sow twice a year. They must irrigate and cultivate the swamps during the rainy season. In this re-afforestation campaign every tax payer must plant at least a fifth of an acre of trees.[8]

By the 1950s the situation in Tanzanian Sukumuland was also of great concern to its British administrators. In that

decade the land area planted to cotton increased from
67,000 hectares to 170,000 hectares, and fears grew of a
long-term decline in fertility. A tough and wide-ranging
conservation programme was introduced as an anti-famine
measure. Farmers were required to make 'tie ridges' which
conserved moisture within the soil, to manure a certain
proportion of their fields, and to plant a specified minimum
acreage of cotton and cassava. This campaign, however,
was never fully effective.

The second approach was the attempt to create a new
class of 'master farmer'. Such individuals were to be the
standard-bearers of an agricultural revolution based on a
farming system which overcame the limitations of African
soils by the scientific rotation of crops and their integration
with livestock. The aim was confirmed for Malawi, for
instance, in a 1958 report which stated:

> It is Government's aim to create a class of full time
> professional farmers with sufficient land to provide a
> reasonable standard of living and, as a corollary,
> gradually to squeeze the subsistence cultivator off the
> land into full time alternative employment ... the
> Master Farmers Scheme was designed to create and
> develop such farmers.[9]

Schemes of this kind enjoyed success only on a limited
front. An 'improved farmer' scheme in northern Nigeria
achieved an average intake of 1,900 farmers a year from
1945 to 1955, with a failure rate of only 20 per cent.
However such farmers were necessarily exceptions within a
farming community where shortening bush/fallow cycles
were retained; they did not provide a solution to the
underlying problem.

One of the most far reaching attempts within the third
approach – the resettlement of large numbers of small
farmers on newly defined farms – was in Zaire. There the
Belgian administration developed a system of 'paysannats'
based on a crop rotation within specially demarcated strips.

These were subdivided into smaller fields and a cropping rotation devised with the objective of moving production up and down the length of the strip. A sufficient proportion of the strip was in fallow at any one time to ensure that yields were, in theory, maintained over a fifteen or twenty year period. Separate designs were evolved for the very different conditions of forest and savannah. In the former, the key cash crop was oil palm, and in the latter cotton.

The first paysannat was established in 1936 and the example, with adjustments, was subsequently widely followed. By 1954, about 1.5 million hectares were under the system, divided between nearly 170,000 farming families. By 1960, progress had been made towards establishing half a million family units. One of the administrators of the scheme summarized its objective as being to

> replace unorganized extensive agriculture, which often entails the irremediable destruction of natural wealth, by an agriculture which will become progressively intensive, at the same time assuring the continuing fertility of the soils.[10]

The key to the paysannat concept, as indicated here, was that it would become more intensive over time. It was recognized that the integration of some kind of livestock farming with crops would ultimately be desirable. It was strongly supported in the 1950s by the companies who purchased the cotton grown as a cash crop in the savannah, because it appeared to be the most effective way to reverse the declining fertility and falling yields which had become apparent by that time.

The development of the system spanned more than twenty years and achieved a degree of success in terms of its defined objectives. It was unpopular politically, as it involved a good deal of compulsion, and did not survive the chaos of independence. However, it was probably the most serious attempt made in colonial Africa to adapt the traditional bush/fallow system to changing economic circumstances and, if sustained, might have provided technical answers to problems which still prove elusive. Only in the 1980s has large-scale scientific work on bush/fallow rotation in the forest belt been revived, at the International Institute of Tropical Agriculture (IITA) in Nigeria.

A successful initiative

A further, far reaching initiative within this approach was made in Kenya immediately after the Mau Mau Emergency of 1954–7. The situation in the Kikuyu areas of Kenya had become particularly acute by the 1950s as a result of the re-allocation from 1910 onwards of over 7 million acres of land to private European settlers. Kikuyu farmers had traditionally farmed several plots which were within easy walking distance but had different characteristics of altitude and soil type. Following the death of a land owner, his land would be divided between his sons; as the population increased the fragmentation which resulted from this approach became increasingly serious. The introduction of cash crops in the 1930s further reduced the amount of land available for food production.

In Meru District by 1950 there was an average of five fragments per cultivator; the maximum was twenty-two. The outermost fragments were as much as 20 miles apart.[11] It was the Mau Mau conflict itself which forced the government to recognize the need to increase the productivity of the Kikuyu areas, and it was the same conflict which facilitated the means. However, the plan for this far-reaching land reform, drawn up by Roger Swynnerton of the Agricultural Department, was imaginative and effective. It envisaged the consolidation of the scattered plots into farms of 7 to 10 acres, supporting an average household of six to eight people. Such farms were to be carefully laid out by agricultural officers on the basis of an arable/grass ley rotation, including appropriate cash crops such as coffee and pyretheum. Following consolidation, farmers would have irrevocable freehold tenure to their land. The work was to be completed over the whole country in fifteen years.

In the District of Kiambu alone, over 500,000 fragmented plots were consolidated into 50,000 farms between 1956 and 1960. Such a far reaching change could ultimately only have been achieved with general Kikuyu support. By 1960 the process had achieved its own momentum so that

> most European officers felt that they were no longer pushing out ideas and standards; in large measures the people themselves had seen the benefits and were doing it themselves.[12]

The success of this approach was reflected in a threefold increase in marketed output from 1953 to 1962 in the areas where land reform had been implemented, without a matching decline in the productivity of food crops. Since that time the productivity of the top 20 per cent of farmers has been sustained with a continuous record of technical improvement; about 40 per cent have maintained a level of productivity which enables them to generate an acceptable income; and a further 40 per cent have continued to produce enough for their own household's subsistence requirements.

Of these three policies adopted by colonial governments to deal with the acute pressure on land, the Kenyan example of land reform was the most successful, and the one whose benefits lasted well beyond independence. Nonetheless, whatever success was achieved within these programmes it was not enough to change the general picture of an agricultural system which could only expand production by having access to more land. The practices of livestock owners had not changed significantly with the spread of veterinary services and they too required more land. In 1960, looking at sub-saharan Africa as a whole, such land was still available since average population

densities were still only about 77 per square mile[13] of
cultivable land,[14] or 3 hectares per head. Much of this land
was uninhabited, and for a variety of reasons ranging from
the incidence of tsetse fly to the competing claims of
different clans, farmers were reluctant to move into it.

The agricultural legacy of the colonial period was
sometimes a modified form of shifting cultivation, sometimes a form of settled agriculture which tended to deplete
the fertility of the soil. The adaptability of African farmers
was not in doubt, but whether they would be given the
means to expand production to meet growing urban and
international markets was an open question.

THE RUSH FOR GROWTH

Most newly independent governments were attracted to an
agricultural strategy which thrust aside the supposed
limitations of the existing agricultural system and adopted
various forms of 'transformation' approach. In some cases
this included a continued emphasis on an elite group of
master farmers; in others it included the development of
settlement schemes where a concentration of supporting
services were supposed to create a group of commercial, if
small-scale, farmers; in others it included the development
of large government-owned estates, managed by parastatal
companies as described in Chapter 8.

With some exceptions, the transformation approach has
not been successful. The reasons for this include both the
design of the projects – ranging from the crops selected to
the land to which people have moved – and the quality of
their management. In the 1960s and 1970s these problems
were consistently underrated by governments. The most
dramatic examples of this approach have included the
massive resettlement schemes in Tanzania and Mozambique in the 1970s, and in Ethiopia in the mid 1980s. In
each case the consequences of moving a million or more
people, in the case of Tanzania, at least five million, were
hardly recognized before the operations began. In Tanzania
in the early 1980s, 90 per cent of agricultural production in

the resettled villages was still geared to subsistence consumption and there had been no long-term increase in the productivity of the farmers involved.[14]

Whatever resources were devoted to the transformation approach, the bulk of agricultural production continued to come from the millions of small farming families who were adjusting their forms of production only slowly. In some cases they received support from government services for the first time. In Zambia, the provision of hybrid maize seed, fertiliser and marketing services to small-scale farmers dated from the mid 1960s; in Kenya the provision of such services was extended for the first time in the 1960s well beyond the Kikuyu. The response was erratic. The local physical environment was not always well matched to these inputs. Unjustified financial risk could be incurred by using fertiliser in an area of erratic rainfall; the labour required on cash crops could conflict with the labour required on food crops. These dangers were matched to the inefficiency of the marketing boards which in most countries were supposed to buy the crop, and to the pricing policies discussed in Chapter 8 which until the mid 1980s consistently worked against the interests of small farmers.

As a result, the majority of farmers continued to concentrate their efforts on the production of food for their own families, rather than for the market. Between 1960 and 1980 the total acreage devoted to food production in Africa increased from about 70 million hectares to about 100 million,[15] or about 2.5 per cent per year, sufficient to sustain a population increase of about 2.7 per cent. Yet during the same period the acreage devoted to export crops grew from only 15.5 million hectares to 17.2 million; of the seven major export crops[16] the production volume of only three: tea, cotton and tobacco, increased.[17] Livestock owners continued to manage their herds primarily as a means of survival and a bank of wealth rather than to maximize the number of animals they marketed. Africa's trade in cereals was seriously skewed. She might, as in 1986–7, have to import 8 million tonnes of cereals, amounting to about 40 per cent of urban consumption,[18] or, as in 1988/9 have a surplus of 3 million tonnes which could not be transported, and thus sold, to deficit countries.[19]

Within this overall picture one approach, when well managed, appeared to combine the potential of commercial large-scale management with the potential of small farmers to achieve an increase in productivity. A number of projects have been successful in which the supply of inputs and the marketing of the product are managed on a commercial basis while the bulk of production comes from small farmers. These include the Smallholder Coffee Authority in Malawi, which supports 4,000 growers, the Mumias Sugar Company in Kenya which supports 30,000 growers, and the Kenya Tea Development Authority, which through a network of forty factories, supports over 150,000 small farmers. All of these are projects in which the government holds a controlling interest and in which it has a strong commercial partner.[20] In each of these cases the majority of farmers have less than 1 hectare under the relevant crop, but most achieve levels of income well in excess of their neighbours who remain outside the projects. Sometimes this success is at the expense of food production, but more often an increase in productivity is achieved across all crops. While projects of this kind can be very impressive they cannot hope to generate an increase in output from the mass of small scale farmers, as their requirement for scarce, high level mangement is too great.

THE CURRENT REALITY

The last thirty years have not therefore established precedents for the future. The rural population is growing at over 2 per cent per year and densities are increasing. The underlying position remains one in which most of the rural population i.e. three quarters of the total, is able to feed itself adequately, but has neither the surplus labour nor the technology to make big strides in productivity. The erratic performance of organizations which are supposed to support farmers, such as input supply companies and marketing boards, only exacerbates the situation. Although some farmers *are* adopting more intensive systems of production this is not yet at a fast enough rate to generate the large increases in marketed output necessary to feed the towns, where the population is growing at over 6 per cent per year.

Areas of critical population density continue to co-exist with areas which are relatively under-populated. In a wide band of west Africa, from Dakar to Kano including the 'sahelian' and 'sudanian' zones, the total population in 1980 was about 30 million at an *average* of 17 people per square kilometre. Forty per cent of the people live in only 6 per cent of the total area, and densities rise to 100 per square kilometre. To the south of this zone, where tree cover becomes more dense in the Guinea-savannah, population densities are particularly low and there is plenty of scope for inward migration. This is occurring spontaneously, but not at a rate which significantly affects the dense clusters further north.[21] Such situations are replicated elsewhere: even in Tanzania, with its 24 million people, as much as one-third of the cultivable area is under-populated.[22]

The facts that much farmed land falls short of its potential and that in large areas of Africa population levels are low, do not alter the fact that innovators in the tradition of Chipimbi continue to succeed in achieving important increases in productivity. On a farm two miles from Ngaoundere, in northern Cameroun, Alhaji Hamayadji Giwa cultivates, with the support of his two wives, three hectares of sweet potatoes, bananas and ground-nuts. The sweet potatoes are all of a specific variety, namely TIB 1, which is the product of breeding work carried out at IITA in Nigeria in the 1970s. The yield of TIB 1 is three to four times greater than that of the local variety of sweet potato and Giwa is able to market about 60 tons of sweet potatoes per year. Maintaining production at this level is back-breaking work. However, the farm is one of the main sources of supply to the Ngaoundere market and use of TIB 1 has enabled Giwa to become an affluent 'yeoman' farmer.

More modest, but important, increases in the productivity of another root crop, cassava, have also been achieved by thousands of small farmers in western Nigeria. Here, too, the cassava variety is the result of breeding work at IITA which has been available to farmers since 1978. Ten years later in Oyo State, which has a total of about 100,000 farming families, nearly half of the land area had been planted with the new variety which out-yields the local varieties by about 25 per cent. As 60 per cent of the cassava grown in this area is marketed in towns, a yield increase even of this order of magnitude has had a positive impact on urban food supplies. An even greater sustained impact on productivity has occurred amongst the thousands of small farmers in the former reserve areas of Zimbabwe. Here, the introduction of the hybrid maize variety SR 52 has had a dramatic effect on yields of maize. From 1979, when the hybrids were distributed on a wide scale, to 1985 yields almost doubled. As production increased farmers had a growing surplus over their household requirements and sold an increasing proportion of their crop, reaching 60 per cent in 1985 and in 1988, and accounting for half of the national marketed production.

Successes of this kind occur where technology, the potential of the farming system, and the market allow it. In some areas these factors have to be reinforced by the provision of seasonal credit to enable farmers to adopt an innovation. Thus in northern Nigeria there has been a long-established practice of Hausa farmers purchasing immature beef cattle at the end of the harvesting season, and feeding them on maize stalks and other crop residues during the dry season, before marketing them at the end of six months. Space on the farm, and lack of finance, restricted the practice to an average of one beefcattle per farmer. From 1976 credit was made available specifically for this purpose and farmers were encouraged to hold more than one animal, and to build stalls and improve feeding materials. Within five years there were over 4000 smallholders participating in the scheme, and their marketed output had increased by nearly three times over previous levels. In this case a strategy of building and strengthening an existing practice had combined with organizational arrangements to increase small farmers' output.[23]

FOOD FOR THE FUTURE

The objectives of farmers in the future will be first, to continue feeding their families and second to take advantage of the expanding urban market. Exports are likely to rank only as a third objective. Whether they can increase production at a rate which allows urban markets to be fed and exports to be maintained depends on several factors. Production systems will have to be intensified in ways which do not deplete fertility; areas which are now underpopulated will have to be used more productively; the organizations which serve small farmers, including **relevant agricultural research institutes, will have to be** strengthened; and finally, agricultural prices will have to be maintained at a level which provides an incentive.

Important policy changes have been adopted by governments in agriculture in the late 1980s as a response to the relative failure of the preceding twenty-five years. These have frequently been made in response to pressure from major international aid donors. The most substantive changes have been considerable upward adjustments in prices paid to farmers, which have had a positive effect on output. It is doubtful, however, whether the changes implemented to date constitute an adequate boost towards achieving a continuous increase in marketed surpluses. The great majority of farmers continue to use minimal quantities of fertiliser although fertility is being depleted; few governments are tackling the question of the use of their under-populated areas on a systematic basis; the organizations which serve small farmers have cut back their operations in response to budgetary pressures and in response to the pressure for privatization; the frequently competent staff of national agricultural research bodies are everywhere starved of funds for transport and field labour.

Those countries which had the best record of increasing productivity in the 1960s and 1970s, such as Kenya and Cameroun, are no longer maintaining their momentum. Irrigation has been shown to have potential on a relatively small scale, but cannot be a solution for the mass of farmers.

In spite of this, innovation by individuals and communities of farmers in Africa will continue, and for the most part will enable rural families to maintain themselves at a reasonable level of nutrition. Food supplies to the one third of the population, or 230 million people, who will be living in towns by the year 2000 will be uneven, and a continued dependence on imports, if they can be financed, is likely. The labour which rural families can devote to export crops will not grow significantly as a proportion of the total and – except where export crops have a very high value, as in the case of horticulture – they will grow only slowly, if at all.

10
Artisans and Entrepreneurs: the Industrial Dilemma

Pre-colonial Africa did not lack entrepreneurs who managed trading companies, in some cases stretching well beyond contemporary national frontiers, and which had the capacity to invest profits from trade in production. As shown in Chapter 4, from medieval times gold was being exported from the Shona-speaking kingdoms centred at Great Zimbabwe through Arab traders at Sofala in Mozambique. The trade was sufficiently profitable for the Portuguese to take over Sofala in the early sixteenth century, and their written accounts confirm that the export cargoes were brought to the coast by African representatives of the Shona king or *monomutapa*. In West Africa trade with the Mediterranean coast and Cairo was continuous from medieval times. The west African goldfields of Mali and Songhay probably produced about one-third of the gold in circulation in late medieval Europe.[1] Leading merchants of the city-states of the savannah maintained important trading links to the north. For instance, Malam Yaroh of Zinder in Niger maintained his own agents on the north African coast in the mid-nineteenth century. This network was so well developed that when Captain Hugh Clapperton 'discovered' Kano in 1824 he was able to obtain cash from a local merchant in return for a bill of exchange on the

British consul at Tripoli. Seventy years later the cloth merchants of Kano, who 'put out' yarn for weaving and organized the dyeing and marketing of the cloth, were exporting as far afield as Alexandria across the desert and Brazil across the sea. A single currency zone had operated in the Islamic states of the central savannah since the eighteenth century.[2]

Further south, the coastal merchants of west Africa had been trading with Europe for several centuries. Such activities were by no means limited to the slave trade. Cash crops were exported from early in the nineteenth century, such as ground-nuts from the Gambia in the 1830s, and oil palm and rubber from Ghana from the 1870s and 1890s respectively. The middlemen who organized supplies of these crops for European traders were not only accumulators of capital but also invested in new opportunities, such as that created by the demand for cocoa in the 1890s. It was the Akwapim people of southern Ghana, exposed to centuries of trading with Europe, who had the capital in the 1890s to hire porters and clear the forest in order to plant cocoa. In Nigeria in the same decade the first cocoa plantations were established by the African traders of Lagos, such as J.K. Coker, using pods from Fernando Po. Thus the pattern of accumulation of capital from trade for subsequent investment in production which was so important in late eighteenth-century Britain had had its roots in Africa before the colonial period.

However, such dynamic and far-sighted traders and producers did not operate in a context which was generally favourable to the development of wage-paid labour or the accumulation of capital. Chapter 3 described the web of relationships of pre-colonial societies in which kinship was the prime determinant of obligation and responsibility. Where large scale production existed it was carried out by slaves, as was the case with gold mining in the Asante kingdom. Among the few exceptions were the cocoa planters of Akwapim. In east Africa wage-paid labour was confined almost entirely to entrepôt ports such as Mombasa and Zanzibar.

Limits to the individual accumulation of capital were also set by, for instance, the Asante state whose long distance trade was shared between state merchants and wealthy private traders. The latter were not fully independent because

> the State both harassed the wealthy commoner with unpredictable exactions when he was alive and claimed a large proportion of his self acquired movable property when he died.[3]

This was so severe a problem that in the early twentieth century a petitioner to the *asantehene* protested against such death duties and said they had

> brought the downfall of the Asante nation and for this reason they had to bury their money underground so that more money was hidden underground than on the earth.[4]

The decay of older loyalties with the onset of the colonial era provided a new social context in which these limitations on entrepreneurs no longer applied. It may, however, be argued that there were deeper reasons for the relative weakness of African entrepreneurs at this time, that is, the absence of the kind of 'worldly asceticism' which Weber described as the key to European capitalism. In contrast

> the norm was certainly frank enjoyment of pleasure amidst a life often harsh and insecure. This hedonistic pragmatism is to be seen moulded for ever in the rolls of fat around the necks of the bronze and terracotta-heads from Ife.[5]

This of course was less true of the Islamic societies of the savannah which were periodically the subject of reform movements, with a strong ascetic bent, and of recurring significance in the twentieth century. In this century Christianity, too, would produce reform movements in which values close to those of the protestant ethic prevailed.

THE ERA OF THE MULTINATIONALS

Capitalist activity in the nineteenth century, for the reasons discussed above, was mainly associated with new types of activity, such as cocoa production or mineral mining, whether these were in the hands of European or African entrepreneurs. This was in the context of a world trading system geared to the industrial needs of Europe: as these intensified, the required scale of production in Africa gave an overwhelming advantage to the Europeans, with their store of skills and technology.

The opportunity was seized by European trading houses such as Lever Brothers, Union Miniere, the British-South Africa Company, and Lebanese, Syrian and Indian merchants. The total real value of exports from a selection of seven African countries[6] rose three and half times from 1907 to 1928, a further five times from 1928 to 1959 and a further four times from 1959 to 1982. Nearly all exported products were primary commodities such as palm oil and cocoa, or copper and gold. The associated investment in production and marketing gave the trading houses commanding positions within African economies.

In 1982 the total stock of that investment in Africa was estimated at about $13 billion,[7] with over half of it still concentrated in the production and export of primary commodities. Since 1976, the flow of new investment has been very modest, and in some years negative. Where there has been new investment it has been financed largely from income generated in Africa and re-invested locally. Consequently, companies from the old colonial powers of Britain and France continue to own about 30 per cent of the stock of foreign investments, with the USA and Japan owning another 50 per cent. In many countries this still gives the foreign investor a position of significance. In both Nigeria and Kenya, for example, foreign investment probably generates about one-fifth of Gross National Product. In these cases individual companies such as BAT in Kenya, Unilever in Kenya and Nigeria, Elf in Gabon, and CFAO in a number of francophone countries are operating at levels of sophistication which have no indigenous counterpart. The processes in use have frequently been heavily dependent on imports, with only a modest local added value, and have been sustained by relatively high levels of protection.

During the colonial period the response of African entrepreneurs to the growing presence of these large companies was varied. In the interstices of the system, particularly in west Africa, the older, established, trading families in cities such as Kano and newcomers to the commercial sector played a significant role. In the Islamic communities of the savannah religious reformation tended to reinforce entrepreneurial skill, as demonstrated by the Murid Brotherhood in Senegal and in the development of the 'Reformed Tijianiya' (a more fundamentalist and anti-colonial Islamic movement) which also originated in Senegal but spread through much of the savannah in the 1930s. In central Africa influential movements such as Jehovah's Witnesses were attractive to those who sought to set themselves apart and to adopt a puritan lifestyle.[8]

THE INFORMAL SECTOR

With some exceptions, the role of individuals influenced by these movements was very limited throughout the colonial period. At independence governments for the most part gave them preference over entrepreneurs from immigrant groups. Such preference as often as not excluded entrepreneurs from tribal groups out of favour with the government of the day, such as the Ibo, Bamilike, waGanda, and waChagga. Nonetheless, members of these communities and many others have developed small-scale enterprises in the informal sector which continue to grow in range and number. Such enterprises now account for more than 60 per cent of industrial employment in countries as far apart as Ghana and Tanzania;[9] more than half of them are located in small towns and villages, and the extended family is their most important source of labour; they contribute at least a quarter of total manufacturing output; and typically they employ between one and ten workers. An informal producer is always difficult to define but it is used here to describe an owner or an employee of a small-scale enterprise comprising less than ten people, operating from an impermanent site, under an ill-defined registration and tax scheme.

Within this sector there is a vast range of experience and competence. In Ethiopia, as in India, the role of the informal producer is not distinct from the mainstream of the economy, but is in fact a key part of it, producing for instance the home-spun cloth worn by most Ethiopian women. In the larger cities of Nigeria traditional clothes and the more basic household goods all continue to be made by local artisans. When imported cloth became more difficult to obtain from the mid 1980s tailors and seamstresses reverted to using a higher proportion of home-spun cloth woven on handlooms. In Ghana at Suame Magazine in the city of Kumasi, about 5,000 craftsmen operating in makeshift sheds, in small garages, and in workshops, offer a complete repair service to Ghana's fleet of ageing vehicles, all suffering badly from a ten-year shortage of spare parts. In Nairobi, most oil cans used in the routine servicing of vehicles are re-cycled to hold oil wicks dipped in paraffin as a main source of domestic light for both urban and rural homes.

In west Africa such small-scale entrepreneurs have long been tolerated, though seldom actively encouraged. The economy of a city of 2 million people, such as Ibadan, has grown on the back of this kind of enterprise. Modern corporate businesses are few and licences for small-scale repair shops and petty street traders provide a major share of city revenue. In contrast, in the European-style cities of east and central Africa such as Nairobi, Lusaka and Harare, the informals have frequently been hounded out of their preferred locations. In Lusaka, small-scale enterprise takes place mainly in the shanty towns three or four miles from the city centre.

In Nairobi, the origins of the several thousand metal workers who produce tin trunks, paraffin lamps, braziers, household utensils and agricultural tools on open sites, lie in both precolonial blacksmithing activities, and in Kenya's immigrant Indian communities, particularly the Sikhs and Bohras. The Sikhs were the main source of artisan skills as European-style buildings sprang up in Kenya from 1900 onwards. By the inter-war years such Sikh artisans had a number of Kenyan assistants adopting their skills; by the 1950s the Sikhs were moving on to the role of investor and entrepreneur in both construction and industry, leaving the way clear for their former assistants to take on the role of artisan. But employment in the building trade is notoriously irregular, and such artisans alternate self-employment with wage-paid work on the building sites.

The significance of the older pre-colonial blacksmith tradition is illustrated in cases from Nairobi brought to light by Kenneth King who examined the origins and experience of Nairobi informals in the early 1970s.[10] He describes the case of Mutang'ang'i one of the leading informals who at that time made foreguards for bicycles, bicycle stands and cutting machines using a series of hand-built metalworking machines which he had designed and built himself. He was the grandson of a traditional Kikuyu smith who made spears and knives in the late nineteenth century in a small village about twenty miles from Nairobi. He had initially made braziers and water carriers on the estate of a European settler, who had persuaded him to manufacture in addition chisels and hammers. Later, after four years in detention during the Mau Mau Emergency, he worked for an Indian workshop in Nairobi establishing himself as the pioneer manufacturer of bicycle carriers and foreguards. In the next fifteen years he effectively trained about forty others, including several step-brothers. They have been the nucleus of several hundred self-employed artisans manufacturing these bicycle attachments who can be seen on open sites across Nairobi. Faced with competition from his own protégés, Mutang'ang'i himself moved his product line to a more specifically agricultural market: maize stalk cutters, fence post nail machines and hand shears.

Observation of the range of products being made in the late 1980s by Nairobi's *jua kali* artisans – those who work under the 'hot sun' – confirm that Mutang'ang'i's story is far from unique. Product differentiation and improvement has been occurring steadily over the years and now includes metal and wooden window frames, doors, storage tanks, household furniture, beds, as well as a much improved range of braziers, and tin trunks. A good third of the stock of any hardware retail shop in Nairobi is now derived from this source. Kenya's one formal window frame manufacturer has been forced to move into a completely different business as the *jua kali* producers have been able to dominate the market with a product which is of equal quality but considerably cheaper. A welding machine designed and produced by *jua kali*s is beginning to compete with the conventional, imported Japanese product.

The individual work histories of Mutang'ang'i's original forty trainees include as many different jobs as were held by Mutang'ang'i himself, since the informal sector is typified by a very high turnover. Its members move in and out of employment, and in and out of Nairobi itself, at a very fast rate. In the 1950s and 1960s this ensured the rapid dissemination of such skills into towns and villages all over Kenya, and this process is being constantly reinforced.

What are the links between such informals and modern industry – not only in Kenya but elsewhere in Africa? First, many of the materials with which they work, such as scrap metal, textile waste, and timber, are recycled, often illicitly, from large scale industry. Second, many informals continue to work in the formal sector for several months at a time. Third, much of the construction industry depends on formal companies subcontracting at least half of a total work programme to informals, many of whom in turn use tools produced by other *jua kali* artisans. These factors suggest that an increase in turnover in the formal sector will ensure a reflected increase in turnover in the informal sector. However, these links do not form a cohesive whole, and there are weaknesses in the development of the informal sector which have tended to disguise its potential.

In practice, many though not all informals have no security of tenure over the site on which they work, have very few means of tying their small workforce to the enterprise for more than a few months, and may run out of their supply of recycled materials (from the formal sector) at any moment. Faced with this level of uncertainty, the response of employers within the sector has been to invest as much of their profits as possible in land or housing, if possible in their home area or within the city, if tenure is reasonably secure. One measure of the weakness of such enterprise is that it would be extremely difficult to ensure, across such a wide range, the quality control necessary for the export market outside Africa. So, while product development has been impressive, and confirms a certain level of re-investment, it does not usually lead to development of medium-sized businesses with tangible assets. Furthermore, although the sector is generating profits which in turn increase the national stock of capital, this is mainly in housing and land, and not in manufacturing capacity.

FORMALIZING THE INFORMALS

Can this be changed? The Peruvian economist Hernando de Soto in his book, *The Other Path*,[11] argues that such change can be brought about in the Latin American context by legalizing the informals. He sees the range of legal and bureaucratic constraints upon them as being the main limitation on their developing into self-sustaining businesses. This argument is partly valid in the African context: Mutang'ang'i was periodically obliged to remove his metal cutting machines from his worksite in Nairobi. On the other hand, a systematic survey by the International Labour Organization has shown that, in a sample of ten African countries, 40 per cent of informal sector enterprises pay some form of tax or registration fee, implying a degree of recognition by government.[12]

By the late 1980s no African government could afford to neglect the significance of the sector for the employment of the hundreds of thousands of primary and secondary school leavers who were joining the labour market each year, and most were making policy statements which indicated some support for it. However, it was also proving difficult to discard old attitudes. In Kenya, a member of a research institute, with a brief to find technology relevant to both formals and informals, could still describe the latter as mainly 'layabouts' in 1989. Despite the 1974–8 Kenya Development Plan stating 'there has been some counter productive harassment of these enterprises, which will be promptly ended',[13] in 1989 a complete informal vehicle maintenance site was abruptly closed down by the city government. In Nigeria, on the other hand, the National Open Apprenticeship Scheme is attempting to support forms of apprenticeship which have been traditional in the Nigerian informal sector, by seeking to upgrade their quality and supplement them with classroom training.

If initiatives of this kind are sustained, and matched by measures which increase the informals' security once they are in business, the sector can certainly gather greater strength and has the potential to generate jobs almost as fast as the urban population grows, but at very low levels of income, and in the form of enterprises where investment and technology is minimal. With exceptions, this is not a training ground for larger-scale entrepreneurs. In fact one of the striking characteristics of the history of Africa's informals during the last three decades is how few of them have managed to launch genuine large-scale businesses, capable of competing with the foreign-owned or -managed enterprises which are still so critical in many countries. Most of the exceptions to this pattern are in Nigeria where several large scale Nigerian-owned businesses have developed with a turnover measured in tens of millions of dollars.

NIGERIA: CRADLE OF ENTREPRENEURS?

A series of studies of such businessmen have been conducted by Nigerian scholars, and these are particularly significant given the fact that Nigeria acounts for one third of 'value added' in manufacturing in sub-Saharan Africa as a whole (excluding South Africa). Elsewhere, Africa's leading industrialists tend to be the chairmen or directors of companies which are owned or managed by multinational companies. The Nigerian studies throw doubt on whether these businesses are really self-sustaining, or revolve too heavily round the personality of their founder. They identify a failure to concentrate on taking a large market share for one product; in contrast they describe a preference for entering a new market before the full potential of the current one is reached. Of course, there is some justification for this: competition is intense and the Nigerian public's purchasing power low, and so returns may be higher from launching a new product in a different market.

A technical explanation of this kind however does not account for the continuing one-man-band nature of many such businesses, which prevents growth for organizational as well as market reasons. In a survey carried out in the mid 1960s of 419 businesses in western Nigeria, 74 per cent said that 'partnerships or joint ventures were difficult or undesirable because of financial untrustworthiness'.[14] Individuals among them went on to say:

—The spirit of cheating reigns supreme amongst us;

—Honesty is still wanting amongst the indigenous
businessmen;
—Most of our businessmen are not honest.

In Ghana one-man proprietorships characterized 75 per
cent of larger, locally-owned firms in the late 1960s.

The most notable exceptions to this pattern are found in
Kano where a 1975 study[15] showed that nineteen of
Nigeria's twenty largest industrial companies were located.
This may be attributed to the fact that the city's traders
were not swamped by the growth of the larger British
companies during the colonial period, that among the
merchant families involved in the kola nut trade, two
generations were common, and that merchant families in
Kano were particularly successful from the early 1960s at
forming links with overseas companies, not least with
those from the Far East. It may also have been connected
with the recurring impact in Kano of the Islamic 'ascetic'
movements, particularly current in commercial circles.

However the situation found in Kano was not typical of
west Africa or even of Nigeria, and the one-man-band was
and is the predominant theme. While it has been suggested
that the absence of a cadre of professional managers is a
major explanation for this situation, the real reasons
almost certainly lie closer to the psychology of the
entrepreneurs themselves. Few of them in Nigeria, as
elsewhere, have more than ten years of schooling. Therefore older rural values relating to power and status, and
especially the ability to redistribute patronage, pre-
dominate. Consequently, the criteria of 'profit maximiza-
tion' and 'efficiency of management' are frequently not
critical.

Whether more and better schooling would in the short
run produce a larger group of efficient entrepreneurs,
capable of making individual businesses more competitive,
is an open question. Akeredolu-ale, one of the Nigerian
analysts of local entrepreneurs, writing in 1975 saw deeper
problems:

Private indigenous entrepreneurs in Nigeria are still
to cultivate the discipline of conserving more than they
consume of their trade surplus and of re-investing such
surpluses to expand the firm. Very limited entrepreneurial ambitions, conspicuous consumption and a
tendency to spread their thin investments over many
ventures [the 'group of companies' mentality], a
tendency ... to only scratch the surface of innovation,
the aversion to teaming up with others, all these and
other motivational factors are likely to continue to
limit the growth of Nigerian enterprises even in those
spheres which are exclusively reserved to them and to
postpone the day when they may hope to take over the
higher reaches of enterprise.[16]

In his earlier analysis in 1969 of Nigerian businessmen,
Kilby reached similar conclusions:

While Yoruba and Ibo patterns of status mobility
based on achieved wealth provide a strong incentive to
establish a business enterprise as a means of obtaining
high social status, once established there are no
antecedent roles conferring respect for efficient managerial performance. On the contrary, because conspicuous leisure is the principal manifestation of
superior status, the carrying out of supervisory functions ... represents a socially degrading activity...[17]

These descriptions of the prospects for Nigerian entrepreneurs are hardly encouraging. If, however, they were
too pessimistic this should have been belied in the
subsequent years since the Nigerian Indigenization Decree
of 1972, implemented from February 1974, which reserved
twenty-six activities in large-scale industry exclusively for
Nigerian ownership; foreign companies operating in these
businesses had to sell out.[18] The results of this measure
were that 50 per cent of total manufacturing activity
(measured by value added) was left entirely in Nigerian

hands. While there was certainly an increase in the output of these businesses in the prosperous years of the late 1970s it is doubtful if they did more than keep pace with the fast growth rate for the manufacturing sector as a whole, estimated by the World Bank to be 12 per cent from 1970 to 1982.[19] Further, they certainly did not succeed in swimming against the deep tide of recession which engulfed Nigeria from 1983 onwards. In theory, during this period their potential to adapt technology to source inputs locally (as had occurred in Biafra during the civil war), rather than to import them might have given them a competitive edge over the large manufacturing companies managed and partly owned from overseas. In practice, the description of the potential of their businesses made by Akeredolu-Ale and Kilby proved to be substantially valid.

The time span which is likely to be required for a generation of more effective large-scale entrepreneurs to evolve is considerable. One of the problems for those entrepreneurs, and other corporate managers, who do seek to act as professional industrialists is that the context in which they operate is dominated by the values described in earlier chapters. For instance, the manager of an airline, however committed he may be to an efficient seat reservation system, may be obliged to withdraw seats already allocated in favour of a minister and his train of attendants. Another entrepreneur establishing a sack-making factory with limited protection, may find a relative of the president given a licence to import freely the same product. Alhaji Abbo is a former truck driver who has successfully developed a 3,000 hectare maize farm and oil extraction plant in northern Cameroun. In 1989 he was obliged to move out of his house to live on the farm in order to avoid the pressure to entertain visiting dignitaries on behalf of local politicians. Thus whether the would-be efficient entrepreneur rises from the informal sector or parachutes into a larger-scale enterprise with a degree from an international business school, he will frequently be trapped into the same style of running a business as the Nigerian enterpreneurs described above.

SMALL IS STILL BEAUTIFUL

Entrepreneurs in pre-colonial Africa were effective in articulating trading relationships between Africa and the rest of the world, and in developing the productive activities which generated the trade. The colonial period ushered in an era of foreign investment which gave the large scale trading houses of Europe a hold on the development of local economies allowing little room for Africa's entrepreneurs to develop their skills. In spite of the nationalizations of the 1960s and 1970s the stock of capital of foreign investors continues to generate about one-fifth of Africa's gross national product.

The many and varied attempts by governments both to take over foreign assets and to set up new state-owned businesses, have seldom been successful. While state-owned and foreign businesses have held the centre of the stage for three decades, tens of thousands of informal sector artisans have been producing a range of goods for use in households, agriculture, transport and construction. Over time, these have both adapted their technologies and developed many new product lines. They have not existed independently of formal industry, but have drawn skills and materials from it. But the constraints on their existence implied by operating from open waste land or shacks have created a situation where they have little security, and the owners of such enterprises are discouraged from reinvesting a high proportion of their profits back into the business. Nevertheless, this sector has the potential to generate employment at a rate close to the rate of growth of the urban population, but at very low levels of income.

One of the weaknesses of most African economies is an absence of large-scale entrepreneurs running manufacturing businesses, whether they have emerged from the informal sector or been trained by the corporate sector. The studies from Nigeria suggest that this failure may be as much to do with the character and personality traits of the generation of entrepreneurs who developed their businesses in the 1960s. It is certain that even those entrepreneurs and managers who seek to act as professional industrialists have to operate in an environment which is hostile to them, and in which the pursuit of marginal returns is an uphill struggle.

Thus at a time when Africa needs to industrialize, to create both exports and jobs, a review of the last thirty years shows how difficult this task has been and will be. A good part of the difficulty is derived directly from the structure of social and cultural values discussed earlier in this book. These are responsible for both the 'power and status' motivation ascribed to Nigerian entrepreneurs, and for the centralizing tendency of governments which until recently have frequently been hostile to the informals. Among the many constraints on Africa's attempts at industrialization, the factors deriving from Africa's pre-colonial social structure must be deemed among the most important.

11
The Aid Machine

The two World Bank men, one German and one British, strode across the tarmac in the steaming heat of Dar es salaam. Clearly men with a purpose, their well-ironed tropical suits and ties contrasted with the colourful informality of the other passengers and the rest of the airport crowd – the men in body length *kanzas* or open neck shirts, and women in black *buibuis* stretching from their heads to below their knees or in multi-coloured *kitenge* dresses proclaiming variants on the theme of *Uhuru na Mwalimu*.[1] The Bank men, their first-class tickets ensuring a place at the front of the queue for immigration formalities, wasted no time in getting through the airport and were quickly ferried by car along the narrow road into the city. Within an hour of arrival they were closeted with the permanent secretary, the most senior civil servant, of the Ministry of Agriculture mapping out the ground for a loan from the World Bank to Tanzania which would put $25 million into livestock production, turning ranching and the export of beef into a major national industry. This was an ambitious objective, but it was 1971 and Robert McNamara had been President of the World Bank for three years, long enough to begin to realize his goal of a leap forward in Bank lending that would take it from $1.1 billion in 1967 to $11.4 billion in 1980, his last year in office.

Only such a leap could have spawned the dynamic activity of the Bank staffers in the field in the early and mid 1970s. The two-man team arriving to promote the concept of a large-scale loan for livestock production in Tanzania in 1971 was a manifestation of McNamara's bold and almost visionary objectives. Their tough activism contrasted with the Ministry of Agriculture's considerable suspicion of the Bank's motives, doubts about whether the government could possibly meet all the conditions of lending that the Bank would require, and sheer reluctance to organize all the preparatory technical studies that would form a part of project preparation.

The civil servants' reluctance would be resolved by a ministerial directive that the project must be supported – some action was always better than none, the project would have an impact in several regions, if it worked it would boost exports and create employment. The snag lay in the price of meat, the Bank wanting it raised to choke off local demand and free meat for export, the government wanting it held at its current low level to keep urban meat-eaters happy. Having flagged the issue and fired the interest of the minister, the Bank duo returned to the cooler, more workman-like atmosphere of life in Nairobi almost certain that sooner or later a project would go to the Bank board, and that it would almost certainly be approved.

In fact it took another two years for the project to be fully studied, for the government to support its formal submission to the World Bank, for the Bank's board to approve it and for the first tranche of funds to flow. The project was highly imaginative, building on a commercial ranching project which already existed. It envisaged the development of other commercial ranches (albeit government-owned); the provision of credit to a selection of pastoral cattle keepers (for water supplies, improved grazing and other facilities); a great improvement in the system by which cattle were transported from grazing areas to

abbattoirs; and the re-equipment and expansion of the
existing export meat-packing plant. In framing the loan
agreement both the government and the Bank had
formally agreed that high-powered international management of the meat plants and ranches was necessary to
success, that pastoral cattle keepers should be given title to
their land (an innovation), and that the meat price should
be raised, thus restraining urban demand.

By the late 1970s, however, it was clear that the project
had failed in nearly all of its objectives. At one level the
reasons were not difficult to see: although government
initially fulfilled the conditions of the loan, in hiring
management and adjusting prices, it later backed out of
the commitment. Contracts were shortened and meat prices
restrained; the meat plant was nationalized and the export
distribution channel lost; the issue of land tenure for
pastoralists became submerged in the much bigger *ujamaa*
re-settlement programme of 1975; and livestock buying at
markets was taken out of the hands of the traditional
Somali buyers and for the most part placed in the hands of
state agents.

But this is not the whole story. The failure was not just
one of execution, nor even one of mistaken concept; it was
more the product of a profound ambivalence in the
relationship between the World Bank and the government.
This was matched by a further ambivalence in the
relationship between the government and the livestock
owners, supposed to be the ultimate beneficiaries of the
project. For the project to be successful it was essential for
each stool of the tripod which supported it – the government, the livestock owners and the Bank – to have an
equal commitment to its success and to perceive the project
in roughly the same terms. In fact, no such harmony of
view existed. The government saw it as a means to
increase the resources under its control; those few livestock
owners who were aware of the project saw it as a means to
acquire more stock and supplies of water, but with no
thought of selling more of their animals; the Bank saw it
as an intervention which would initiate a commercial

livestock industry in Tanzania, a means of increasing resource utilization and exports. Such differences in emphasis and even objective were the fatal flaw in the project, a flaw which saddled Tanzania with a $17 million commitment to repay the Bank's soft loan wing, the International Development Agency (IDA).[2] Today the majority of Tanzania's current total debt of $5 billion consists of obligations contracted in many similar projects financed by a wide variety of donors, many of which have similar ambiguities surrounding them.

DO BORROWERS HAVE A STRATEGY?

Such ambiguities are not unique to Tanzania but run right through relationships between development agencies and African governments. Chapter 3 argued that ambiguity was an underlying characteristic of African society. Historically, this was driven by a complex web of lineage lines in which one set of loyalties was hedged against another. Today, when facing the outside world, the strategy of senior civil servants is also frequently one of hedging; programmes are often put up to three donors simultaneously, so that the influence of one can be offset against the influence of another. As a result, African governments seldom have a concerted strategy for dealing with donors.

This is confirmed by the fact that there are very few serious statements about aid made by senior Africans on behalf of their country, or their region. A ridiculous proportion of the public debate on aid takes place exclusively within the donor countries, and is generated by articles written mainly by western and Third World academic observers. It is as if those who know aid best from the viewpoint of the recipients fear that an outspoken critique will turn off the tap rather than improve the quality of the flow. Not even Julius Nyerere's collected speeches, which range across almost every aspect of the problem of development, contain a serious reflection on the role of aid in Tanzania or Africa in general. The reports of international commissions such as that of Brandt do not make up for this gap. Since aid is becoming more, not less, important in Africa there is a crying need for a more outspoken analysis of the problem, not only from the recipients' point of view, but by the recipients themselves.

These kinds of problems were not envisaged in the seminal work of economists such as Walt Rostow, writing in the 1950s, and Hollis Chenery, writing in the 1960s, whose work played a key role in justifying the early stages of development assistance. At that time, economic thinking on development was very much influenced by the success of the Marshall Plan in financing the rehabilitation of Europe, and by the effect of parallel U.S. aid to Japan. Rostow's *Stages of Economic Growth*[3] identified a key role for external concessionary finance, i.e. to increase the rate of investment without reducing the level of domestic consumption. Given certain other conditions such as a high rate of growth in at least one manufacturing sector and a favourable institutional environment, an increase in the rate of net investment from say 5 to 10 per cent of national income could put a country on the path to self-sustaining growth. The underlying assumption was that, if other factors were reasonably favourable, capital formation and exports would within, say, a generation reach the level where concessional finance was no longer necessary.

The African experience has not justified this assumption. In the 1980s, aggregate Gross Domestic Product (GDP) has been roughly static,[4] and per capita GDP has been falling at a time when net aid flows have been rising.[5] The reasons for this should not be obscured by the fact that the short term objectives of aid have undergone several changes over the last thirty years. Most notably these have included, first, a concern with income distribution and the need to combat 'absolute' poverty, triggered by McNamara in 1973; and second, the need to finance the trade deficits, and consequent 'adjustment', of the many African countries for whom the second oil price rise of 1979 was a near fatal

blow. The IMF, the World Bank and bilateral national aid
donors have all allocated an increasing proportion of their
annual commitments to lending of this type. In the case of
the World Bank, this proportion was as high as 30 per cent
of total loans to Africa approved in 1988.[6] Such changes in
the target areas of lending not only make its impact more
difficult to assess, but have not yet led to a sustained
improvement in the rate of economic growth achieved by
recipient countries. Nevertheless, in-flows of aid have been
increasing. In 1970 they totalled $1.0 billion, in 1978 $4.7
billion and in 1987 $11.1 billion.[7]

It can be argued that the increase rather than the
reduction in the need for aid is due to a series of
weaknesses in its composition and nature. It can also be
argued that the economists' justification for aid has never
been its real rationale, but that political considerations of
strategic security by the donors have conditioned its
distribution and nature, in some cases even allowing
military support to be classified as aid. However, the
quality of economic decision-making in most African
countries over the last thirty years suggests that this is
inextricably linked to the relative failure of aid. The
important role which larger donors have come to play in
'supporting' African economies has not prevented governments from retaining their entrenched political priorities.
To make matters more complicated, where aid programmes
have sought to channel funds to small-scale farmers, or
small businesses, the real priorities of the target beneficiaries have seldom been identical to those of the donor
or the government.

Even so, donors have also used aid to pursue their self-
interest regardless of whether or not it was compatible
with that of the recipient. This has led to the tying of aid to
a large extent to inappropriate or unduly expensive goods
from the donor's country, to sharp annual variations in the
volume of aid flows and to a lack of commitment to real co-
ordination with other donors. Thus, in examining the more
specific factors which have contributed to the aid machine's
lack of success, it is frequently the case that both donor and

recipient carry a part of the responsibility. These issues will be discussed below.

A POOR MATCH

There is plenty of opportunity for the general sense of ambiguity discussed above to manifest itself at the level of individual projects. There are often three related questions: do recipient governments really want the project? do the target beneficiaries (such as smallholders) within the country really want the project? do the donor(s), the recipient government and the beneficiaries expect roughly the same from the project?

The environment within which projects have been planned and executed has frequently allowed these questions to remain unanswered in reality, if not on the paper on which loan agreements are written. It was created in good part by the situation in the 1970s when a poor match developed between the pressure to lend from donors, and the administrative ability of the borrowing countries to 'receive'. Overwhelmed by the number of donors pushing their desire to lend, recipient governments were frequently unable to sort out their own priorities in a meaningful way. This is hardly surprising. In the early 1980s Kenya was trying to cope with 600 projects from 60 donors; and even a mini-country such as Lesotho was dealing with 321 projects from 61 donors.[8]

The gap between the willingness to lend and the capacity to receive is partly due to the fact that the majority of donors have country lending, or granting, targets. The staff members they deploy in the field to identify projects are under pressure from their senior management to turn such targets into reality. Working within an embassy office or the regional office of a multilateral bank it is not difficult for donors' staff to come up with a list of potential projects which can be presented to a recipient country's ministry of finance for discussion.

Overworked officials in finance ministeries rarely reject a

whole list of potential projects; they are much more likely to identify a few priorities at random, and pass on the donor to the line ministry, hoping for the best if and when the project is financed. Once a project is on a donor's priority list it takes on a life of its own, and may become unstoppable. Only a very few civil servants within the recipient government understand what the project is really about. Numerous conditions may be attached to the donor's disbursement of funds, such as the allocation of manpower to the project, or a change in pricing policy. Once the loan agreement is signed the donor may have a much more precise view of these conditions than the recipient, especially at the level of the line staff who are actually supposed to manage the project. As the donor becomes more and more concerned at lack of action the recipient country staff become more and more dubious that the project is really in their national interest, and may even start discussions with another whose conditions may be perceived as less onerous.

To these dilemmas must be added the differing perceptions of a project by potential beneficiaries such as farmers and small-scale businessmen. In an agricultural project farmers have to understand the potential benefits of the inputs (say, fertiliser and seed) financed by the project, to find them relevant, and to be sure that their produce will find a market, before committing themselves to participation. In many agricultural projects this has not been the case. The irrigation schemes in the Sudan, including the Gezira project, provide an example of a case where a poor response from tenant farmers, for a variety of reasons, has consistently dogged the major rehabilitation projects financed by the World Bank and other donors in the early 1980s.

There are many projects where farmers have seen potential benefits from a project, but where these have not been the same as those anticipated by the project designers. Thus in integrated rural development projects, such as those financed by the World Bank in many Nigerian states in the 1970s, fertiliser ear-marked for cash crops was frequently spread on food crops. In livestock projects credit designed for fencing and water supplies has been chan-nelled into domestic buildings, for which similar materials are required. In projects designed to support small (and larger-scale) entrepreneurs various forms of 'leakage' are frequent: credit funds ear-marked for a particular purpose are deployed for entirely different purposes, or for the purchase of domestic assets.

The frustrations for the donor arising from these differences of perception and interest are great. But even when they are recognized, his options are limited. To cancel a project is to set back a country's loan or grant programme and perhaps risk political problems between recipient and donor. Consequently, changes in project objectives are much more frequent than cancellations. The World Bank's 1985 review of project performance indicated that 'only 42 per cent of its projects were implemented as agreed, and 58 per cent were changed significantly during the implementation process'.[9] Even changes of objective within the period in which funds are being disbursed may still leave pressure for additional change, especially if there is a ministerial reshuffle.

In an attempt to try to contain the pressure for such changes donors adopted in the 1970s a strategy of establishing semi-autonomous project units, which were nominally attached to national ministries, but in fact were more or less independent of them. In Juba, southern Sudan, the agricultural rehabilitation[10] project jointly financed by the British government and the World Bank in 1978 had an annual budget in excess of that of the Ministry of Agriculture of the regional government. Such project 'islands' created additional suspicion within recipient governments and the approach has been largely abandoned.

The problems described above will not be easily resolved. The ambivalence surrounding project aid is likely to continue. The situation will only improve if first, recipient governments are able to allocate a higher proportion of the time of capable civil servants to the allocation of in-coming aid; second, if donor governments and agencies dovetail their country lending programmes more closely with the medium-term budgetary plans of the recipient countries; and third, if recipient governments are more careful in interpreting the priorities of their own small farmers and other small-scale producers.

The move away from project loans and towards structural adjustment loans in the 1980s does not diminish the main thrust of this argument. The main aim of these more recent loans is to assist governments in making major policy changes (such as abolishing price controls and freeing interest rates) and creating new institutional arrangements (such as privatising government-owned companies). Such changes may receive support from cabinet ministers and senior civil servants, but may also be accepted not from conviction but from necessity; nominal support is essential to ensure finance for a minimum quantity of imports. Even if they are accepted from conviction, perhaps more often the case than political statements would imply, major vested interests have to be combatted to implement them. Some of this comes from urban consumers, concerned with rising food prices, or trade unions concerned with falling real wages. Some of the opposition to liberalization may come from multinational companies used to low interest rates and to a protected local market. Faced with such effective local opposition civil servants in charge of delivering on policy conditions may indeed feel ambivalent about the desirability of an individual structural adjustment loan.

SWITCHING RESOURCES

Some of the ambivalence shown by recipient countries towards aid is explained by its utility as a means of freeing local resources to finance projects which otherwise might get squeezed out, but which might have important political attractions. Donors frequently finance projects, or chunks of government expenditure such as part of the health service, to which recipient countries would in any case have to give a high priority, and this relieves government of that particular commitment. Revenue can then be switched to other items, such as military hardware, or so-called prestige projects.

Only a minority of African countries spend a high proportion of their annual government expenditure on defence – as much as 19 per cent in Burkina Faso and 13 per cent in Tanzania in 1986.[11] It is difficult to believe that many of the prestige projects discussed in Chapter 8 would have been contemplated in the absence of the very high volumes of aid reaching countries for other, more mundane, purposes.

More difficult to determine is the extent to which aid has freed resources for consumption, and so done little to increase investment levels in the manner envisaged by Rostow or Chenery. In fact the extent to which this happens, and to which aid itself directly finances consumption, for instance paying the salaries of local staff, has been a matter of controversy among economists. Keith Griffin is one who takes an extreme position believing that

> aid is essentially a substitute for saving and . . . a large fraction of foreign capital is used to increase consumption rather than investment.[12]

This statement is clearly true in the context of food aid. In 1986, 40 per cent of the nearly 9 million tons of cereals imported by Africa was financed under food aid projects, at a cost to donors of approximately $0.5 billion.[13]

In fact it is now widely recognized that some consumption expenditure of this type, in so far as it combats malnutrition, should be considered as equivalent to investment. But consumption does not directly create capital assets whether financed internally or externally, and investment levels in most countries have not risen significantly as a proportion of GDP in Africa over the last twenty years, and remain 6 or 7 per cent lower than in both the rest of the developing world and in the industrialized world. During this period, domestic savings rates have fallen significantly (with some exceptions such as Kenya and Cameroun) and therefore the inevitable

diversion of some aid finance from investment to consumption is accentuating a negative trend, however necessary it
may be in years of famine and drought.

TEA MONEY

Corruption is always a two-way process. The mushrooming
of aid budgets in the 1970s turned aid into a fairly important
source of business for some small and medium-sized
companies in Europe and elsewhere, indicated by the
formation of pressure groups in many European Community (EC) countries to ensure that an increased proportion of national aid budgets ended up in the hands of that
country's exporters. In Britain, the Confederation of British
Industry (CBI) regularly convenes seminars and con-
ferences on this topic. In the 1970s, this kind of pressure
led to the prevalence of an increasing pool of funds
allocated to soft or mixed commercial credits, which some
EC governments were able to describe as aid. Much of this
now forms part of Africa's stock of debt as the recipient
countries have been unable to service their export credits,
and has become a burden on the export credit guarantee
agencies of the EC governments. In fact export credits form
37 per cent of the total stock of African debt.[14]

Recipient countries have, however, generally played the
leading role in the process of allocating contracts between
suppliers, whether of equipment, contracting services or
consultancy services. This process has regularly been the
subject of corruption as civil servants or ministers connected with the award of the tender have sought back-
handers for themselves and their associates.

Projects financed by multilateral agencies, such as the
World Bank, were and are far from immune from this
process. While the bidding for contracts may nominally be
through international competitive bidding arrangements
between suppliers and members of a government, the
award may in practice be carried out in ways which
make it impossible for the Bank and other donors to police
it. Such arrangements have to be seen in a wider

context. Corruption is now largely acknowledged as an actual or past practice. President Houphouet Boigny, of Ivory Coast, is on record as saying that a minister who cannot enrich himself is not worth his salt. President Mobutu of Zaire has publicly objected to not being acknowledged as the seventh richest man in the world.

There is a good argument for presenting these forms of corruption as consistent with past African practice, in which the chief's position was acknowledged in tribute, as was the eighteenth-century practice in Europe, and nineteenth-century practice in the USA. However, they are difficult to defend in the context of aid when cultural values are different in donor countries and recipient countries, and when public opinion in the donor countries perceives aid as having a moral justification. Even more importantly, they obviously lead to bad, poorly planned projects perhaps with inadequate or inappropriate equipment. A significant, though not decisive, part of the low return to aid projects in Africa can be attributed to corruption in the award of contracts. Such corruption has played some part in building up the funds held in international bank accounts or other forms of investment by African citizens, recently estimated to total $20 billion between 1974 and 1985.[15]

These examples of ambiguity, of the switching of resources, and of corruption explain some of the failures of aid which can be attributed primarily to the recipients. Other explanations of failure are more clearly attributable to donors. These include lack of co-ordination, volatility in aid flows, the serving of the national interest of donors (particularly through its tying to national suppliers), ineffective evaluation, and the assumption of greater wisdom.

WORKING TOGETHER

The numbers of projects and donors in individual countries is a source of confusion for which donors themselves are almost entirely responsible. Even the World Bank regularly despatches different missions to an individual country unaware of each others' presence, or who may meet by accident in a permanent secretary's outer office. The consequences for the country, especially in the many cases where the recipient government is not able to sort out the resultant confusion, can at worst be disastrous.

There is, for example, the problem of matching finance in local currency, which governments are generally required to commit to each donor-assisted project. In effect governments take on a commitment to support a part of the costs of several hundred projects at any one time, such 'counterpart funding' in countries like Kenya or Tanzania frequently amounts to a nominal commitment of about $200 million per year. In reality it becomes almost impossible to find this amount in the budget, and projects have to limp along on an underfunded basis or with the overseas donor financing an increasing proportion of the total costs. Commitments to matching finance are seldom adequately analyzed, and although the recipient governments may carry a good deal of the responsibility for this, donors are also at fault in assuming that the counterpart funds for their projects will have priority.

A second dimension to real co-ordination involves only the donors, whose policies outside the aid arena may conflict with those within it. The most crucial example of this is trade policy, for access to markets in the industrialized world may be critical to a recipient country's export programme. Thus the EC remains highly sensitive to the origins of garments made up within African countries when the woven fabric is imported from elsewhere, and may reject such imports on the grounds that they are not wholly manufactured within the exporting country. Another example is the need for co-ordination between national aid agencies and national export credit agencies, where the latter may be seeking to guarantee finance for, say, a large steel mill[16] which is clearly out of line with national development priorities agreed in different agencies between the donors and recipient governments.

PEAKS AND TROUGHS

Volatility in aid flows is notoriously difficult from the recipient's point of.view, and the US Congress has made American aid a dangerously-poisoned chalice to the recipients. Short-term changes in the volume of flows to a particular country can ruin the effectiveness of a particular programme or project. For example:

> US aid commitments to Zimbabwe began at $24m at Independence in 1980, rose to $84m in 1982, fell to $59m in 1984 and were set to fall well below $20m in early 1986 prior to a decision in September 1986 to cancel all future aid programmes ... US aid to Sudan stood at $64m in 1981, rising to $121m in 1984; in 1986 total US military and economic aid to Sudan stood at $158m prior to total suspension in late February with only $50m of food aid being disbursed following Sudan's developing relations with Libya.[17]

The ability of donors to turn off the tap is often cherished as a means of enforcing economic discipline, or more specifically the sets of policies now associated with structural adjustment. However the 'correct' economic policies are at best subjective and in any case other political considerations frequently come into play. As effective economic policy can hardly be judged in less than a three year period, and political affiliation is also a long-term question, it seems entirely reasonable that aid should be committed over a three year period.

PROMOTING THE DONOR

Given the political rationale lying behind these sharp changes in the volume of aid directed to particular countries, it is clear that the promotion of the donors' perceived national self-interest is closely bound up with aid. Nearly 80 per cent of French and British aid, excluding that which is channelled through multilateral organizations, is given to their former colonies.[18] A very high proportion of nearly all industrialized countries' aid is tied to their own goods or personnel. On average this is about 33 per cent, although it ranges up to about 60 per cent in the case of Italy, and is over 40 per cent for Britain, France and the United States.[19] Detailed studies of the cost of such tied aid have indicated that the resultant prices to the recipient country are typically 20 per cent more than they would have been if the country had a free choice in its supplier.[20] While tying is not necessarily incompatible with the fundamental economic objectives of aid, it reduces its potential benefit to the extent that goods are over-priced, or that they are less appropriate – and sometimes much less appropriate – for the job.

SELF-ASSESSMENT

Criticism of aid from both left and right, particularly in recent years, has led to the establishment of evaluation units within most of the major donor agencies. The assessments made by these units, frequently based on the work of so-called objective consultants, are increasingly available in edited form. As with other institutional innovations in the aid field, the World Bank has been the most consistent, and perhaps rigorous, of self-assessors publishing an annual review of in-house project audits. Taking the donor agencies as a whole, about 9,000 evaluations of individual projects have been made since 1970, probably accounting for about 12 per cent of all projects launched since that time.[21]

Although this would normally be an adequate sample, the results are much less significant than they appear, even were they to point conclusively in one direction, which they do not. Projects need to be assessed over time; there are very few whose benefits can be seriously assessed in less than ten years, and a period of fifteen to twenty years would be more meaningful. On this basis the rural development projects which became fashionable among most donors in the 1970s, and which were supposed to have a direct impact on the rural poor, are only now coming to the stage where a meaningful evaluation can be conducted. Yet the World Bank has conducted and published project audits on average seven years after the first disbursement of funds, and three years after the final year of disbursement. This is too short a time frame to be meaningful.

The assessment of structural adjustment loans is even more problematic than the assessment of rural development projects. There are any number of reasons why such loans may be successes or failures, which go well beyond the conditions for the disbursement of the loans. For instance, if an economy grows at 5 per cent per year following a two-year disbursement of a structural adjustment loan, if the international price for the country's commodity exports has risen by at least 5 per cent in the same period of time, can the loan be regarded as justified? Conversely, if state-owned companies have been offered for privatization but few bidders have come forward, is this a 'failure' if the firms continue as loss makers in the public sector? The analysis of a group of such SAP projects will be meaningful only in about ten years after they became fashionable – that is in about 1995.

While the factors of time and the sheer difficulty of analysis partly explain the relative failure of donors to provide a meaningful public assessment of aid programmes, they do not explain the cumulative inadequacy of the results which are available to date. First, there are inherent limitations in looking only at individual projects, which do not pick up some of the key problems discussed above, such as fungibility and co-ordination. It is more appropriate to examine the impact of aid programmes and projects in aggregate on a particular country. Pioneering work of this kind is quite recent. A study commissioned by member governments of the World Bank in 1985 conducted seven such case studies.[22] Similar studies of five countries were carried out for USAID in 1983. Taking these and studies commissioned by donors in countries where they are the predominant donor into account, it appears that only about ten African aid recipients have been studied in this way. Reviewing national programmes, however, raises key and difficult questions for both donors (why did they not co-operate more effectively?) and recipients (how could they justify a range of prestige projects? why are they more dependant on aid than ever?) Yet without such country reviews the performance of aid will not improve more than marginally.

Second, few of the evaluations discuss the donors' own role in promoting some of the weaknesses in project design. A classic case is the pressure brought to bear by the World Bank in agriculture in the 1970s in support of island projects, the efficiency of which would be ensured by hiving them off from executing ministries, and appointing expatriate (mainly European) managers to run them. The duplication and friction thus created was palpable. The World Bank has subsequently identified this as a major weakness in the design of projects, but has not acknowledged its own role as the prime engineer of the approach.

The unsatisfactory nature of project evaluation work and the inconclusive lessons which can be drawn from it provide little justification for the donor 'omniscience' which continues to characterize their negotiations with recipients. There is no suggestion of possible error of self-doubt when World Bank missions meet a fifty-year-old permanent secretary in a Ministry of Finance, even if he has been receiving similar missions, offering rather different policy prescriptions, for the previous twenty years. Donors, including the EC and the World Bank, have been trying to persuade the Kenyan government to privatize grain marketing since 1984. There is good reason to ask to whom can the assets of the grain marketing board be sold? Yet the World Bank has continued to press this issue, at one stage moving the permanent secretary in the president's office to angrily rebuke the young leader of the Bank's team, and to the president himself being moved to recount to the team the Biblical story of the seven fat and seven lean years. There are no easy answers to African development, and an appropriate degree of humility on the part of donors is a necessary condition for developing a serious dialogue with recipient governments.

PUMP PRIMER OR DRIP FEED?

The confidence displayed by the World Bank men and other donors in the early 1970s has clearly not fulfilled its promise. Neither Africa nor the donors carry the prime responsibility for this. The premise on which the donors worked was that large amounts of capital could be absorbed by small African countries because their need for productive investment was demonstrably high. It would seek to twist Government's arm to ensure that appropriate management was bought in. The premise on which African governments worked was that if capital could not be had on highly concessional terms it was better to accept it on terms more or less defined by the donors.

These compromises on both sides left important issues of policy, and responsibilities for execution, unresolved. Supervision teams from the donors frequently laid bare basic differences in the perception of projects. However, when these differences were revealed it was difficult to know which side feared cancelling the project most – ironically it might be the donor with its vested interest in a cumulative increase in annual disbursements, rather than the government with several hundred projects of which at least a half could be in the same state. The move to lending in the 1980s for 'adjustment', and away from projects, has replaced a set of conditions closely tied to projects with a set tied to broader conditions affecting a whole economy, or large sectors within it. This has not removed the scope for profound disagreement about the relevance of such conditions.

The problems of 'switching resources' and corruption have to be added to the issue of a basic ambiguity. In the first case aid has frequently freed government revenue for purposes very different to those the donors would support (a new presidential palace, a larger army, a new capital city); in the second case corruption has affected the allocation of contracts in ways which damage project execution. The donors are at fault on the issues of co-ordination, volatility, tying of aid to a donor country's goods and blinkered evaluation of the impact of aid as a whole.

The evident conclusion is that the policy basis on which aid has been given to Africa has not been fulfilled. Aid is now essential to Africa as any kind of external finance is essential: it is a means of paying for imports which would otherwise not be bought, about half of which are capital goods necessary for the maintenance of assets, badly depreciated after years of neglect. This seldom adds up to a coherent investment plan, but may be more simply described as a way of keeping things going until better days arrive. We cannot confuse the kind of economic drip-feed which aid has become with its bold objectives as originally conceived; self-sustaining growth is a mirage which is now more elusive than ever.

12
The Prospects for Progress

Africa is now littered with the discarded blueprints of the last quarter of a century. These have ranged from the emotional, continent-wide vision of Kwame Nkrumah ('Africa must unite'), to Julius Nyerere's target of 'socialism in one country', to the hard boiled 'Africa needs Europe' school of Houphouet Boigny and Kenyatta. Each of these visions has left its own particular legacy, some transparently more successful than others, but all falling short of their original promise. There are still visionaries in Africa, even on the grand scale, but they are increasingly on the sidelines of political life. Contemporary blueprints focus on the next three years, and their targets are modest, if not downright pessimistic.

This book has concentrated on the political and social values of Africa today, and traced their evolution over more than a century. It has also shown that they are only a part of the explanation of Africa's problems; a difficult agricultural base, the inequalities of the world trading system, the sometimes exploitative role of multinational companies have also had a major part to play. However, the relevance of these technical, physical and economic problems to development is discussed infinitely more frequently than the political and social context in which

they are found. Leading African civil servants entrusted
with the day-to-day execution of policy over the last
twenty years know that these are not necessarily the
major problems. Philip Ndegwa is a highly respected
former governor of the Central Bank of Kenya. In 1986 he
wrote:

> There is no magic in the process of economic and social
> development of nations which enables instant transform-
> ation. Development can only be achieved over time,
> and more often than not along a difficult path. This is
> because ... the process of development involves not
> only the production of more goods and services but also
> the transformation of the society itself, including the
> establishment of new institutions, social systems, rules
> and values.
> ... This means that the social traditions, values and
> attitudes which exist in any society cannot be brushed
> aside.[1]

The open discussion of these issues in Africa is difficult,
since they reach into the heart of political life. Furthermore, their policy implications may be quite limited since
they define the environment, and condition people's behaviour within it, but are frequently outside the area of
influence of planners, civil servants and aid-donors. Nonetheless, they have to be embraced as a first step in
understanding the limits to where Africa may be in
another twenty-five or even fifty years.

THE CURRENT POLITICAL DYNAMIC

Economic recovery is not at the top of the political agenda
in African countries today. It is secondary to the political
priorities of preserving specific presidents in power and the
patronage system associated with them. These priorities
imply, on the domestic front, the attempt to maintain a
continuing powerful role for the state, the economic

dominance of a fairly small elite and an indifference to the welfare of rural peasant farmers, complicated as this may be by political loyalites to certain tribal groups. In relation to the outside world they imply a wariness to foreign investors, and an ambivalence to foreign aid in so far as investors and aid donors may undermine the autonomy of the government.

The result is that major segments of the population – sometimes a majority, sometimes a minority – will continue to experience a sense of deprivation, and to be in permanent opposition to the government. The Ibos in Nigeria and the Bamilike in Cameroun are both groups who in the 1950s and 1960s respectively made a bid for predominant national power; they failed, and continue to feel excluded from the political mainstream of their countries. The identity of such marginal groups has sometimes changed, as presidents change: the Kikuyu were 'in' under Kenyatta and are 'out' under President Moi; the Bemba were 'in' under President Kaunda in the 1960s, but have been 'out' since Simon Kapwepwe broke away in 1971. A sense of deprivation of a different kind continues to smoulder amongst the immigrant groups of Indian, Lebanese and Europeans, especially in Kenya and Zimbabwe, who feel that their economic position may be attacked, or re-attacked, at any time. Though not in permanent opposition, their loyalty to the government of the day is shallow.

This sense of deprivation has spilled over into civil conflict or war a sufficient number of times for it to be a continuing threat, or an on-going reality as in Chad, Sudan, Ethiopia, Burundi,[2] Uganda and Somalia. The civil war between Renamo guerillas and the government in Mozambique also reflects this sense of deprivation – Renamo has been particularly strong amongst the Makonde of the north, who were most affected by the communal village programme of the 1970s. In Angola the support for Jonas Savimbi's UNITA has been stronger amongst the Ovimbundu people of the central plateau than amongst the rest of the population. While civil conflicts of this kind should diminish in the next twenty-five years as African states mature, they will not disappear. For what is now at stake is not the acceptance of the artificial boundaries imposed by the colonial powers, but the distribution of opportunity within them.

No African country has managed to escape from the pattern of its past history, but in the late 1980s certain common characteristics can be seen among the more successful countries, notably Kenya, Cameroun and Botswana. First, the leadership has been consistently tough and pragmatic. Kenyatta and Ahidjo were nationalists first, and localists second although both went to great lengths to secure their political base amongst their own ethnic group. In the 1960s Kenyatta manipulated sales of formerly white-owned land and businesses in such a way as to create a new class of Kenyan capitalists to replace the old white capitalists, in a no-nonsense determination to both preserve the private sector and to transfer its ownership into African hands. This was the decisive factor in determining Kenya's subsequent political and economic direction. In the early 1960s Ahidjo considered that he faced two key problems in Cameroun: first, preventing the economic hegemony of the Bamilike; and second, preventing a breakdown between the English- and French-speaking parts of the country. He tackled the first by systematically awarding government contracts to northern businessmen (former traders) from his own area of Garoua and the second by insisting that schools and the civil service must be bilingual, a policy which has been extremely successful. These policies were pursued with great determination and consistency, and Ahidjo was remarkably successful in holding Cameroun, with its 300 recognized languages, together. This success was built on a medieval system of security and detention which caused numerous 'disappearances'.

The second characteristic of these more successful countries follows from the first: government has been strong, and has continued to function. A necessary condition of this is that there has been sufficient money to enable it to function (barely true for instance in Zaire, and parts of Nigeria and Tanzania in the 1980s), and that civil strife has been contained, sometimes ruthlessly. Ensuring sufficient money to finance the government machine has been a by-product of the third characteristic: maintaining savings and investment, which in all three cases (Kenya, Cameroun and Botswana) have risen substantially since 1960, to about 25 per cent of the output of the economy in 1986.[3] This is because government has never lost sight of the primacy of production, and has been able to avoid excessive borrowing to pay for it – in Cameroun because of the availability of oil, and in Kenya as a result of the low-key transfer of assets into African hands without any disruption in production. In Botswana, government has consistently decided to live with the mining companies, rather than nationalize them or even seek to control them. Instead it has, for instance, taken a $400 million shareholding (6 per cent of issued share capital) in the traded stock of DeBeers Consolidated the diamond marketing company, and two seats on DeBeers' Board, thus indirectly giving it a shareholding in the giant Anglo-American mining house.[4]

The fourth characteristic of each of the three countries is that they have had the luck to avoid the worst of the droughts which have badly affected agriculture and hydro-electric power supplies in many African countries in the 1970s and 1980s. While the north of Cameroun has been badly affected, its key productive areas lie in the high rainfall zones of the western highlands; in Kenya the old colonial rule-of-thumb that one year in five will be a year of drought has been sustained, and lean years have been followed by bumper crops. In Botswana, the negative effects of low rainfall years are offset by the consequent increased sale of livestock, much of which is exported to high-value EC markets, since Botswana's urban meat-eating population is small.

Do these three relatively successful countries provide any kind of signpost to the rest of Africa? The answer can be only a muted 'yes' since the economic foundations of most African countries, and the size and distribution of their population is very different to the situation prevailing in the early 1960s. Most countries now have to build on an economy in which the productive assets are very run down, and even more importantly, in which a political consensus remains elusive.

THE INDIVIDUAL FUTURE

An awareness of politics grows out of individuals' perception of the world around them, and earlier in this book some of the main contributing factors to an African perception of the world, notwithstanding Africa's great diversity, were sketched. The political future will largely depend on how these perceptions develop, and it is not impossible to gauge that development.

At the level of the individual the following trends are likely. First, much more variety and less conformity and subservience in individual views. Respect for elders, already severely weakened, will further diminish. In the rural areas, family and tribal loyalties will continue to be important and religion and superstition will continue to play a major role. In the urban areas, where a third of Africa's population will soon live, tribal loyalties will for the most part diminish, but will for many years exist in parallel with other loyalties. These loyalties are increasingly to a myriad of individual community groups and associations, concerned with religion, education, savings and credit, trade and various forms of self-help. Sometimes they are organized on a tribal basis, sometimes they embrace people from a number of different tribes. They cut across class and gender, though women's groups almost certainly out-number those of the men. Trade unions play a part within these associations but, since their function is nearly entirely within the formal sector – which employs only a small proportion of the population – they play a relatively minor role. Purely tribal loyalties will eventually be neither more nor less than the regional loyalties of Europe, of the Scots to Scotland or the Bavarians to

Bavaria. They will last longest where tribal life has always been urban, for instance amongst the Asante in Kumasi, or the Yoruba in Ibadan.

Commitment not only to the extended family but also to the nuclear, two-parent family will diminish as men fail to adjust to the aspirations of educated women, and more women follow the long-established practice in coastal west Africa of running their own households. As tribal culture weakens, status and power will come to be less connected with an outward demonstration of wealth, and this may pave the way for a more powerful generation of entre- preneurs as specific commercial objectives come to supersede those of status.

THE ECONOMIC FUTURE

The key to future economic growth in Africa lies in the markets which are being created as towns and cities expand. Most estimates suggest that such urban centres are growing at five or six per cent a year. At this rate a third of the population will be living in towns by the year 2000. Such concentrations of population are frequently regarded as a burden on food supplies, and as a factor likely to worsen the balance of payments as consumer goods and food are sucked in from abroad, either openly or clandestinely. In fact, the individual migrants who par- ticipate in this urban migration manage to generate income which is more attractive to them than the income they would have earned by remaining in the rural areas. Furthermore, the goods they consume, from food to furniture, are either currently produced by informal sector artisans, or have the potential to be produced in this way. In a great city like Ibadan a flour made from cassava, known as gari, is the basic foodstuff and armies of hard working women perform the task of transforming the cassava into *gari*; clothes and basic furniture, as discussed in Chapter 10, are all made by local artisans. The result of the migration process is therefore a steady increase in the demand for *purchased* products, since most rural families will grow their own food, and make much of their domestic equipment. The value of this market today is probably about $30 billion per year; by the year 2000 it will be $70 billion.[5]

The ability of small-scale producers, whether farmers or artisans, to meet this market has become much clearer in the economic conditions of the 1980s. The rural community has produced more food than ever before, although not yet enough. Significant shifts of production have occurred from export crops, such as coffee and cocoa, to food crops for the domestic market, and the trend towards such shifts is likely to continue. This can be seen in countries as different as Tanzania and Cameroun. An expansion of production will also come from the use of land which is now sparsely populated. Artisans will develop their ability to diversify their products and achieve limited improvements in their technology. As the urban economy grows the official export of primary agricultural commodities will increase only at a very modest rate, if at all.

The principal characteristic of African economies in the next fifty years will then be an urban market which will in aggregate be very valuable but will have a low income per head. This market will be appropriate to the skills and operating style of both the farmers and artisans who will meet its demands. For the most part, the scale of production will not expand into larger-scale corporate enterprises because of the cultural factors which make larger-scale business organization difficult throughout Africa. The output of such small-scale producers will not only be sold on local markets but also across national frontiers. Cross-border trade in both foodstuffs and consumer goods is a growing phenomenon, though still largely unrecorded and outside the influence of official regional economic associations, such as the Preferential Trade Area, which now nominally embraces seventeen countries of central and east Africa.

Inside this framework the existing modern sector may well struggle for survival. Large-scale, publicly-owned enterprises will breathe their last gasp and wither away well before the state which spawned them. Large-scale, private businesses in manufacturing, geared to relatively high-value consumer products, will find little room for expansion as the incomes of most urban consumers continue to be very modest. This situation will not prove attractive to multinational companies or other sources of off-shore private investment, and the current trend towards disinvestment is likely to continue. Projects where a specific commodity is in international demand will prove an exception to this; such demand may prove to be strongest in other parts of the developing world, particularly Asia. In general multinationals will be on the defensive, and they will seek to minimize their risk by continuing to negotiate management and royalty contracts which guarantee a minimum income. This will leave entrepreneurs from local minority communities in a strong position as the owners of existing fairly well managed productive assets, and as the suppliers of intermediate goods to small-scale producers.

In those countries where there is no political backlash against them, such entrepreneurs are likely to continue to be key players in the domestic economy. In this situation it will be difficult to generate manufactured or processed exports since the expertise to produce competitively for international markets will be in short supply, though some countries such as Zimbabwe will be able to build on their existing export base. The unfavourable prospect for exports is perhaps the most damaging of Africa's economic weaknesses since it implies continued dependence on unstable, and on the whole, unfavourable commodity markets. Behind this instability lies the simple fact that for many commodities such as coffee and ground-nuts, demand in the industrialized world with its stable population has probably reached saturation point.

These developments will continue to leave governments in an increasingly exposed position. The difficulties of collecting taxes from millions of small-scale urban and rural producers will ensure that revenues continue to be inadequate in relation to the expectation of services such as universal primary and secondary education, health services, and transportation. An increasing proportion of these services will be provided by local communities on a fee-paying basis. Such groups are also likely to reinforce their existing role in the mobilization of savings, and it will be in mutual savings organizations, rather than formal financial institutions, that small-scale producers will find access to credit.

As a result of the limited increase in exports most governments will continue to experience serious balance of payments difficulties, although in some countries sometimes offset by earnings from minerals such as oil and diamonds. Nonetheless, unofficial exports between neighbouring countries are likely to continue to increase, but to go largely unrecorded. Economies will gradually become more interdependent, particularly between food deficit and food surplus countries, and the migration of labour between countries is likely to increase.

THE POLITICAL FUTURE

The growth of this economy of small-scale urban production will, over fifty years, change the face of African politics. The prevalence of many countervailing centres of influence to government, in the form of local associations will in the long-term make it increasingly difficult for governments to concentrate all power in their hands. Thus the regime of one-party states, nearly always achieved at considerable cost to those out of sympathy with the dominant party, will cause increasing resentment. As a greater range of individual views prevails, so the poverty of policy choices made by a virtually self-selected group of politicians will become less and less acceptable. However, the response of governments is likely to be more and more dogmatic, and be driven by considerations of 'security'; there will be little willingness by those in power to defer to differing views even when these are held by a majority.

Current experience from countries as diverse as Kenya and
Mozambique confirms this. In 1988 the Kenyan government openly considered abolishing the secret ballot in
order to dissuade opposition voters from declaring their
position. For ten years Frelimo, the ruling party in
Mozambique, has operated a system by which party
members are publicly elected by each community in a
manner which effectively rules out those who may have
opposing views. In the 1988 elections to the National
Assembly in Cameroun, the two alternative lists of
candidates, under a proportional representation system,
were consistently doctored to make them indistinguishable
from each other.

The basis of support for this pattern of continued
authoritarian government will become less localist, simply
because of the size of the urban population, and because
tribal identities will continue to break down in an
urban environment. In rural areas politics will continue to
be highly localist, but the tribal connotations of localism
will gradually be reduced. For some time threats to
governments will continue to come primarily from those
already close to power. As with the pre-colonial
chitumukulu of the Bemba, heads of state will fear
members of their senior council more than the dispossessed
of the shanty town or the rural hamlet. Neither will they
hand over power gracefully to an elected successor; the
transfer of power will continue to be an abrasive, coup-
ridden business.

To the public at large faith in the political process,
already at a low ebb, will diminish further. Strong
individual faith in Islam and Christianity will provide an
outlet for social energies rejected by formal politics. Since
women's role in politics will be restricted by the same male
attitudes which militate against equality in the home, the
Christian churches will continue to be particularly attractive to them. With Islam, however, there will be important
links between the strength of the mosques and the political
complexion of government, as has always existed between
the Murid Brotherhood and the government of Senegal,

and as the introduction of Sharia Law in Sudan in 1983, and the strength of fundamentalist movements in northern Nigeria indicates. Eventually, as has already occurred with Islam in some countries, these countervailing centres of power will challenge governments and sometimes gain control over them.

Changes in these attitudes and practices will be the result of a long political process which will certainly take more than a century to work out, and even then will probably compress the time which it took Europe to work through comparable processes. Democratization will come gradually as the new urban interest groups flex their muscles as alternative centres of power. In this respect Nigeria may be the key reference point, because its enormous population of more than 100 million will continue to force it into constitutional experiments, because its press has seldom been effectively muzzled, and because its leaders have never acquired the absolute power of many neighbouring heads of state.

The uneven course of this process of political evolution, and the fact that neighbouring countries will be at different stages within it, will continue to make official regional co-operation between countries very difficult. So long as a head of state – and thus his circle of patronage – can change quite unexpectedly, multi-country regional groupings will have to overcome major political as well as economic problems. In southern Africa, such regional groups will do little to counteract the internal political frailty of the countries in the area, and as a result South Africa will have plenty of opportunity to pursue malevolent policies of destabilization if it chooses to do so.

IMPLICATIONS FOR AFRICA'S DONORS

The aid programme, as it has developed over the last thirty years, has failed in terms of its original objective, i.e. the promotion of a pattern of economic growth in which the injection of external finance on soft terms was no longer necessary. Together with the credits provided by export credit agencies, much of it for military hardware, this policy has culminated in the late 1980s in the accumulation of a mountain of debt which cannot be serviced on the original schedule of payments. The underlying causes of Africa's economic weakness imply that the current pattern of structural adjustment lending will also not break the cycle of dependency on aid. The latter has become a form of economic drip-feed of dubious value to the patient, although it has maintained economic activity at a higher level than would otherwise be the case.

Should donors continue to lend? Recognition by creditor institutions and governments of the impracticability of Africa servicing its accumulated debt has led to very significant rescheduling arrangements since 1985. In that year about 21 per cent of all Africa's earnings from exports were accounted for by payment of principal and interest on debt; by 1987 the figure had fallen to 14 per cent and was likely to decrease further.[6] This has cleared the way for a re-appraisal of aid policies. Aid has created such artificial divisions within what should be normal national programmes of health care or agriculture that it now obstructs the development of such programmes on a country-wide basis.

It would be much more constructive for a consortium of donors to sit down with governments and review their need for aid finance over, say, the next three-year period. Such a review would cover the direction of government policy in all important areas of the economy, including its view of the role of the private sector. If the consortium agreed to support the overall programme funds would be given, on an agreed schedule, providing the strategies were retained. They would not be tied to the goods of donor countries, and all funds from national sources should be in the form of grants (already the case for a majority of donors). It would be far more useful to Africa to have a smaller amount of total aid on this basis, than to retain the present system where thinking and strategy is dominated by donors, to the extent that national governments have almost lost control over public initiatives in their own countries.

THE INTERNAL STRUGGLE

It is likely that Africa is now moving into a phase in which the rest of the world is less interested in her affairs. The problem of servicing debt is already, in practice, less severe than it was in the early and mid 1980s. Relaxation of the international cold war has meant that military intervention by powerful countries from either the western or eastern blocs – from Cuba to France – will be much less frequent. Even South Africa may decide that the returns from supporting such organizations as Renamo in Mozambique are extremely slim.

Africa will, then, be thrown increasingly inward on herself, and have increasingly less reason to blame the rest of the world for her problems. These will only be resolved in the course of an internal struggle, which will eventually produce governments neither more nor less enlightened than, for instance, those which have ruled over western Europe for the last five hundred years. In the course of this struggle African governments will deal harshly with their opposition, keep power at the centre, and entertain corruption as a normality. While advised to look outwards, and open their economies to trade and investment, they will feel compelled to look inwards as the competition on international markets appears unequal. Attempts by both India and China to open their economies in the 1980s have resulted in a tug-of-war between their economic liberals and economic conservatives, which shows every sign of ending either in stalemate or in a victory for the conservatives. If these richly-endowed giants of the developing world are barely equal to the task of liberalization, Africa is much less equipped for the challenge, and much less prepared to face it. She can only equip herself to face the world from a secure position when she has developed an internal strength which will come from the accumulation of power by centres of growth which lie far outside the existing bureaucracies of government, party and presidential palace. Then out will go the difficult legacies of hierarchial government, clan loyalties, arbitrary succession and the adjustment to a money-based, urban-led culture. In this way, in as little as a hundred years, Africa's doubts about herself – now so prevalent – may finally be removed.

Notes

Chapter 1: Introduction

1. W.E. Smith, *Nyerere of Tanzania*, London, Gollancz, 1973, p.156.

Chapter 2: The Peopling of Africa

1. D.W. Phillipson, *African Archaeology*, Cambridge CUP, 1985, p.109.
2. Ibid., chap. 6.
3. Parsons, D. St. John, *Legends of Northern Ghana*, London, Longmans Green, 1958, quoted in W.H. Allan, *The African Husbandman*, London, Oliver and Boyd, 1968, p.286.
4. D. Nurse and T. Spear, *The Swahili: Reconstructing the History and Language of an African Society 800–1500*, University of Pennsylvania, 1985, p.37.
5. D.W. Phillipson, *African Archaeology*, p.171.
6. Allan, *The African Husbandman*, p.286.
7. Ibid., p.286.
8. As evidenced by artifacts from sites such as Acasus in southern Libya and Tamaya Mellet in Niger.
9. A. Obayemi, 'The Yoruba and Edo-speaking peoples and their neighbours before 1600', in A. Ajayi and M. Crowder (eds), *History of West Africa*, London, Longman, 1985, p.260.

Chapter 3: Patterns of Allegiance

1. J.S. Mbiti, *African Religions and Philosophy*, London, Heinemann, 1969, p.109.
2. J. Kenyatta, *Facing Mt Kenya*, London, Secker and Warburg, 1938; reprinted Mercury, 1961, p.115.
3. Mbiti, *African Religions and Philosophy*, p.182.
4. C. Laye, *The African Child*, London, Fontana, 1959, p.104.
5. K.A. Busia, 'The Ashanti', in D. Forde (ed.), *African Worlds*, London, International African Institute and OUP, 1954, p.204.
6. Mbiti, *African Religions and Philosophy*, p.153.
7. S.F. Moore, *The Chagga and Meru of Tanzania*, London, International African Institute, 1977, p.50.
8. B. Davidson, *The Africans*, London, Longman, 1969; reprinted Penguin, 1973, p.70.
9. M. Kingsley, *Travels in West Africa*, London, Macmillan, 1897; reprinted Virago Press, 1982, p.526.
10. Mbiti, *African Religions and Philosophy*, p.208.
11. M. Wilson, *For Men and Elders*, London, International African Institute, 1977, p.138.
12. Ibid., p.136.
13. A. Richards, 'The Bemba tribe of Northern Rhodesia', in M. Fortes and E. Evans-Pritchard (eds), *African Political Systems*, London, 1940, p.106.
14. M. Gluckman, 'Essays on the ritual of social relations custom and conflict in tribal Africa', p.65, quoted in Davidson, *The Africans*, p.75.
15. A. Richards, 'The Bemba tribe of Northern Rhodesia', *Tribal Government in Transition*, supplement to journal of Royal African Society XXXIV, 1935, p.12.

Chapter 4: States Beyond the Clan

1. N. Levitzion, 'The early states of the western Sudan to 1500', in Ajayi and Crowder (eds), *History of West Africa*, Longman, 1985, p.135.
   The practice of relating geographical areas to contemporary state boundaries is followed throughout.
2. J. Hunwick, 'Songhay, Bornu and the Hausa states 1450–1600', in ibid., p.347.
3. Ibid., p.338.

4. M. Last, *The Sokoto Caliphate*, London, Longman, 1967, p.32.
5. Ibid., p.72.
6. W. Wallace, 'Notes to a journey through the Sokoto empire and Bornu in 1894', *Geographic Journal*, VIII, 1896, in ibid., p.224.
7. Ibid., p.232.
8. The subject of a novel by Kwasi Armah, *The Healers*, London, Heinemann, 1978.
9. J.K. Flynn, 'Ghana-Ashanti', in M. Crowder (ed.), *West African Resistance*, London, Hutchinson, 1971, p.19ff.
10. I. Wilks, 'The Mossi and Akan states', in Ajayi and Crowder (eds), *History of West Africa*, pp.498–502.
11. K.A. Busia, 'The Ashanti', in D. Forde (ed.), *African Worlds*, International African Institute, London, 1954, p.201.
12. A. Obayemi, 'The Yoruba and Edo-speaking peoples and their neighbours before 1600 AD', in Ajayi and Crowder (eds), *History of West Africa*, p.315.
13. B. Davidson and B. Ogot, *East and Central Africa to the Late Nineteenth Century*, London, Longman, 1967, p.52.
14. E. Steinhart, 'The emergence of Bunyoro', in A.I. Salim (ed.), *State Formations in East Africa*, Heinemann, 1984, p.74.
15. M.S. Kiwanuka, *History of Buganda*, London, Longman, 1971, p.100.
16. Ibid., p.103.
17. M. Horton, 'The Swahili corridor', *Scientific American*, vol. 257, no. 3, September 1987, p.76–84.
18. Phillipson, *African Archaeology*, p.205.
19. J.D. Omer-Cooper, 'The Nguni Outburst', in J.E. Flint (ed.), *Cambridge History of Africa*, Cambridge, 1976, vol. 5, p.319.
20. R. Oliver and G. Matthew, *History of East Africa*, Oxford, Oxford University Press, 1963, p.189.

Chapter 5: The Colonial Impact

1. Kingsley, *Travels in West Africa*, Appendix 1, p.658.
2. Kenyatta, *Facing Mt Kenya*, p.129.
3. Busia, 'The Ashanti', p.207.
4. Ibid., p.208.
5. Kenyatta, *Facing Mt Kenya*, p.133.
6. Ibid., p.251.
7. Allan, *The African Husbandman*, p.337.
8. Wilson, *For Men and Elders*, p.184.

9. Ibid., p.74.
10. Ibid., p.179.
11. M.G. Smith, 'A Hausa kingdom: Maradi under Dan Baskore', in D. Forde and P.M. Kaberry (ed.), *West African Kingdoms of the Nineteenth Century*, London, p.108.
12. Kingsley, *Travels in West Africa*, p.472.
13. Wilson, *For Men and Elders*, p.140.
14. Ibid., p.140.
15. H. Powdermaker, *Copper Town: Changing Africa*, New York, Harper and Row, 1962, chap. 11.
16. Ibid., p.190.
17. Ibid., p.203.
18. B. Davidson, *The African Awakening*, London, Jonathan Cape, 1955, p.132.
19. Translation from G. Baladier, *Sociologie des Brazzaville Noires*, Paris, Presse de la Fondation Nationale des Sciences Politiques, 1955; reprinted 1985, p.14.
20. Mbiti, *African Religions and Philosophy*, p.234.
21. B. Davidson, *The Africans: An Entry to Cultural History*, Penguin, London, 1969, p.289.

Chapter 6: Torn Between Two Worlds

1. Wilson, *For Men and Elders*, p.141.
2. Discussion between author and a lawyer in Douala with high proportion of such cases, 1984.
3. Wilson, *For Men and Elders*, p.136.
4. S. Msefya, *The Wicked Walk*, Dar es salaam, Tanzania Publishing House, 1977.
5. Editions-ICAD, *Love is Love*, Guerchy, France, 1987, p.10. (Transcription and translation from kiSwahili of video film material recorded in Mbambara Village, Tanga Region, Tanzania in 1972.)
6. Okot p'Bitek, *Song of Lawino*, Nairobi, East African Publishing House, 1966, verses from pp.13, 17, 52.
7. J. Ngugi, *Barrel of a Pen*, Trenton, New Jersey, Africa World Press, 1983, p.83.
8. Mbiti, *African Religions and Philosophy*, p.221.
9. Information given to the author in the village concerned in August 1985.
10. To the author while 'on trek' with Man O'War Bay Citizenship and Leadership Training Centre, Kurra Falls, Jos, Nigeria, 1962.

Chapter 7: Chiefs Without a Tribe

1. M. Meredith, *The First Dance of Freedom*, London, Hamish Hamilton, 1984, p.335.
2. Kenyatta, *Facing Mt Kenya*, p.310.
3. D.A. Low, *Buganda in Modern History*, London, Weidenfeld and Nicholson, 1971, p.105.
4. For instance, in the 1975 election there were 184 candidates for 92 seats; of these candidates only 86 were former MPs, and of these only 43 were re-elected.
5. According to Amnesty International and released detainees it was at one time over 1,000.
6. A. Wilson, *US Foreign Policy and Revolution: the Creation of Tanzania*, London, Pluto Press, 1989, p.135.
7. J.K. Nyerere, *Freedom and Development*, Dar es salaam, 1973, p.67.
8. J. Karimi and P. Ochieng, *The Kenyatta Succession*, Nairobi, Transafrica, 1980.
9. K. Armah, *The Beautyful Ones Are Not Yet Born*, Heinemann, London, 1969.
10. C. Achebe, *Antills of the Savannah*, Heinemann, London, 1988.

Chapter 8: The Politics of Development

1. Meredith, *The First Dance of Freedom*, 1984, p.48.
2. O. Obasanjo, *Nzeogu*, Spectrum Books, Ibadan, 1987.
3. Specifically Ethiopia, Zaire, Burundi, Uganda, Somalia, Ruanda, Sudan, Chad, Mozambique, Mauritania, Nigeria, and Angola.
4. *Tanzania Daily News*, 1 September 1988, p.4.
5. Rahad (300,000 acres), New Halfa (400,000 acres), Assalaya, Sennar, Kenana and Guineid (240,000 acres).
6. From an average of 224kg of ginned cotton per acre in 1970–4 to an average of 138kg in 1975–9.
7. C. Coquery Vidrovitch, *Afrique Noire*, Paris, Payot, 1985, p.158. Quotes speech by S. Machel at inauguration of Frelimo Party School, September 1975.
8. Ibid., pp.199–200. Based on information collected from students of villagization in Mozambique.

9. World Development Report, World Development Bank, |WDR/WDB| 1986, p.74.
10. A fact later confirmed in an enquiry commissioned by the British Government itself – the 'Bingham Enquiry' – conducted in 1978.
11. O. Teribe *et al.*, *Industrial Development in Nigeria: Patterns, Problems and Prospects*, Ibadan, University Press, 1977, p.89.
12. C. Leys, *Underdevelopment in Kenya*, London, Heinemann Educational Books, 1975, p.132.
13. J.K. Nyerere, 'Economic nationalism', in J.K. Nyerere, *Freedom and Socialism*, Dar es salaam, OUP, 1968, p.262.
14. Both sets of figures from 'Investment in the ACP states and related financial flows', unpublished study for the EC/ACP, Brussels, May, 1988.
15. Ibid.
16. Tanzania Government Annual Plans for 1970–1 and 1977–8.
17. Central Bank of Nigeria Annual Reports 1977–86 and ILO Mission on Employment in Kenya, 1972.
18. Central Bank of Nigeria Annual Reports, 1981–6.
19. A.E. Ekukinam, 'Management problems, public accountability and government control of public enterprises in Nigeria', in *Proceedings of the 1973 Annual Conference of the Nigerian Economic Society*, Ibadan, 1974, p.125.
20. O. Aboyade, 'Nigerian public enterprises as an organisational dilemma', ibid., p.30.
21. *Tanzania Daily News*, 30 August 1988, p.5. In local currency this amounted to Tsh 510m.
22. E. Ayeh-Kumi, *West Africa Magazine*, London, March 1966, p.330, quoted in T. Killick, *Development Economics in Action*, London, Heinemann, 1978.
23. Leys, *Underdevelopment in Kenya*, p.120.
24. In a speech delivered in 1972 in kiSwahili, and so not for international consumption.

Chapter 9: The Elusive Surplus

1. Allan, *The African Husbandman*, p.162.
2. C. Clark, *Population Growth and Land Use*, London, Macmillan, 1967, p.64.
3. Or 13 per sq. km – assumes an area suitable for some cultivation of 740m hectares.
4. Allan, *The African Husbandman*, pp.354–355.

5. From 16.2 to 29.4 people per sq. km of cultivable land.
6. 15.5m hectares out of a total 70m hectares. Source: FAO Production Yearbook, 1970.
7. Allan, *The African Husbandman*, p.391.
8. N. Farson, *Behind God's Back*, London, Gollancz, 1940, p.318.
9. R.W. Kettlewell, 'The master farmers scheme and the village lands improvement scheme in Nyasaland', in *Report on Conference of Directors of Agriculture*, London, Colonial Office, Misc No. 931, 1958.
10. J. Henry, 'Les Bases theorique des essais de paysannat indigene' in *Bulletin Agriculture du Congo Belge*, XLIII, 1952.
11. A. Thurston, 'The intensification of smallholder agriculture in Kenya: the genesis and implementation of the Swynnerton Plan', PhD thesis, 1984, quoting V.E. Burke.
12. Ibid., quoting R. Otter.
13. 30 per sq. km.
14. P. Collier, *Labour and Poverty in Rural Tanzania*, Oxford, Clarendon Press, 1986, p.92.
15. FAO Production Yearbooks, 1960–80.
16. Cocoa, coffee, tea, ground-nuts, cotton, rubber and tobacco.
17. FAO Production Yearbooks, 1960–80.
18. Cereal imports and urban population (100 million) from WDR/WDB, 1981, p.171; annual average consumption per head of all cereals and tubers was 200kg.
19. FAO Early Warning System data, 1989.
20. In each case the Commonwealth Development Corporation of the UK is one of the overseas partners; in the case of Mumias they are joined by Booker Tate of the UK.
21. J.E. Gorse and D. Steeds, *Desertification in the Sahelien and Sudanian Zones of West Africa*, Washington, World Bank Technical Paper, No. 61, 1987, p.8.
22. Bureau of Land Use and Resource Planning, University of Dar es salaam, 1980.
23. Project proposed by the author in 1972, financed by the World Bank and managed by C.M. Chisholm and Associates.

Chapter 10: The Industrial Dilemma

1. P.D. Curtin, 'The External Trade of West Africa to 1800', in Ajayi and Crowder (ed.), *History of West Africa*, p.627.
2. J. Iliffe, *The Emergence of African Capitalism*, London, Macmillan, 1982, p.9.
3. Ibid., p14.

4. Ibid., p.14
5. Ibid., p.81.
6. G. Hunter, *New Societies of Tropical Africa*, London, OUP, 1962, p.54; and *Towards Sustained Development in sub-Saharan Africa*, Washington, World Bank, 1984, p.63. Export values relate to Kenya, Tanzania, Uganda, Ghana, Zaire and Nigeria. Total in 1907 was £St9.5m; in 1982 £St494m at 1907 prices based on *The Economist* index of value of pound sterling.
7. J.R.M. Cantwell, *The Directory of International Investment and Production Statistics*, London, Macmillan, 1987.
8. N. Long, *Social Change and the Individual*, Manchester, Manchester University Press, 1968, chap. VIII.
9. C. Liedholm and D. Mead, *Small Scale Industries in Developing Countries: Empirical Evidence and Policy Implications*, Michigan, Michigan State University, 1987, p.15.
10. K. King, *The African Artisan*, London, Heinemann Educational Books, 1977.
11. H. de Soto, *The Other Path*, London, I.B. Tauris, 1989.
12. *Sub Saharan Africa: from Crisis to Sustainable Growth*, Washington, World Bank, 1989, chap. 6.
13. 1974–8 Kenya Development Plan, Nairobi, Government of Kenya, 1974.
14. S. Schatz, *Nigerian Capitalism*, California, University of California Press, 1977, p.87.
15. Iliffe, *The Emergence of African Capitalism*, p.75, quoting survey by Dr Idemudia.
16. E.O. Akeredolu-Ale, *The Underdevelopment of Indigenous Entrepreneurship in Nigeria*, University of Ibadan Press, 1975, p.101.
17. P. Kilby, *Industrialisation in an Open Economy: Nigeria 1945–66*, CUP, 1969, p.342.
18. Including most of the well-established trading houses such as CFAO and the United Africa Company which had a majority of their share capital owned locally.
19. *Towards Sustained Development in sub Saharan Africa*, Washington, World Bank, 1984, p.58.

Chapter 11: The Aid Machine

1. 'Uhuru' meaning freedom in kiSwahili, and 'mwalimu' meaning 'the teacher' – Julius Nyerere was and is frequently known as 'the teacher'.

2. International Development Association – funded by the World Bank's profits and from grants from its major shareholders.

3. W.W. Rostow, *The Stages of Economic Growth*, Cambridge, CUP, 1963.

4. WDR/WDB, 1988, Washington, End Table A4. Indicates that sub-saharan Africa's GDP declined by 1.5% from 1980 to 1984, increased by 5.8% and 2.6% respectively in 1985 and 1986 and declined by an estimated 1.4% in 1987.

5. Ibid., Table 22; from $6.9bn in 1980 to $10.0bn in 1986.

6. *World Bank Annual Report 1988*, Washington, Tables 5-1 and 6-2 pp.65, 84; indicates $977m out of a total $2.9bn.

7. *World Bank Development Report*, 1989, Washington, p.20 and *Financing Adjustment with Growth in sub Saharan Africa 1986–90*, Washington, World Bank, 1986, End Table 16.

8. Development Assistance Committee of the OECD, *Twenty-Five Years of Development Co-operation: A Review*, Paris, 1985, p.195.

9. R. Riddell, *Foreign Aid Reconsidered*, London, James Currey/Overseas Development Institute, 1987, p.193.

10. i.e. Rehabilitation after the civil war of 1966–72.

11. *World Development Report*, 1988, Washington, World Bank, Table 23.

12. K. Griffin, *International Inequality and National Poverty*, London, Macmillan, 1978, p.61. Quoted in R. Riddell, *Foreign Aid Reconsidered*, London, James Currey/ODI, 1987, p.133.

13. *World Development Report*, Washington, World Bank, 1988, Table 7.

14. P. Mistry, *African Debt: the Case for Relief for Sub Saharan Africa*, Oxford International Asociates, 1989, p.30 and *External Debt of Developing Countries*, Paris, OECD, 1988.

15. T.E.M. Deppler and M. Williamson, *Capital Flight: Concepts, Measurements, and Issues*, Washington, IMF, August 1987. Assumes private assets are 70 per cent of total national offshore assets.

16. The two steel mills in Nigeria are financed by export credits from West Germany and the USSR and operate at about 25 per cent of potential capacity.

17. Riddell, *Foreign Aid Reconsidered*, p.207.

18. OECD, *Development Co-operation*, Paris, 1987, Table 18, p.254.

19. Ibid., Table 13, p.241.

20. Riddell, *Foreign Aid Reconsidered*, p.209. Refers to studies on Zimbabwe and Kenya.

21. R. Cassen, *et al*, *Does Aid Work?*, Oxford, OUP, 1986.
22. *World Development Report*, 1988, Washington, World Bank, Table 13.

Chapter 12: The Prospects for Progress

1. P. Ndegwa, *The African Challenge*, Nairobi, Heinemann, 1986, pp.169–170.
2. Where between 5,000 and 20,000 Tutsi were killed by, mainly, Hutu, Government soldiers in August 1988, echoing the even larger massacres of 1964.
3. *World Development Report*, 1981, Washington, World Bank, 1981, p.142; World Development Report, 1986, p.230.
4. *African Business*, London, August, 1987.
5. Population growth estimates based on *World Development Report*, 1989 World Development Bank, Table 31. Assumes urban population growth from 100m to 230m, and constant real income per head of $300.
6. *World Development Report*, 1989, Washington, World Bank, pp.239, 211. These are actual rather than scheduled debt service payments.

Glossary

age sets: peer groups, usually of boys rather than girls, that cut across family lines

asantehene: king of the Asante

Asante: dominant people of central Ghana

askia: king of Songhay

Babito: people of the dominant clans of the Bunyoro kingdom (of present-day Uganda)

Bamilike: a people of Cameroun who are largely on the periphery of political power

Bantu: a generic term for tribes with a common origin close to present-day Cameroun, but who migrated throughout central, eastern and southern Africa

Bemba: a tribe of northern Zambia

changamire: paramount chief of Urozwi, a kingdom of the Shona people (of present-day Zimbabwe)

chitumukulu: paramount chief of the Bemba (of Zambia)

Fulani: originally a cattle-rearing people, particularly of northern Nigeria, but with related clans throughout the Savannah regions of West Africa

Hausa: a people of northern Nigeria

Ibo: a tribe of south-eastern Nigeria

induna: military leader of the Zulu people (of present-day Zululand and South Africa)

213

jihad: holy war engaged in by followers of Islam

jua kali: used in Kenya to describe those who work in the 'hot sun', ie the artisans working in the informal sector

kabaka: king of Buganda (of present-day Uganda)

Kikuyu: a leading people of Kenya

litunga: paramount chief of the Lozi

Lozi: a people of western Zambia

Luo: a people of western Kenya

Malinke: a dominant tribe of Mali

monomatapa: king of the Shona tribe

mugabe: senior chief, effectively king, of the Banyankole tribe of present-day Uganda

Mwanamatupa: northern part of Urozwi kingdom, independent of Urozwi from c.AD1500 (in present-day Zimbabwe)

Ndebele: an off-shoot of the Nguni peoples. Ndebele occupied Matabeleland in south-western Zimbabwe in the 1830s

Nguni: a Bantu people of Natal

Nyakyusa: a people of south-western Tanzania

Rozwi: dominant clan of the Shona people

Songhay: a people who built the Songhay empire of the sixteenth century

sudan: savannah area of west Africa, stretching from Dakar to Khartoum

uhuru: a ki-swahili word to denote post-colonial freedom

ujamaa: ki-swahili word for 'familihood', used in Tanzania to describe self-managing productive units, especially villages.

Index

Abbo, Alhaji 165
Abdullah, Emir of Zaria 46
Academie Française 115
Accra 50
Achebe, Chinua 118
'Action group' (Nigeria) 100
Adae celebrations 66
Addis Ababa 123
adultery fines 75–6
African Capitalism (Iliffe) xi
African Husbandman, The (Allan)
    xi
African Mine Workers' Union 101
African National Congress
    (Northern Rhodesia) 101
African Religions and Philosophy
    (Mbiti) xi
African Watchtower Movement 79,
    80
*Africans, The: an Entry into New
    Cultural History* (Davidson) xi
*Afrique Noire: Ruptures et
    Permanences* (Vidrovitch) xii
age sets: and family groups 22;
    loyalty to 30; hierarchical basis
    32; military 59, 60; girls' 59
agriculture: unsuccessful attempts
    to transform 7, 8; marketing
    boards 7, 125–6, 133, 146, 148;
    pioneering 11–12; movement of

seed and crops 16–17, 135;
    improved technology 19; and Lozi
    25; and traditional power
    structure 65; and migrant labour
    76; pricing 124, 125, 126; fertility
    136, 137, 141, 142, 145, 150; and
    population changes 136–8,
    147–8, 151; imperial
    intervention 138–45; rush for
    growth 145–7; fertilizer 146, 150,
    175–6; breeding work 148, 149;
    seasonal credit system 149–50;
    important policy changes 150;
    aid projects 175; and 'island'
    projects 176, 185; and drought
    192; aid obstructs programmes
    200; *see also* farming
Ahidjo, Ahmadu 113, 114, 115, 191
aid/aid donors: statistics 1; and
    political adjustment 1–2; and
    economic adjustment 2; as
    economic 'drip feed' 8, 187; and
    negligence of completed
    investments 122; and exchange
    rates 125, 126; and agricultural
    policy changes 150; projects
    168–71, 174–87; ambiguities
    between agencies and
    governments 171–4, 180, 186,
    190; changes in short-term

215

objectives 172–3; volatility in aid flows 173, 180, 182, 187; serving national interest of 173, 180, 182–3, 187; structural adjustment loans 177, 184, 200; switching resources 177–9, 180, 186; food 178, 182; corruption 179–80; lack of co-ordination 180–181, 187; ineffective valuation 180, 183–6, 187; assumption of greater wisdom 180; failure of original objective 199; reviewing need for aid finance 200
Akan gold fields 40
Akeredolu-Ale, E.O. 163–4, 165
Akwapim people 153
Albert, Lake 52
Alexandria 153
Alhaj Muhamed I 41
Ali Ber, Sunni 41
Alikawa clan 47
Allan, William H. xi, 68–9, 139–40
Almoravid movement 39, 65
ambivalence/ambiguity 30, 31, 34, 82, 171, 176, 177, 180, 186, 190
Amin, Idi 89, 105, 121, 132
ancestors: identification with 21; loyalty to 22, 24; as guardians of clan's welfare 23–4, 69; contact with 23; and rituals 24–5, 66; and chiefs 27, 35, 50–1, 73; and supernatural protection 29; and Islam 65; loosening of links with 85
Angola x, 68, 190
Ankole, kingdom of 26, 35
Ankole people 35
Anthills of the Savannah (Achebe) 118
apprenticeship 161
Arab: traders 14, 33, 55, 152; scholars 44
Arabia 45
archaeology 52, 57
Armah, Kwasi 118
army, colonial experience of 6
art 65
artisans: undermined by colonial regime 2; growth of 7–8; in Nigeria 157; Sikh 158; jua kali 159, 160; informal sector 157–60,

162, 194; diversification and improved technology 195
Arusha Declaration (1967) 107, 128, 132
Arusha textile mill 130
Asante kingdom 5, 37, 49, 50, 51, 54, 59, 61, 63, 66, 73, 154
Asante people 22, 26, 27, 30, 49–51, 73, 121, 153, 194
asantehene (Asante kings) 49, 50, 51, 54, 61, 63, 73, 154
Asia 3, 196
askias 41
Atlantic Coast 37
Attahiru 1, Caliph 48
authoritarianism: and pre-colonial societies 2, 3, 103; and Latin America 3; and clans 5; and power 32; and Sokoto Caliphate 48; of colonial regime 86; and Banda regime 99; drift towards 103–9, 110, 118; in Uganda 104–6; and localism 104, 105, 110; in Tanzania 106, 108; politics dominated by 119, 198
authority, destruction of 71–4
Awolowo, Chief Obafemi 100
Azikiwe, Dr Namdi 100

Babangida, General 100
Babito people 54
Babu, A.M. 107
Bacwezi people 14, 52, 54
Bahuma people 54
bakabilo 72
al-Bakri 37, 39
Baladier, G. 78–9
Balewa, Tafawa 100
ballot, and Latin America 3
Balovale 85
Bamba, Amadu 117
Bambuk gold field 40
Bamilike people 7, 134, 136, 157, 190, 191
bananas 16, 135, 138, 148
Banda, Aleke 97
Banda, Dr Kamuzu (Hastings) 97, 99, 119
Bani River 40
Bantu people: expansion 4, 13–14, 16–20, 37, 135; language of 10, 13, 14; invaded 52; tradition

combining religious and political power 57; trade in Great Zimbabwe 57; diaspora 57, 62
Banyanankole people 26, 74, 110
barley 11
BAT 156
Batumbezi people 52
beads, imports of 57
Beautyful Ones Are Not Yet Born, The (Armah) 118
Belewa, Tafawa 74
Belgium/Belgians: reliance on forced labour 72; in Ruanda 140
Bello, Muhammed 45, 47
Bemba people 33, 34, 70, 72, 101, 102, 190, 198
Benin 18, 52, 61
Benue River 18
Berber peoples 44
Biafra 165
Birnin Gazargamo 44
Biya, Paul 113, 114, 115
black market 109
blacksmithing 158
Bokassa, 'Emperor' Jean-Bedel 123
Bongo, Omar 126
Booker McConnell 127
booty 55, 71, 75
Boran 96
bori (spirit worship) 74
Bornu 42
Bosumpra 11
Botswana: and production/politics priorities 3–4; and transfer of power 110; leadership 191; strong government 191–2; maintenance of savings and investment 192; and drought 192
bourgeoisie 88, 89, 96; Kenyan Asian 131
BP 127
Brandt, Willy 172
Brazil: and slaves from Mwanamutapa 57; exports to 153
bribes 96–7
bride price 91, 92
Britain: invasion of Sokoto Caliphate (1902) 45, 48; military confrontation with Asante (1823–96) 49; occupation of Buganda 58; attempts at indirect rule through chiefs 66; and

chiefly power 72; and Islam 84; and Ugandan constitution 104; and quasi-federal Ugandan state 106; and company investment 155–6; company growth in Nigeria 163; and aid 182, 183
British Plastics Window Group 183
British South Africa Company (BSA) 63, 72, 85, 126, 127, 155
Buganda 5, 54, 55–6, 58, 61–2, 69, 104, 105, 121
building 57, 158
Bukhari, Muhamed 46
Bukoba 125
Bukubwe 70
Bunyoro 54, 55, 61, 104
Bure gold field 40
bureaucracy 201; in Buganda 49; and *kabakas* 56, 62; and informal sector 161
Burkino Faso 95, 178
Burundi 14, 121, 190
bush/fallow cycle 136, 138, 141, 143
Busia, Kofi A. 50–1, 66
businesses, modern 2, 3

Cairo 40, 152
Calabar district 31
Cameroun 14, 19, 165; and production/politics priorities 3–4; migrant movement from 4; tribal languages 9; and Bantu people 14; succession problem 113–15; high growth rates in 1970s 113–14; coup attempts 114, 115; and roads 122; and prestige projects 123; and agricultural productivity 150; domestic savings 178; leadership 191; strong government 191–2; maintenance of savings and investment 192; and drought 192; changes in crop production 195; elections to National Assembly (1988) 198
Canada 122
cannibalism 31
Cape Coast, Ghana 69
Cape of Good Hope 57
capital: international 7; from financial markets 8; accumulation of 153, 154; used to

increase consumption 178; and investment 186

cash crops 5, 68, 69, 70, 73, 84, 122, 129, 138, 142, 143, 153, 175

Casimance, Senegal 116

cassava 16, 135, 140, 141, 149, 194

cattle 139; and Fulani 18; dispossession of 63; and cash crops 70; and marriage 91; Zebu 135; and Hausa 149; and Tanzanian project 169, 170

Central African Federation 101

Central African Republic 123

Central Bank of Kenya 189

cereals 11, 146–7, 178

ceremonial 65, 66, 74

CFAO 127, 156

Chad 121, 190

Chama Cha Mapunduzi (CCM) 106

changamire (Urozwi king) 58, 62

'Change the Constitution' movement 112

Chenery, Hollis 172, 178

chiefs/chieftaincy: and traditional systems 2; institution of 17; loyalty to 21; and succession 21, 30, 34–5; role of 24, 25–6; power of 24; and supernatural 27; hierarchical structure 32, 103; killing of sick 35, 67, 110; European attempts to rule through 66; resentment of alienation of Christian converts 66; weakened chiefly power 71–3, 85; teenage girls as additional wives 86; status 122–3; and tribute 180

children: and establishment of new villages 22; and wives' subordinate position 32–3; and single mothers 88; and international culture 93

China 57, 201

Chipimbi 17, 135, 148

chitumukulu 33, 34, 72, 198

Christianity: introduction of 5, 64, 65; and clan loyalties 22, 23; and personal spiritual uplift 26; primary message of 65; synchronization with trade activities and colonization 65; Coptic 65; conversion to 65, 67;

and Mau Mau 81; reform movements 155; women's role 198

Christiansbourg Castle, Accra 50

Church, the 72–3

Church of New Zion 80

Church of Scotland 67

Church of the Cherabim and Seraphim, Nigeria 79

churches 79, 82

circumcision 26

civil service/servants: and class structure 88; corruption 96, 179; in Malawi 99; allocated contracts 132; and aid 168, 169, 171, 175, 176, 177, 179; and development policy 189; bilingual 191

clans/clan system: social character of 5; value system of 5, 6; loyalties 19, 21, 22–3, 30, 37, 47, 60–1, 62, 89, 99, 201; antagonisms 19; and tribes 22; coalitions of 23, 58, 61; dominant 36; as base of social structure 37; and Mali 40; and marriage in Sokoto Caliphate 47–8; and centralised kingdom 48–52, 54–6; and lineage lines 50; efforts to develop alternatives to 62; and introduction of cash crops 69; and localism 99

Clapperton, Hugh 46, 152

class allegiances 88–9

clitoridectomy 26, 67

cloth, trade in 33, 157

cocoa 69, 138, 153, 155, 195

cocoyam 16

coffee 73, 125, 138, 139, 144, 195, 196

Cohen, Sir Andrew 104

coinage 68

Coker, J.K. 153

colonial period: and 'nation building' x; briefness of xi; prevention of continuity in development of African society 2; innovations of 5–6; states become independent 62; resistance to colonialists 63; establishment of key western institutions 64; and religion 64–7; and commerce 67–71; destruction of authority

71–4; position of women 74–9;
new forms of expression 79–82;
difficulties for emerging
independent nations 82–3;
authoritarian nature of 86
Comité de Dévélopement de
Jeunesse de Yabi à Douala 90
community/communities: values
and chief's office 26; and
individual morality 26; and life
force 28; as closed societies 29;
lack of formal judicial system 29;
and secret societies 30–31;
intolerance of the individual 32;
and hierarchy 32; obsession with
supernatural 32; consciousness of
death 32; chief's role in 35; and
gold empires 37; relations with
ancestors/gods 51; king as
symbol of unity 51; role of land
changes 69; and migrant labour
76; change in women's role 77;
and development of money
economy 84–5; urban classes
links with 89; and fee-paying
services 197
community groups 193, 197
companies: state-owned 7;
overseas-owned 7; multinational
155–6, 177, 188, 196
Confederation of British Industry
(CBI) 179
Congo 68
Congo-Kordofanian language
family 10, 18
contracts: bidding for 179; and
corruption 180; government 191;
management 196; royalty 196
Convention People's Party 73
co-operative societies 72, 73
copper 121, 155; and Great
Zimbabwe 56, 57; and northern
Rhodesia 70, 72, 77; Zambian 85,
89
corporal punishment 124
corruption 95–6, 120, 134, 179–80,
186–7
cotton 69, 122, 138, 139, 141, 142,
146
credit: and exports 179, 181,
199–200; and community groups
193, 197

crop rotation 137, 141, 142
crops: cash 5, 68, 69, 70, 73, 84,
122, 129, 138, 142, 143, 153, 175;
adoption of new 16–17, 135; food
176, 195; export 195
Cuba 201
cultivators/cultivation: take-over
from hunter-gatherers 11–12, 14;
and Bantu expansion 13, 14
cultural differentiation 18
culture 92–4, 202
currency, local 125, 181
currency zone 153
curse, and death 28
Cushites 14

Dahomey 51, 52, 61
Dakar 117, 148
Dan Fudiye, Uthman 44–7, 73
Danes 50
Dar es salaam x, 91, 168
Davidson, Basil xi
death: and causation 28–9, 95;
community consciousness of 32
DeBeers Consolidated 192
debt statistics 1
defence expenditure 178
deities, and life of community 27
democratization 199
despotism 52, 55
destabilization 199
development agencies 171
Diagne, Blaise 117
diamonds 197
Dingane 60
Dingiswayo 59
Dinka 137
Diop, Abdou 115, 116
divination 65
divorce 75, 76, 90
Doe, Samuel Kanyon 132
Douala 90
dress 76
Drobo (Asante god) 27
drought x, 54, 135, 179, 192
Dutch (on Gold Coast) 49
duty, ties of 29
Dyenkira people 49, 50

education: introduction of western
5, 72, 83; social 26; and
conversion to Christianity 65;

impact of missionary 67; available mainly to males 77, 85; creation of education service 120; training in informal sector 161; and entrepreneurs 163; and community groups 193; paying for 197; *see also* schools

Egbo people 31

ekyihumba (temporary king) 35

Elf 156

Elisabethville (Lubumbashi) 78

Elmina 50

Enfant Noir, L' (Laye) 27

entrepreneurs: undermined by colonial regime 7; as potential countervailing power to government 7; 'power and status' motivation 8, 167; investment in production 152; reasons for relative weakness of 154; response to presence of multinationals 156; and informal sector 156–60, 161; Nigerian 132, 162–5; and schooling 163; and manufacturing businesses 166; in the future 196

Eremon 12

Eritrea 121

estate workers 70, 76, 84

Ethiopia 14; and racial types 10; early stone tool 'industries' 11; Coptic Christianity of 65; civil conflicts 121, 190; resettlement schemes 145; and informal producers 157

Europe/Europeans: rising economic powers of 49; Bugandan contacts 55; and gold trade 57; years of rule 62; apparent invincibility of 63; industrial needs of 155; sense of deprivation among immigrant groups 190

European Community (EC) 179, 181, 185, 192

exchange rates 124, 125, 126

exports: and agriculture 7, 150, 151; diversification 119; Uganda 121; Sudan 122; and exchange rates 125; cash crops 153; statistics 155; and informal sector 160; credit 179, 181, 199–200; access to markets 181;

commodity 184; unfavourable prospects for 196, 197; and payment of debt 200

extra-sensory perception 29

Facing Mt Kenya (Kenyatta) xi

family: identifications of 21–2; and age sets 22; and introduction of cash crops 69; and land 70; loyalties 193; weakening commitment 194

family, extended: and colonial period innovations 6; and migrant labour 6, 76; and founding in new units 19; and children 88; weakening links 89, 194; and localism 99; as source of labour in small-scale enterprises 157

family planning 87, 90

famine 179

Far East 163

farming: and ancestors 23–4; and religious beliefs 24; and Lozi 25; and community 32; cash crop 70; substance 87; and superstition 95; and increased cattle numbers 139; and seasonal credit 149–50; *see also* agriculture

father, and loyalties 22

femmes libres 77, 78–9

Fernando Po 153

fetish rites 66, 81

fishing 13

Flame Trees of Thika (TV production) 93

folklore 12, 16

food production: levels 1; women take over burden of 6; and urban demand 7; shift from export crops to food crops 195

foot-and-mouth 138

For Men and Elders (Wilson) xi

Foreign Aid Reconsidered (Riddell) xi

forest 142, 143; and Bantu migrants 13; and crops 16; and bush/fallow cycle 136

France: conquest of Senegal and Mali 63; attempts at indirect rule through chiefs 66; and chiefly power 72; and Islam 84; contact

with Senegal 117; planning
experience 120; and company
investment 155–6; and aid 182,
183; reduced military
intervention by 201
free churches 79, 82
Freetown 77
Frelimo 123, 124, 198
French National Assembly 115,
117
Friendship Textile Mill 130
frontier fighting 54, 55
Fulani people 10, 137; ethnic
origins 18; as semi-nomadic
pastoralists 18; expansion 19;
alliance with Hausa states 42,
45; scholars 44; based in
countryside 44; power in Sokoto
47, 61; urban settlement of 48
Fulbe people see Fulani people

Gabon 123, 126
Gambia, the 153
Gao 37, 40, 41, 44
gari 194
Garoua, Cameroun 191
Germany: faces major resistance in
south-west Africa 63; use of
forced labour in Tanganyika
71–2; Tanzanian resistance to
German colonialism 103
Gezira Scheme 122, 175
Ghana 50, 61; secondary
settlement in 4; nascent states of
5; and early stone tool
'industries' 11; and Fulani 18;
and clan loyalties 22–3; and gold
empire 37, 39, 40, 61; and Islam
39, 41, 65; markets of 49; and
success of cash crops 69; and
nationalism 73; military regimes
110; and prestige projects 123;
hostility to immigrant groups
132; export of cash crops 153; and
cocoa 153; and small-scale
enterprises 157; one-man
proprietorships 163
Gidado, vizier 47
Gikuyu, Embu and Meru
Association (GEMA) 112, 113
Giwa, Alhaji Hamayadji 148
glass 57

Gobir, Sultanate of 44, 45
God: loyalty to 22; view of 23;
clan's links with 24; and life
force 25; and chiefs 25, 35; and
death 28; loosening of links with
85
gods, relations with community 51,
69; see also deities
gold 68, 155; empires of 37–42; and
Asante kingdom 49, 50, 153; and
Great Zimbabwe 56, 57, 152;
South Africa 70
Gold Coast (later Ghana) 49
gold empires 37, 39–42
Goree 117
government, post-independence:
dominant role of state 2;
diversifying of exports 119;
creation of local industries 119;
creation of educational and
health services 120; economic
planning 120; corruption 120;
unplanned leaps 121; civil strife
121; accumulation and
distribution of wealth 121–2;
prestige projects 122–4;
disregard for village
communities 123–4; centralizing
the economy 124–6; foreign
investment 126–9; state
enterprise management 129–31;
citizen entrepreneurs 131–2;
hierarchical 201
Great Zimbabwe 56–8
Griffin, Keith 178
Gross Domestic Product (GDP) 172,
178
Gross National Product 156, 166
groundbeans 137
groundnuts 17, 117, 135, 139, 148,
153, 196
'Group of Forty' 81
growth rates 3–4
guerrilla wars x

Harare 158
Hausa: as majority in Sokoto
Caliphate 47; farmers 149
Hausa states 37; origins 42; and
Fulani 44; and Sokoto Caliphate
45, 47
Hausaland 46

health services 120, 177, 197, 200
hierarchy, and community 32
'Holy Ghost' movement 81
hospital treatment, and bribery
    95–6
Houphouet-Boigny, President 123,
    180, 188
human sacrifice 64
hunting and gathering 11, 12, 13,
    14, 20
husbands: status of 32; wives'
    subordinate role to 32–3; and
    polygamous marriage 33;
    common grounds for friction with
    wife 76; as migrant workers 76
hydro-electric power 192

Ibadan 157–8, 194
Ibn Battuta 37
Ibo-land 16
Ibo people 7, 100, 134, 136, 157,
    164, 190
Ife 52, 154
Igala 18
Ijeba 52
Ikun people 31
Ila people 101
Iliffe, John xi
imports: and local industries 119;
    Uganda 121; value of 125;
    dependence on 151, 156;
    ensuring finance for 177; EC
    rejection of 181; and aid 187
income: levels 1, 161, 196; and
    family 89; distribution between
    expatriate companies and
    individuals 120
independence ix, x, 82, 104, 111;
    confusion of social and moral
    values 96; and nationalism 100
India/Indians: extent of trade and
    production 3; entrepreneurs 7,
    155; and informal producers 157,
    158; British attitude to existing
    values 64; planning experience
    120; as immigrant investors 126;
    sense of deprivation among
    immigrant groups 190; attempts
    to open economy 201
individual: community intolerance
    of 32; unprecedented opportunity
    85; and sick relatives 88; and

authoritarianism 103; future of
    193–4
Indonesians 16
indunas (military leaders) 59
informal sector 156–60; formalizing
    160–2; links with modern
    industry 159–60
initiation: into age sets 22, 59;
    ceremony 26–7
inter-marriage 19, 61
International Development Agency
    (IDA) 171
International Institute of Tropical
    Agriculture (IITA) 143, 148, 149
International Labour Organization
    161
International Monetary Fund
    (IMF) 89, 173
intrigue 29, 30, 35, 99
investment: and aid 8, 178; and
    government 122; foreign 126–9,
    155–6, 166; in production 152,
    153, 155; and informal sector
    161; and capital 186; statistics
    192
iron 11, 13, 42
irrigation 122, 135–6, 140, 151, 175
Ishaq II, *Askia* 41
Islam ix; and Cushites 14; and
    Fulani 19; and clan loyalties 22,
    23; and spiritual uplift 26; and
    clitoridectomy 26; and succession
    question 35; and trade 36, 37, 39,
    40; expansion of 39; and Ghana
    39; and pagan faith 39, 42, 48,
    65; and Mali 40; as an
    integrating religion 40; and
    Songhay 41; and alliance of
    Hausa and Fulani states 42,
    44–8; and Sokoto Caliphate 45–8;
    women's role 74; and clash of
    cultures 84; single currency zone
    153; reform movements 155, 156;
    and government 198–9
Italy 183
ivory, trade in 33, 50, 56, 71
Ivory Coast 50; government role in
    economy 119; and prestige
    projects 123; share capital 127;
    transfer of ownership 128

Japan 156
Jehovah's Witnesses 156
Jenne 40
jihad 19, 45, 46, 48, 74
Johnston, Sir Harry 136
Jos 77
Jos Plateau, Nigeria 11
jua kali artisans 159, 160
Juba, Sudan 176

Kabaka Yekka (KY) Party 105
kabakas 54–6, 61–2, 104, 105
Kalahari desert 56
Kalema, Kabaka 55
Kambona, Oscar 107
Kamwana, Kenan 80
Kano vii, 42, 46, 148, 152, 153, 156, 163
KANU 111, 112
Kapulu, Mwata 85–7
Kapulu, Pezo 86–7, 91
Kapwepwe, Simon 101, 102, 190
Karagwe 138
Karanga 56, 58, 62, 67
Kariuki, J.M. 113
Karonga (of Mulavi tribe) 16
Karonga, Malawi 70
Karume, Abeid 107
Karume, Njenga 112
Kasomo 80
Katanga 77, 127
Katerega, Kabaka 55
Katsina 42
Kaunda, Kenneth 80, 86, 101, 102, 190
Kebbi clan 47
Kenya: and production/politics 3–4; tribal languages 9–10, 14; and racial types 10; and Luo people 14; colonization by Babito 54; dispossession of land 68; and Mau Mau 81; transfer of power 110; and succession issue 110–13; and population 139; land reform 143–4; government support for small farmers 146; and agricultural productivity 150; foreign investment in 156; informal sector 158–9, 161; Development Plan (1974–8) 161; domestic savings 178; counterpart funding 181; and

immigrants 190; leadership 191; strong government 191–2; maintenance of savings and investment 192; and drought 192; considers abolition of secret ballot 198
Kenya, Mount 4
Kenya African Union 81
Kenya Land and Freedom Army 81
Kenya People's Union (KPU) 9, 112
Kenya Small Traders' Society 90
Kenya Tea Development Authority 147
Kenyatta, Jomo xi, 6, 9, 64–5, 83, 111, 112, 113, 118, 188, 190, 191
Keyta dynasty 40
Khadre, Abdoul 117
Khartoum 11, 69
Khoisan people 10–11, 14
Kiambu District, Kenya 144
Kibaki (Kenyan Minister of Finance) 112
Kikuyu 20, 64, 81, 82, 143, 144, 146, 158, 190; movement of 4; and age sets 22, 30; and ancestors 24; and clitoridectomy 67; and political succession 112, 113
Kilby, P. 164, 165
Kilimanjaro 16, 125
Kilimanjaro Native Co-operative Union 73
Kiltex textile mill 130
Kilwa 57
King, Kenneth 158
kingdoms, and clan strength 48–52, 54–6
kings: and traditional systems 2; seen as holy 25; killing of sick 35; and Islam 39, 40, 41; variable power invested in 48–9, 51, 52; as symbol of community unity 51; and succession 52, 55; loyalty to 55, 56
Kingsley, Mary 30–1, 64, 77, 84
Kinshasa 78
kinship: and loyalties 2, 21, 50, 153; and Europeans 64
Kisumu 112
kiSwahili 9, 103, 106
Kiwewa, Kabaka 55
Koinange, Mbiyu 111
kola nut trade 163

Kongo, Angola 58
Konni clan 47
Kumasi 49, 63, 157
Kumbi Saleh 39
kuomboka ceremony 25
Kwamaan people 49, 50

labour: migration of 68, 70–1, 76,
    140, 197; wage 68, 153; volunteer
    68; forced 71–2; agricultural 76;
    and informal sector 161
Lakwena, Alice 81
Lamba people 17, 135
Lambaland 17
land: availability xi, 7; settlement
    of 4; redistribution 22;
    exhaustion of 23; competition for
    54, 59, 70; dispossession of 63,
    67, 68; family 70; individual
    acquisition of 85; sale of Kenyan
    191
land reform 143–4
language, secret 34
languages, tribal 9–10, 14, 18, 39,
    47, 54, 103, 191
Last, Dr Murray 47
Latin America 2–3; *see also* South
    America
Laye, Camara 26–7
Lealui 25
learning centres 40, 44, 45
Lebanese 7, 155, 190
Lenshina, Alice 6, 80–1
'leopard' societies 31
Leopoldville (Kinshasa) 78
Lesotho 174
Lever Brothers 155
Leys, Colin xi
Liberia 77, 110, 126; and prestige
    projects 123; creole population
    132
Libya 182
life force 23, 25, 28
lineage lines 3, 5; and tribes 22;
    and loyalty 22, 30, 47, 49, 51, 56,
    61, 171; and gold empires 37; in
    Mali 40; in Asante 49, 50, 51;
    and commemoration of ancestors
    50; and primogeniture 61
litunga (paramount chief) 25, 34,
    85
livestock 18, 136, 137, 139, 142,

146; diseases 138; and pressure
    on land 139, 144; projects 168,
    169–71, 176; and drought 192;
    see also stock keeping
Lobengula 60
local industries, creation of 119
localism 134; nationalism v
    localism 99–103; and
    authoritarian government 104,
    105, 110; in Uganda 104–6;
    Senegalese avoidance of
    problems 117; Nyerere's defeat of
    118; politics dominated by 119;
    reduction of tribal connotations
    198
Lovale people 85, 86
Lozi kingdom, Zambia 85, 137
Lozi people 25, 32, 34
Lualuba River 17
Luba people 17
Lubaland 17
Lubumbashi 78
Lukuku people 31
Lumpa Church 80, 81, 82
Lunda people, Zaire 58, 70, 85
Luo peoples 9, 14, 54, 111
Luo-land 111
Lusaka 158
Luweru Triangle, Buganda 105

Machel, Samora 124
McNamara, Robert 168–9, 172
Madagascar 16
magic/magicians 6; and life force
    23; and death 28; and Mau Mau
    82; *see also* sorcery/sorcerers;
    witchcraft
Mahgreb 39
Maitu Njugira (Ngugi) 93
maize 16, 17, 135, 146, 148, 149,
    165
'Maji Maji' war (1905–7) 63
Makonde people 190
Malawi: and labour migration 70;
    and Watchtower 80; Banda
    regime 97, 99; and prestige
    projects 123
Malawi, Lake 70
Malaysia 3
Mali: and Fulani 18; and gold
    empire 37, 40–1, 61, 152; French
    conquest of 63

Malinke people 40, 61
Mansa Musa 40
manufacturers: undermined by colonial regime 2, 7; consumer goods 69; encouraged by governments 119; lack of imported materials 129; immigrant groups 131; and informal sector 157, 158, 159, 160; in Nigeria 164, 165; lack of large-scale entrepreneurs 166, 196; and aid strategy 172; and export of garments 181
Maradi kingdom 74
market opportunities xi
marketing, and agriculture 7
marketing boards 7, 125–6, 133, 146, 148
markets, European 2
markets, financial 8
markets, international: undermining in colonial period 2; unstability of 119; and agricultural production 145; EC 192
markets, local 177, 195; undermining in colonial period 2; of Ghanaian coast 49; women's role on west coast 77
markets, urban: expansion of 4, 194–5; international 145; and agricultural production 145, 150
marriage: exogamous 30; hierarchical basis 32; wife's subordinate position 32–3, 75, 79; polygamous 33; urban version of traditional 77–8, 90–2; monogamous 77; missionaries support withdrawal from 85
Marriage Law (1971) 91
Marshall Plan 172
Masai people 137
Master Farmers' Scheme 141
Matabeleland 60, 63
Mau Mau 6, 81–2, 93, 111
Mau Mau Emergency 143, 158
Mauritania 11, 39
Mazrui, Ali xi
Mbau people 42, 48
Mbau state 42, 44
Mbiti, John xi, 25–6, 28–9, 79–80, 94

Mbopha, *induna* 60
Mboya, Tom 9, 20, 111
Mediterranean: trade in 36, 42, 152; supply of gold to 61
Meru District, Kenya 143
Middle East 57
migration: Bantu 4, 13–14, 16–20; urban 194
millet 11, 69, 137
minerals 155, 197
mines/mining 84; on copperbelt 6, 72; as innovation 68; development as major colonial objective 70; contracts 76; and development of inland towns 77; Zambian control of 121
mission schools 86
mission stations: colonial experience of 6; and education 65, 67; influence on marriage and family 75; and women's role 75
missionaries: failure to accept African philosophy 64; and Watchtower movement 80; and clash of culture 84; and marriages 85; paternalism 87; and nationalism 87
Mitchell Cotts 127
Mobutu, Sese Seko 123, 180
Modern History of Tanganyika, A (Iliffe) xi
Moi, Daniel Arap 111, 112, 113, 190
Mombasa 153
monarchy 40–1; *see also* kings
money, introduction 68, 84–5; rapid development of money economy 84–5
Mongu 25
monomutapa (Shona king) 152
morality, personal 26
Moravian Church 75
Morocco 41–2
Mozambique 60, 62; independence x; and rural areas 7; land appropriation 68; civil war 99, 190; and rural families 133; resettlement schemes 145; public elections 198
mugabe (senior chief) 35, 74
Muganda clans 54
Mulavi tribe 16

Mumias Sugar Company 147
Mundia, Nalumino 102
Mungai, Dr Njoroge 111
Murid Brotherhood 117, 156, 198
Museveni, Yoreveni 81, 105, 106
Mushala Gang 102
Mushiri, Wilson 90
Muslims *see* Islam
Mutang'ang'i 158–9, 161
Mutex textile mill 130
mutilation 33–4, 72
Mwanamutapa 56, 57
Mwanga II, *kabaka* 55
Mwatex textile mill 130
Mwinyi, President Hassan Ali 110
Mzilikazi 5, 60, 62

NaChagga people 29
Nairobi 90, 157, 158, 159, 169
Nairobi University 93
Naivasha 82
Natal: and Bantu expansion 14; and Nguni 58, 60
National Council of Nigeria and the Cameroons (NCNC) 100
National Liberation Movement 73
National Theatre, Kenya 93
nationalism: and chiefs 73; and Mau Mau 82; inadequacies of 87; and localism 99–103
Nationalism and the New States in Africa (Mazrui) xi
nationalization 127–8
Ndebele kingdom, Zimbabwe 5, 60
Ndegwa, Philip 189
Near East 57
negroid peoples 10, 11
ngambela 34
Ngaoundere 148
Ngonde people 66–7, 69, 73, 75, 110
Nguni people 58–9, 60, 62, 137
Nguni wa Thiongo (James Ngugi) 93
Niger Delta 31, 51
Niger River 18, 37, 40, 41
Nigeria 192; and independence ix, 100; Emirates brought into confederation 5; coexistence of old and new systems 6; population 16; chiefs in first independent government 73–4; expulsion of Ghanaian immigrant workers 89; trade unions in 89; coup (1966) 89, 120; constitution (1979) 100; rivalry between major tribal groups 100; localism 103, 110; and military regimes 110; civil conflicts 121; and prestige projects 123; foreign-owned companies 127, 128; state enterprise management 129; and indigenous entrepreneurs 132, 162–5; groundnut production 139; and cocoa 153; foreign investment in 156; and informal producers 157, 161; National Open Apprenticeship Scheme 161; recession 165; strength of fundamental movements 199; and democratization 199
Nigerian Indigenization Decree (1972) 164
Nile River 135
Nilo-Saharian languages 14
Nilotic languages 54
Njonjo, Charles 112–13
Nkrumah, Kwame 7, 73, 119, 131, 132, 188
Nkumbula, Harry 101, 102
Nok people 11
Northern People's Congress (NPC) 73, 100
Northern Rhodesia 17; and land appropriation 68; and migrant labour 70; Government seeks to revive chieftainship 72; women's life in inland towns 77
ntoro groups 22
Nuer people 30
Nyakyusa people 22, 32–3, 35, 66–7, 69, 70, 75, 90, 91, 110
Nyanja Ya Malawi 16
Nyasa, Lake 17
Nyasaland 80, 101
Nyerere, Julius 6, 110, 127, 132, 171–2, 188; on state of Africa 1; and nationalism 103, 106; and *ujamaa* villages 107–8; reputation as an individual 109; defeat of localism 118
Nzeogu, Chukwuma 120

Obasanjo, General 120

obligation 29, 30, 32
Obote, Milton 104, 105, 106, 121, 132
Odinga, Oginga 9, 20, 111, 113
oil 127, 197; price rises 172–3
oil palm 138, 142, 153
oral history 32, 52
oral tradition 14, 52, 57, 58
Organization of African Unity meeting of African Heads of State (1966) 1, 123
Oru people 31
Other Path, The (de Soto) 160
Ovimbundu people 190
Oyite-Ojok 105
Oyo State, Nigeria 51, 52, 149

Pakistan 3
palm oil 139, 155
Parti Africa d'Independence (PAI) 116
Parti Democratique Senegalais (PDS) 116
Parti Socialiste (PS) 116
paysannats 141, 142
p'Bitek, Okot 92–3
peer groups 32
Persia 57
Peter, Kyungu of the Ngonde 73
Pinto, Pia Gama 113
Planned Parenthood Association 90
Plymouth Brethren 85
poetry (of Sokoto Caliphate) 47
poison test 72
political parties, and class 89
political systems: problems in development of 7; in western sudan 18; and succession 21; and the clans 21, 56; and characteristics of states 36; expansion and consolidation 36; and Asante 51; and Buganda 56
poll tax 68, 71, 86
polygamy 33, 75
Poorah people 31
population: drift to towns 4; urban 7, 161, 166, 193, 194, 198; expansion 16, 69, 70; statistics 138, 139, 148, 151; growth 147
Portugal/Portuguese: and Latin America 3; introduction of new crops 16; and Mwanamutapa 57; reliance on forced labour 72; and gold trade 152
Portuguese territories x
pottery 11, 13, 57
Powdermaker, Hortense 78
power: and authority system 32, 71–3; and status 32; precariousness of 35; passing from one leader to another 36; variable power invested in kings 48–9, 51, 52; and kabakas 55; weakened chiefs' 71–3; governmental 118, 197; party 118; transfer of power in future 198; and new urban interest groups 199; accumulation by centres of growth 201
pre-colonial societies 121; authoritarianism 2; concentration of loyalties within kinship groups 2, 153; system of succession 2; nature of African societies in 4; entrepreneurs 152
Preferential Trade Area 195
pricing, and agriculture 7
primogeniture 52, 61
prisoners of war 49–50
private sector investment 8
productive system, changes in 5, 67–71
prostitution 78–9
puberty: and age sets 22; and initiation ceremony 26
public good 95–6
pygmies 11
pyretheum 144

radio-carbon techniques 11
railways 122
rain forest 11
rainmaking 95
Rand 77
re-afforestation 140
recycling of materials 160
Reformed Tijianiya 156
relatives: identification with 21; loyalty to 24
religion, traditional: common forms 19; and practical affairs 24; mystique surrounding leaders 56, 58; Islam's ability to co-exist with 39, 40, 42, 48, 65; new form of

expression 79–82; and economic
    change 94–5; role of 193
Renamo 124, 190, 201
resettlement schemes 145–6
Richards, Audrey 34
Riddell, Roger xi
rinderpest 138
ritual: and ancestors 24–5, 26; and
    chiefs 24, 25; and initiation
    ceremony 26–7; and supernatural
    power 27
roads 122
Roman Catholic Church, and
    Church of New Zion 80
root crop cultivation 13
Rostow, Walt 172, 178
Rozwi, clan 56, 57
Ruanda: and oral tradition about
    Tutsi people 14; and population
    16, 139
rubber 153
Rufisque 117
Rungwe District 70
rural areas, investment in 7
rural development projects 183–4
Ruvuma Development Association
    (RDA) 107

Sahara 11, 18
Sahel 10, 18
St Louis 117
Sambo, Emir of Zaria 46
San people 56
Sarki Umar, Emir of Kano 42, 44
savannah 142; and Bantu migrants
    13; and crops 16; Islamic societies
    of 36, 154–5, 156; Nigerian 42;
    city-states of 152; single currency
    zone in 153
Savimbi, Jonas 190
savings, domestic 178, 192, 193
School of Oriental and African
    Studies (University of London) xii
schools 67, 84; see also education
secret societies 30–1
self-help 193
Selya 70
Senegal 118: French conquest of 63;
    and national identity 103;
    constitutional transfer of power
    110; tackling of succession
    problem 115–17; avoidance of

localism problems 117; contact
    with France 117; and Murid
    Brotherhood 117, 198
Senegal River 37, 39, 40
Sene-Gambia 18
Senga people 17
Senghor, Leopold 6, 115–18
Shaka 5, 58–60, 62
Shamwana, Edward 102
sharia law 44, 45, 199
Shell 127
Shilluk people 110
Shimanjemanje, Kawanda 17
Shona language 152
Shona people 56, 57, 60, 62
Sierra Leone 77; creole population
    132
Sikhs 158
silver 42
slavery/slaves 68, 153; chiefs right
    to enslave own people 33; on
    farms in Emirates 46; and Islam
    48; and urban settlement of
    Fulani 48; and Asante economy
    49–50, 53; exchanged for weapons
    50; and lineage lines 51; as
    reward 55; and Portuguese 57;
    and Urozwi 58; dependence of
    Sokoto Caliphate on 61;
    prevalence in courts 72; and
    Swazi Queen Mother 74;
    descendents of returned slaves on
    west coast 77; and population 138
Smallholders Coffee Authority 147
Smith, Ian 127
social education 26
social services 4
socialism 107, 109
society see community
Sofala 56, 57, 152
soil: erosion 135, 140; fertility 11,
    16, 145; conservation 137; and
    crop rotation 141; and
    bush/fallow cycle 136
Sokoto, Sardauna of 73–4
Sokoto Caliphate 5, 42, 44–8, 49, 61,
    62
Sokoto people 37
Somali people 170, 190
Somalia 121
Song of Lawino (p'Bitek) 92–3
Songea 107

Songhay 41–2; and Fulani 18; and clan loyalties 22–3; and gold empire 37, 61, 152; and Mbau people 42

Soninke people 39, 61

sorcery/sorcerers 95; and life force 23, 28; and human fortune/misfortune 28; and pagan faith 39; *see also* magic/magicians; witchcraft

sorghum 11, 17, 135, 137

Sotho people 60

Soto, Hernando de 160–1

South Africa: and majority government x; stone tool industries 14; land appropriation 68; migrant miners 70, 71; and destabilization policies 199; and Renamo 201

South America 3, 16; *see also* Latin America

southern Rhodesia 63, 68

Spain 3, 39

spirits: groups 22, 30; ancestral 26; competing influences in 31; and recently dead 35; worship of 65, 74; and Islam 65; and destruction of traditional authority 71, 73; and economic change 95

Stages of Economic Growth (Rostow) 172

state: centralizing tendency of 6–7; loyalty to 24

'states': characteristics of 36; weaknesses of underlying structure 36–7; and Islam 36–37

status, and power 32

sterility, fear of 32

stock-keeping 13; *see also* livestock

stone building 57

stone tool 'industries' 11, 14

structural adjustment programmes (SAP) 125

Suame Magazine, Kumasi 157

subordination: of wives 32–3; to chiefs and kings 33–4

succession system 2, 21, 30, 34–5, 110–17, 118, 202

Sudan, 54, 84; success of cash crops 69; and military regimes 110; civil conflicts 121, 190; and Gezira Scheme 122; and aid 182; and Libya 182; introduction of sharia law 199

sudan 18, 37

sugar cane 16

Sukumaland, Tanzania 139, 140

Sulayman, Sunni 41

Sullebawa clan 47

Sunguratex textile mill 130

supernatural: common understanding of 20; and rituals 27, 66; and causative explanation 29; community obsession with 32

superstition 6; and Mau Mau 82; and causation 95; role of 193

suspicion 28, 29, 30, 99

Swahili peoples 37; settlements of 14; and trade 57, 71

Swazi people 74–5

sweet potatoes 140, 148

Swynnerton, Roger 143

Syria/Syrians: as immigrant investors 126; as merchants 155

taboos of traditional religion 65

Taghaza salt mine 41

Tanganyika 58, 60, 71, 101

Tanganyika, Lake 16, 17

Tanganyika African National Union (TANU) 106

Tanzania ix, 121, 192; and rural areas 7; and Bacwezi 14; and 'Maji Maji' war 63; labour migrants 70; and co-operative societies 73; marriage law 91; and corruption 95; and national identity 103; resistance to German colonialism 103; authoritarianism 106; stages to centralized socialist state 107; and *ujamaa* villages 107–8, 109; split between pragmatists and socialists 109; and railways 122; and roads 122; and prestige projects 123; and coffee 125; Arusha Declaration 107, 127, 128, 132; theft from parastatal companies 129; textile mills 120–31; and rural families 133; resettlement schemes 145; population 148; and small-scale enterprises 157; livestock project 168, 169–71; defence expenditure

178; counterpart funding 181; changes in crop production 195

Tanzanian Parliamentary Public Accounts Committee 129

tax/taxation: illegal 44, 46; and labour migration 70; rigorous collection of 68; from prostitutes and cult specialists 74; difficulties of collecting 196

tea 146

technology 165; agricultural 19; choice of 130; European 155; for formals/informals 161; artisans 195

textiles 130–1

Tie, Ghana 12

'tied' labour 50

Timbuktu 40, 42, 44

tin 42, 77

tobacco 146

Togo 50, 123

Tolbert, William 126

Tonga peoples 58

Toola family 12

trade: insignificant share in world 1; chiefs' monopolies 33; with Mediterranean 36, 152; and Islam 36, 37, 39, 42; and Mbau kingdoms 42; and Great Zimbabwe 56–7; and Christianity 65; and mining 70; accumulation of capital 153; with Europe 153; era of the multinationals 155–6; and community groups 193

trade routes 40

trade unions 177; weakness of 89; in Kenya 111; and community groups 193

transportation 197

Transvaal, and Bantu expansion 13, 14

tribal orientation 3

tribes: as groups of clans 22; loyalty to 24, 89, 99, 193–4; and localism 99

tribute 180; and Asante economic strength agricultural 54; and Bemba 72; Kapalu rejects 86

Tripoli 153

tsetse fly 145

Tuareg people 10

Tubman, William 126

Tunka Memin 39

Turay, Samori 63

Tutsi people 14

Tutu, Osei 49

twin babies, killing of 64, 75

Uganda 61; oral tradition about Bacwezi 14; and Babito peoples 54; success of cash crops 69; and co-operative societies 73; Asian expulsion 89, 132; authoritarianism 104–6, 110; localism 104–6, 110; constitution 104; Obote governments 104–5, 106; civil strife 105–6; Amin's rule 106; Tanzanian invasion 106; nationalization 121; civil conflicts 121, 190; cotton production 139

uhuru (freedom) x

Uhuru na Mwalimu 168

ujamaa villages 107–8, 109, 123, 170

Ukuku people 31

unborn: identification with 21; loyalty to 24

Underdevelopment in Kenya (Leys) xi

Unilever 127, 156

Union for the Total National Independence of Angola (UNITA) 190

Union Minière 127, 155

Union Nationale Camerounaise (UNC) 114

Union Progressiste Senegalais (UPS) 116

United National Independence Party (UNIP) 86, 87, 101, 102

United People's Congress (UPC) 104

United People's Party (UPP) 101–2

United States: African investment 156; and tribute 180; and aid 182, 183

urbanization 5, 77, 87, 90, 96, 193, 194, 195

Urewe 13

Urowzi 56, 57, 58, 62, 121

Urua 16

USAID (United States Agency for International Development) 184 usury 44

veterinary services 139, 144
Victoria, Lake 13, 14, 52
Vidrovitch, Catherine Coquery xii
villages: new, and children 22;
    ujamaa 107–8, 123, 170; in
    Mozambique 123–4
violence, 'licensed form' of 35
Volta River 51

waChagga people 71, 72, 73, 103,
    125, 134, 136, 137, 157
Wade, Abdoulaye 116
waGanda people 157
wages, falling real 177
waHaya people 103, 125
waKara people 136, 137
Wallace, W. 46
Wamara (Bacwezi king) 54
waTengo people 136, 137
Weber, Max 154
West African Pilot, The (newspaper)
    100
Wicked Walk, The (Msefya) 91–2
Wilson, Monica xi, 69–70, 75–6, 91
witchcraft 95; and death 28; and
    defensive tactics 29; and Islam
    65; and Church of New Zion 80;
    see also magic/magicians;
    sorcery/sorcerers
wives: subordinate role of 32–3; in
    polygamous marriage 33; friction
    with 76; problem of migrant
    workers 76; heavier workload 76;
    teenage girls as 86; mistreatment
    of 87, 90–1
wizardry *see* magic/magicians;
    sorcery/socerers
Wolsey, Sir Garnet 63
women: and undermining of
    extended family 6; greater
    freedom of 71; ritualized position
    74–5; servitude to husbands 75,
    78; dress 76; key trading role on
    west coast 77; *femmes libres* 77,

78–9; position changes 85;
    aspirations of educated 194
World Bank 125, 165, 168, 169, 170,
    173, 175, 176, 179, 180–1, 183–6
World War Two 76

Yameossouko 123
yams 16
Yaroh, Malam 152
Yasi people 31
Yemen 18
Yoruba people 18, 51, 52, 100, 137,
    164, 194
young/old: increased power of young
    71; and authoritarianism 103

Zaire x, 192; and Lumpa Church 81;
    civil conflicts 121; palm oil
    exports 139; cotton production
    139
Zambezi River 25, 56
Zambezi Valley 16, 58
Zambia ix; mining 6, 121; stone tool
    industries 14; and Chewa people
    16; and Watchtower 80; and
    Lumpa Church 81; trade unions
    in 89; localism 101–3; coup
    attempt 102; drift towards an
    authoritarian system 102; and
    railways 112; and indigenous
    entrepreneurs 132; government
    support for small farmers 146
Zambia River 85
Zanzibar ix, 107, 153
Zaria 46
Zimbabwe 60, 62; majority
    government x; independence x;
    migration of Shona into 56; and
    Watchtower 80; corruption
    scandals 120; and population 139;
    agricultural productivity 149;
    and aid 182; and immigrants 190;
    exports 196
Zulu people 58
Zululand 58–60